"This carefully crafted book presents detailed narratives of spiritually sensitive clinical practice that stretch across various worldviews and life challenges of clients. It integrates professional knowledge and values with insights from the very personal spiritual journeys of the authors. Case presentations are matched with deep reflective questions and podcast interviews with professional helpers. Thus, this wise book encourages close, empathic listening and communicating, both within clinical encounters and in readers' own personal and professional development."

— **Edward R. Canda, PhD,** professor, School of
Social Welfare, The University of Kansas

"This beautiful book embraces the tensions that exist when doing clinical practice with spiritually diverse populations. Centering the stories of clinicians, students, and clients, the rich phenomenological narratives remind readers that storytelling and the art of listening are pathways to spiritually sensitive practice. The imagery and attention to the details of lived experiences and settings fertilize the ground for deepening empathy, creating more participatory forms of knowledge, and strengthening opportunities for transformational change."

— **Loretta Pyles, PhD,** professor, School of Social Welfare,
State University of New York at Albany

SPIRITUALITY IN MENTAL HEALTH PRACTICE

This key text presents an accessible and diverse exploration of spirituality in mental health practice, broadening the definition of spirituality to comprise a variety of transcendent experiences.

Chapters include a brief history of the tensions of spirituality in mental health practice and consider a range of emerging topics, from spirituality among the elderly and energy work (Reiki), to spirituality in addiction recovery, incarceration, and hospice work. The book offers a close examination of the limits of the medical model of care, making a case for a more spiritually sensitive practice. Rich case examples are woven throughout, and the book is paired with podcasts that can be applied across chapters, illuminating the narrative stories and building active listening and teaching skills.

Suitable for students of social work and counseling at master's level, as well as practicing clinicians, *Spirituality in Mental Health Practice* is an essential text for widening our understanding of how spiritual frameworks can enrich mental health practice.

Miriam Jaffe, PhD, LSW, is an associate teaching professor of graduate composition in the Rutgers University Writing Program. She specializes in life-writing and narrative activism. She is the lead editor of casebooks on K-12 schools as therapeutic communities, sexual trauma, and LGBTQ sexual trauma.

Widian Nicola, LCSW, DSW, is a clinical social worker, qualitative researcher, and assistant professor at Seton Hall University.

Jerry Floersch, LCSW, PhD, is an associate professor of social work at Rutgers University. He is the author of *Meds, Money, and Manners: The Case Management of Severe Mental Illness* and the co-author of *Qualitative Methods for Practice Research*. His clinical practice focuses on adolescents and adults.

Jeffrey Longhofer, PhD, LCSW, is an associate professor of social work at Rutgers University. He is the author of *A-Z of Psychodynamic Practice* and the co-author of *On Being and Having a Case Manager*. His clinical practice focuses on children, adolescents, and adults.

SPIRITUALITY IN MENTAL HEALTH PRACTICE

A Narrative Casebook

Edited by Miriam Jaffe, Widian Nicola,
Jerry Floersch, and Jeffrey Longhofer

Routledge
Taylor & Francis Group

NEW YORK AND LONDON

First published 2020
by Routledge
52 Vanderbilt Avenue, New York, NY 10017

and by Routledge
2 Park Square, Milton Park, Abingdon, Oxon, OX14 4RN

Routledge is an imprint of the Taylor & Francis Group, an informa business

Library of Congress Cataloging-in-Publication Data
Names: Jaffe, Miriam, editor.
Title: Spirituality in mental health practice: a narrative casebook / Miriam Jaffe, Widian Nicola, Jerry Floersch, Jeffrey Longhofer.
Description: New York, NY: Routledge, 2020. | Includes bibliographical references and index. | Identifiers: LCCN 2019057597 (print) | LCCN 2019057598 (ebook) | ISBN 9780367442811 (hbk) | ISBN 9780367442828 (pbk) | ISBN 9781003008781 (ebk)
Subjects: LCSH: Social service—Religious aspects. | Mental health—Religious aspects. | Psychotherapy—Religious aspects. | Mental health personnel—Training of.
Classification: LCC HV530 .S669 2020 (print) | LCC HV530 (ebook) | DDC 204.088/3622—dc23
LC record available at https://lccn.loc.gov/2019057597
LC ebook record available at https://lccn.loc.gov/2019057598

ISBN: 978-0-367-44281-1 (hbk)
ISBN: 978-0-367-44282-8 (pbk)
ISBN: 978-1-003-00878-1 (ebk)

Typeset in Bembo
by codeMantra

Visit the eResources: www.routledge.com/9780367442828

CONTENTS

EDITORS

Miriam Jaffe, PhD, LSW, Director of the Rutgers Doctorate in Social Work Writing Program for six years, holds a PhD in 20th-century American literature based in cultural theory and ethnic studies, a dual certification in composition, and an MSW. She focuses on issues of life-writing and autoethnography in literature. From Routledge Press (2017–2019), she has developed casebooks on social work in K-12 schools, sexual trauma, and LGBTQ sexual trauma. Jaffe served as a therapist at The Center for Therapy and Counseling in New Jersey, specializing in complex trauma and attachment theory, and she serves as Associate Teaching Professor of Graduate Writing in the Rutgers University Writing Program, where she engages in narrative activism.

Widian Nicola, LCSW, DSW, is a clinical social worker, qualitative researcher, and assistant professor at Seton Hall University. Dr. Nicola is interested in narratives of the lived human experience, particularly those affected by social inequalities. With an interest in phenomenology, Dr. Nicola combines clinical social work practice with qualitative research to unveil the often complex nature of the shared human condition. As such, to disseminate new knowledge that complement, challenge, or expand relevant studies in social work, Dr. Nicola created, produced, and published the *Lived Experience Project*, a narrative social work podcast show that explores unique and evocative stories rarely heard in mainstream media. In the classroom, Dr. Nicola invites students to bridge clinical theory to practice and practice to theory as a means of honoring the unique nature of individual experience.

Jerry Floersch, LCSW, PhD, Associate Professor, Rutgers University School of Social Work, is a 1998 graduate of the School of Social Service Administration at the University of Chicago. After earning the master's degree in social work from the University of Kansas, he worked as a social worker in drug and alcohol, hospital, mental health, and community settings. He administered a mental health crisis service and played a key role in developing and implementing housing policies and programs for the adult severely mentally ill. He is the author of *Meds, Money, and Manners: The Case Management of Severe Mental Illness*, published by Columbia University Press (2002), where, utilizing ethnographic and socio-historical methods, he examined the rise of community support services, the rise of the case manager and case management, and the limits of management models in providing services. He is a recent NIMH K08 recipient (2004–2009) for training in and development of qualitative methods to study youth subjective experience of psychotropic treatment. His work on psychotropic treatment focuses on the meanings adolescents and young adults make of their medication treatment, including social and psychological "side effects." In 2008, he was recipient of a Case Western Reserve University Presidential Research Initiative award, where, as the PI, he led a two-year investigation of college student use of mental health services, including psychiatric medications. His new book, with Jeffrey Longhofer and Paul Kubek, *On Having and Being a Case Manager*, builds on earlier work in this field by exploring a clinical method for case management practice. He is currently conducting a multisite study of college student use of psychiatric medications. He has a new book with Oxford University Press: *Qualitative Methods for Practice*.

Jeffrey Longhofer, PhD, LCSW, is an associate professor of social work at Rutgers University. He is a clinical social worker and applied anthropologist whose research focuses on health and mental health practice, the cross-cultural study of mental illness, mental health case management, and the roles stigma and shame play in the social and psychological dynamics of practitioner/patient interactions. His recent ethnographic research has been in childcare settings and among children with parents suffering from life-threatening illnesses. His research has appeared in journals including *Psychiatric Services, Culture, Medicine and Psychiatry, Transcultural Psychiatry, Journal of Aging Studies, Qualitative Social Work: Research and Practice, Families, Systems and Health, Social Work and Mental Health, Ethnohistory,* and *Theory and Society*. His books include *On Having and Being a Case Manager: A Relational Method for Recovery* (2010) and *Psychoanalysis from A-Z* (2015). He has served as the associate editor of the Society for Applied Anthropology journal, *Human Organization*, and the editor of the American Anthropological Association journal, *Culture and Agriculture*.

CONTRIBUTORS

Cristina Blasoni, LCSW, ChT, DSW, earned her MSW at Hunter University and her DSW from Rutgers University. Along with the traditional clinical skills, Blasoni incorporates Reiki and hypnotherapy to assist those under her care with holistic modalities. Blasoni has 30 years of experience with the psychiatric and co-occurring disorders. The focus on Blasoni's practice is the state of the clinician's presence in the pained person's healing space; she focuses on changing stigmatizing language to innocuous language and finding the humanity in the pained person. Through the training and implementation of techniques learned via the Hearing Voices Network, Blasoni assists those who experience the phenomenon of voices and visions to find inner strength, healing, and peace utilizing unconditional positive regard and radical empathy.

Bianca-Ramos Channer, LCSW, DSW, is an assistant professor at Kennesaw State University (KSU). Prior to KSU, Dr. Channer was an assistant professor and Director of Field Education at the College of Saint Elizabeth. She developed a BSW program and was instrumental in getting the program accredited by the Council on Social Work Education. Dr. Channer received her Doctorate of Social Work from Rutgers University in 2016. Her dissertation examined the identity struggles incarcerated youth. Dr. Channer completed her Masters in Social Work at Rutgers University in 2010. After completing her MSW, she worked for the New Jersey Juvenile Justice Commission (JJC). Starting out as clinician in a medium security detention center, Dr. Channer provided individual, group, and family therapy to a case load of dually diagnosed youth. Dr. Channer worked on re-entry policies and helped the JJC establish release planning procedures for residents identified as being a high risk of recidivism. She worked as an interagency liaison between the Juvenile Justice Commission,

Children's System of Care, and the Division of Child Protection and Permanency. Dr. Channer has established trainings for social workers, advocated for changes in policies, and developed and implemented new policies and programs. Dr. Channer's research interests include re-envisioning social work education by scaffolding courses with evidence-based practice and mindfulness techniques, professional identity development in BSW/MSW students, and infusing art and technology into social work education.

Lynda Fabbo, DSW, LCSW, received her Bachelor's degree from Seton Hall University and her Masters and Doctorate in Social Work from Rutgers University. She began her career working as a crisis intervention therapist with children and families involved in the Passaic County Family Court. She then went on to provide school-based therapy for at-risk children in several North Bergen Elementary Schools. She is currently on a Child Study Team in a high school and middle school, working with children and young adults who have learning and developmental disabilities. Dr. Fabbo is also a Certified Field Instructor for social work graduate students and a Clinical Supervisor for social workers in the process of procuring licensure. In her private practice as a psychotherapist, hypnotherapist, and Usui Reiki Master/Practitioner, she provides help to those looking to improve their health, lives, and relationships. She believes we all have the potential to be successful and possess the tools we need to achieve our goals. Treatment is viewed as a journey taken together to find this potential within, and Dr. Fabbo uses a holistic approach to mental health counseling and wellness with her clients. She is also a passionate teacher and provides classes and seminars on Mindfulness and Energy Healing.

Michael Garbe, LCSW, DSW, has worked in the field of trauma, substance abuse, sexual offenses, and private practice. Having experienced, processed, and integrated, a spiritual crisis of his own, he now specializes in working with individuals who would like to have spirituality integrated into their therapy. Along with his clinical work, Michael has dedicated himself to increasing spiritual competence within the helping professions. In addition to the authored chapter in this textbook, his latest research, at Rutgers, has developed into a framework on how to assess and provide treatment for individuals who have had a "spiritually transformative experience." He has presented his research at the American Center for the Integration of Spiritually Transformative Experiences (ACISTE) national conference, and he hopes to inspire current and future helping professionals to join in on this important conversation.

Michael Jarrette-Kenny, LCSW, DSW (Rutgers University, New Brunswick), is a clinical social worker and psychotherapist. He is currently employed as a clinician in Wyckoff, NJ, providing individual and group counseling services for adults, couples, children, and families. He started his social work career in

1998 as a support counselor for developmentally disabled adults at The Arc of Bergen and Passaic counties. Upon completing his MSW in 2004, he began working on an acute inpatient psychiatric unit at Bergen Regional Medical Center and as a screener for Care Plus NJ's Psychiatric Emergency Screening Program. He has completed advanced training in hypnosis at the New York Milton H. Erickson Society for Psychotherapy and Hypnosis (NYSEPH) and in EMDR. His areas of interest include the integration of hypnosis and mindfulness approaches in the treatment of complex trauma.

Anthony Nicotera, JD, DSW, LSW, is an associate professor in Seton Hall's Social Work Program, Department of Sociology, Anthropology, and Social Work. He is a clinical social worker and directs NYU's post-master's program in Spirituality and Social Work. He consults with the Fellowship of Reconciliation. He worked with Vietnamese Zen Master Thich Nhat Hanh, nominated for the Nobel Peace Prize by Dr. Martin Luther King, Jr., to help create the mixed-media films *Planting Seeds of Mindfulness for Children* and *The 5 Powers*, which won best film at The People's Film Festival in Harlem, NY. He helped found Newark New Jersey's Cristo Rey High School. He served as Chaplain to the College of Law and School for New Learning via DePaul University's Center for Spirituality and Values in Practice, which he co-founded. He also helped found DePaul's peace and justice studies program. He has led numerous workshops, retreats, and healing circles, and presented on panels pertaining to spirituality, social justice, and social work. He has been arrested or detained some 20 times for nonviolent civil disobedience. He spent six years as a member of the Society of Jesus, a religious order in the Roman Catholic tradition. As a Jesuit, he completed the Ignatian Spiritual Exercises, a 30-day silent retreat, and worked internationally and domestically in prisons, hospice facilities, inner-city parishes and schools, and legal and social service centers. He also lived in Latin America, working with community organizations and victims of war and violence, and he lived and worked in India with Mother Teresa.

Kanako Okuda, LCSW, DSW, is a licensed clinical social worker and has been actively involved with social work education, having served as an education coordinator, field instructor, and lecturer in social work schools in New York City. Currently, she serves as the Director of Field Education at Silberman School of Social Work at Hunter College, City University of New York. Prior to joining Silberman, Okuda specialized in Pediatric Oncology at New York-Presbyterian Hospital as a senior social worker. Additionally, she has held lectures and workshops addressing social justice and inclusion practices in the United States. In her early career, Okuda worked with multi-stressed families in the child welfare system in New York City, as well as Japanese-speaking children and their families through New York City Department of Education, to address cultural and language barriers. She also provides psychotherapy via online working with individuals a wide range of concerns. Her work also extends to East Africa, Kenya, working with a community of tea farmers for sustainable economic empowerment. Okuda received her Bachelor of Arts in Sociology and Social Work from Lehman College, City University of New York, her Master of Science in Social Work from Columbia University School of Social Work, her Post-Master's Certificate in Palliative and End-of-Life Care from NYU Silver School of Social Work, and her Doctor of Social Work from Rutgers School of Social Work, the State University of New Jersey.

Joan Ordille, LCSW, DSW, has extensive experience in end-of-life care and grief counseling, and is a part-time lecturer at Rutgers University Graduate School of Social Work. She has experience in direct practice, supervision, program development, leadership development, and administration and policy. With varying experience in direct service experience with individuals, groups, and families, Joan has spent the last several years working in the hospice setting. Her engaged scholarship and clinical interests include multiple aspects of end-of-life care, phenomenology, care of the practitioner, and expanding holistic approaches to health and well-being through a lens that encompasses Eastern and Western philosophic principles and practice modalities. She is active in issues related to peace and social justice and is a Certified Hatha yoga teacher and Reiki master. She is the author of "Phenomenology in End-of-Life Care: Implications for Philosophy and Clinical Practice" in *Clinical Social Work Journal.*

Debra Ruisard, LCSW, LCADC, DSW, holds a BA in Recreation Administration from the University of Alberta, Canada, an EdM from Temple University, and an MSW and DSW from Rutgers University. She is the Consultant for Trauma Informed Care at The Center for Great Expectations, a non-profit agency in Somerset, NJ, that provides trauma-informed residential treatment to pregnant and parenting women who struggle with mental health and substance use issues. Dually licensed as an LCSW and LCADC, she has extensive clinical experience in simultaneously treating trauma and addiction issues primarily with child welfare involved women. In her work she seeks to develop a greater understanding of the relationship between trauma and addiction in order to improve recovery outcomes for her clients. Dr. Ruisard is a part-time lecturer at the Rutgers School of Social Work and has a private practice providing traditional and sensorimotor psychotherapy specializing in the treatment of adults with complex trauma.

Robin Wiley, MSW, DSW, is a licensed clinical social worker who received a BA in Social Work from Virginia State University and an MSW and DSW from Rutgers, The State University of New Jersey. Dr. Wiley has over 24 years of experience serving individuals and families who are addressing various emotional difficulties and life stressors. Much of her work with older adults focuses on bringing attention to specific concerns they encounter and informing professionals and family members about how to be supportive. For more information, check out her website theexperienceofaging.com, or contact Dr. Wiley via email at theexperienceofaging@gmail.com.

PREFACE

Miriam Jaffe

One early afternoon during a January not long ago, as I lay on top of my covers for a quick nap, a voice and a face popped into my head. My eyes were open, and I was lucid enough to remember all the details. The face was that of my husband's uncle on his dad's side: a big, round but still oval face popping through what I can only describe as something like the butcher block paper background of an elementary school bulletin board. His face popped through this artifice from some other realm, probably of my imagination, I thought. But his voice had the same Washington Heights Jewish accent that he had in life, one that I don't think I could replicate on my own, even in my own head. It is a voice that I know when I hear it, but not one I could hear in my head willingly or recreate in any way. He—his English name was Harvey—spoke to me in a rush: "You wanna have another baby?" Then he sort of implied wordlessly that the baby would be in his name, or maybe the baby would be a sort of reincarnation of him. "Sure," I responded tacitly. "As long as I don't die." I fell asleep. I thought nothing of the experience, as if it hadn't happened.

Just a week earlier, we had participated in a memorial for Harvey. In honor of their father, Harvey's children dedicated a Torah scroll to him. His Hebrew name, Chazikyahu, *Strength of God*, was embroidered in gold upon the blue velvet cover of the Torah. We paraded in song with the Torah scroll in one-degree weather from Harvey's son's house to the synagogue where the Torah would have its place in the holy ark. It was an overwhelming gesture that demonstrated the family's love for Harvey, and I was quite moved even though I had met Harvey just a handful of times and didn't know him very well at all.

Moreover, if I chalked up the experience of his apparition to anything, it was that I had just turned 40, and I was confronting my future infertility. After my fourth emergency C-section, at age 38, which was considered "a high risk geriatric pregnancy," I was told, supine on the operating table with a bright light shining in my eyes, "You're done."

Another pregnancy, the doctor told me, would kill me. Either my uterus would pop or the baby would grow into my bowels, and she said something else complicated about the scar tissue.

"Okay," I said. What else do you say when you've survived four deliveries during which you would have otherwise died if not for the obstetric surgeon making this call? "That's okay."

It was okay for me. My three previous children were from another marriage. This fourth baby was my husband's first. He was over-the-moon to have our healthy daughter, but he also felt a pang of loss that we would have no more children.

A week after Harvey popped into my head, I missed my period. I told my husband. He said, "Do you ever miss periods when you're on the pill? I thought not." Right. The pill had made my cycle clockwork. And even if I missed a pill here or there, the likelihood of a 40-year-old getting pregnant on a dime like that is pretty low. At least that had been my own experience back at 38. Then, I recalled to him the scene with Harvey popping into my head, and he froze up and melted all at once. He said, "Everyone says that *Esti is a reincarnation of Harvey's wife's mother like it is fact."

Overnight, my body changed in all the ways that bodies change during the first months of pregnancy, except on overdrive. No one talks about these things, but I will: my nipples changed, my breasts were extremely sore, I had implantation bleeding, my stomach swelled, and the smell of chicken made me vomit. It wasn't in my head. My husband noticed my enlarged areolas and the appearance of lactiferous ducts before I did.

We bought a pregnancy test. The good kind, with the digital screen. But it flashed in error. So we bought a six pack of pregnancy texts. And then all different kinds. And every single test flashed in error. Each morning was a twilight zone. It lasted two weeks.

I called my doctor for a blood test. She said I had to wait to take a test blood until two missed periods. The anxiety of the uncertainty was causing me to dissociate. My husband was excited and regretting that we had donated the baby swing. I was excited, too, and forecast what my life would be like with a fifth child at this stage in our family dynamic. Moreover, I was terrified. I suddenly started watching my older children glide around the house as if they were ghosts, except I would be the ghost if I died in childbirth, a fate I would not have escaped in round one if I had been born just a hundred years earlier. It was the fate my great, great grandmother had succumbed to when my great grandmother was born. I could not imagine leaving my children to bring another child into this world. I did not trust that I would not die in childbirth, in spite of the "agreement" between Harvey and me.

I was driving to work—to work as a psychotherapist—when I could not take it anymore. I gripped the steering wheel really tight with both hands and yelled out: "I can't. I can't do it." *I can't reincarnate you, Harvey. I'm sorry.*

I caught my supervisor in the hallway; rather, she pulled me into her office when she saw the look on my face. I said cryptically, "There's a squatter in my building, but the place has been rendered uninhabitable. So, either I'm gonna have to kick him out, or he's gonna die on his own, or he's going to be the end of me." She told me to go home. By the time I got there, a gush of red blood, like I never saw except during a previous miscarriage, had stained everything.

Relief... and then intense guilt and grief. That's what I felt. My husband and I cried. And I stayed in my bed for a few days. I'd only sort of told one other person, my sister-in-law, and I hadn't given any Harvey-related details.

The thing that got me out of bed was that I consulted a medium. A medium is someone who can channel the souls of dead people. This medium was an old friend who could not help but to channel. It had plagued her, especially since her mother, similarly gifted, had deemed their channeling as something akin to devil's work. Moreover, when my friend tried to shut out the voices, she couldn't. She came close to death herself when she tried to "turn off" her special power. We'd actually only spoken about it once, years earlier. It wasn't something she advertised, and our relationship was totally full of the stuff of life, mostly professional.

But my guilt and grief were all consuming. I stayed in my bed, wondering if all of this was real. Finally, I asked my husband if I should ask my friend, the medium, about the situation. After all, we try to live as Torah-observant Jews, and the Torah forbids communication with the dead through a medium. To my surprise, my husband said, "do what you have to do." I dialed her number.

"I'm calling because I heard a voice." I was crying. "I want to know if I'm crazy."

"You didn't kill anybody." That's what she said, soothingly.

"What? I didn't even tell you what happened."

"So, tell me what happened, but I can do this from a foreign country if necessary." I told her the story in shock at her abilities.

"Well, who has black hair? A big guy! I mean, not portly... but... round." She said this as if not wanting to insult me about this person's weight.

"I don't know. My husband's dad? But he's alive, and he's not portly." I didn't know Harvey when he had hair. I found out later that his hair had been black; he had battled cancer for as long as I knew him. But he remained pretty "round" until the end.

"Well, he says, 'don't worry about it.' And anyway, you didn't kill the soul. You can't do that. It just went back up. If you want to have more babies, there's a line of them ready to come your way, but maybe go to a special doctor." All of that was spoken in a "matter-of-fact" in tone. And then her tone switched back to her regular voice. "Wait, maybe you were pregnant!" It was like there was a disconnect between what she had told me from somewhere else and what she herself was slowly coming to realize.

I was overcome. We got off the phone quickly and then resumed our normal relationship. I've thought about what happened that January everyday since, and I still have not come to any conclusion about what this experience meant. I still catch myself imagining the name Chazikyahu in my head, imagining the nicknames I would have called my baby. I also imagine that the virtually pregnancy proof IUD I immediately installed after this incident could malfunction if God so willed it. I imagine so many more possibilities about the way life works, generally.

★ ★ ★

I have always been open to my psychotherapy clients' "ghost stories," as they sometimes referred to them because my mother told me that her father, after his early death, had "visited" her and my grandmother. She said, for example, he would turn on the faucets when they would try to leave the house so as to jokingly delay them, and when my grandmother would yell out "C'mon, Jack!" and sigh, the faucets would magically stop running. I had no reason to disbelieve my mother when she described this scene.

However, it struck me during my MSW internship at a psychotherapy practice; during clinical group supervision, my colleagues—therapists from a variety of cultural backgrounds and levels of experience—were very closed if not openly judgmental of clients who, say, burned sage to exorcise bad spirits from the house, followed their horoscopes, visited psychic mediums, or expressed a belief in their special powers. One of my first case presentations as a clinician in training was about a man in his mid-20s who had been in and out of therapy—and stable housing, gangs, sobriety—for most of his life. The first time I met him, he told me he could see through things—like, he could see inside the metal casing of the lamp post next to me and could see the wires inside. I wrapped myself tightly in my cardigan and jotted down "psychotic delusions?" on my intake form.

Then, a month into our work together, as we were ending a session, he said to me, "there's a pair of glasses in the chair." He motioned toward the crack in the cushions where I had been sitting. I reached my hand way down into a tight, narrow crack in the pleather upholstery and pulled out my own pair of glasses that I had lost two weeks prior. I looked at him in astonishment. "And there are two nails, askew, holding up that picture on the wall." I pried down the picture to check to find two nails askew, indeed. He gave a few more spot on examples, and said,

> Sometimes, I can just see things that are hiding. I know what people are trying to hide. I know it sounds delusional or whatever it's been called on my insurance. But this hyper-sensory experience is what gives me crippling anxiety.

When I brought up my awe-filled curiosity about my client's hyper-sensory, empathic experience, with my recovered glasses in evidence, everyone in my supervision group laughed loudly. Even my supervisor smirked. No one could believe that I believed him. The group was immune to the possibility that he had a superpower. The only acceptable diagnosis was that there was something wrong with him.

Therefore, I felt pressured to hide my array of other clients' supernatural experiences: the Italian divorcee whose dead relatives were supporting her through her struggles from the other side; the grieving daughter who took a photo of her recently deceased father's house before selling it only to find his reflection, clear as day, in the front door, next to an apparition of her dead mother; the ones who dreamed things about other people that ended up coming true. And me, the one whose husband's uncle was wondering if I might be up for another baby. When I told my own dear therapist about the medium in my life—and the stories of my clients, since I wouldn't dare share them in supervision—I sensed her doubt. Of course, it is natural to doubt.

★ ★ ★

About a year before his death, my father announced to most of the family that he had experienced a premonition: he believed that he had one year to live. He wrote a letter to us about the premonition, and he told us where the letter would be hidden in case his premonition came to pass. Naturally, we all thought he had succumbed to prednisone-induced mania or psychosis. He had always been so scientific, practical, and matter-of-fact, and he hated the fanatical and divisive nature of religion. He was still young and had no signs of dementia.

On the anniversary of his premonition, my dad rejoiced and announced that he was living on borrowed time. He bought a BMW convertible; he went to Costco and strolled up and down every aisle, buying whatever he fancied; he took my mom on an expensive vacation and smothered her with gifts. One day he called me and said that his mother, who passed 15 years prior, appeared to him and engaged in him in five-minute conversation. He was shaken by that experience, calling it "foreboding." And then—it felt so sudden and out of thin air—he was killed by a drugged-up driver who decided to go the wrong way down a highway on purpose. When we opened the letter he left us, we found that he pointed to the fact that we might need to contact a lawyer given whatever circumstances caused his death. I have no doubt that his premonition was real. And if his premonition was real, if I saw with my grieving client the clear reflection of her dead father in a photo, if I had no reason not to trust my mother's ghost stories or those of the Italian divorcee, then I am open to exploring lots of other ways that spiritual energy guides us.

★ ★ ★

I think that few therapists are equipped to imagine these types of experiences as real for their clients. The tendency toward disbelief is grounded in the good intentions of grounding one's client in reality; however, if it is not crazy to believe in God and to observe mainstream spiritual practices, then it should not be laughable to believe in a broader range of spiritual practices.

In fact, we must be curious enough to reframe spiritually sensitive mental health practice in our time; after all, mainstream religion is losing steam in the United States. Freeman (2019), in her study of time use for millennials and non-millennials in the United States, found that millennials spend 0.09 hours per day on religion and spirituality, while the generation before spent 0.16 hours per day on religion and spirituality. Pew Research Center data revealed that along with waning attendance at houses of worship, "17% of Americans now describe their religion as 'nothing in particular'" (2019). Yet "We still want relationships and transcendence, to be part of something bigger than ourselves… Some of us are turning to convenient, low-commitment substitutes for faith and fellowship: astrology, the easy 'spiritualism' of yoga and self-care" (Emba, 2019). Without mainstream religion, which serves to connect and comfort people, many folks find themselves alone, depressed, and anxious. If mental health practitioners, who may serve as modern-day spiritual guides, do not value the "substitutes for faith and fellowship," which are not, in fact, "easy," then we are blind to reality—not trying to protect reality or trying to ground our clients in reality.

We present this volume of case studies to explore various perspectives about the spiritual realities of our time and how these realities apply in the work of mental health clinicians. Anthony Nicotera, in the first chapter "Spirituality, Religion, and Social Work," lays out a historical overview of the challenges that spiritually sensitive practices have endured in the field of mental health. He calls for more inclusive understandings of the roles that spirituality plays in his work as a mental health educator and practitioner. Kanako Okuda, in "The Spiritual Call to Social Work," finds her calling to help others in and of itself a type of spiritual journey; Okuda's journey from the Buddhist practices she grew up with in Japan into the "New Age" spirituality she found in the United States guides Okuda in her role as a fieldwork director, where she helps her MSW students make meaning through spiritual job crafting.

While the first two chapters are rooted in the ways we train early career clinicians in spiritual practices, the rest of the chapters offer examples of clinicians who encounter and employ non-mainstream spiritual practices in their work. Michael Garbe, in "Spiritual Emergence and Spiritual Emergency," offers the case of a client he guided through a kundalini awakening: when life force energy located at the base of the spine spirals through the activation of all of one's chakras, which can be an overwhelming experience at best. In Chapter 4, Cristina Blasoni, a clinical social worker who runs "hearing voices" groups for clients who are considered both mentally ill and chemically addicted, demonstrates her de-stigmatization of voice hearers by practicing radical empathy. Michael Jarrette-Kenny, in Chapter 5, examines meditation practice and an Ayahuasca/plant medicine ceremony to find that these practices and "the attendant experiences of spiritual awakening are extremely powerful, regardless of the neurobiological substrates."

In juxtaposition to Jarrette-Kenny's description of plant medicine and psychedelic "trips," we present Debra Ruisard's "A Power Greater: Exploring Spirituality in Addiction Recovery" as our sixth chapter. Ruisard finds that while the 12-steps' foundations in mainstream religion are helpful to some, many of her substance-addicted clients find sobriety from spiritualties that do not depend on a God figure. Similarly, Bianca Channer's case study on "The Spirituality of Incarceration" explores the spiritual power that develops when one is taken from mainstream society and forced to reckon with his belief system out of desperation and in isolation. The spirituality of isolation is clear in Chapter 8, where Robin Wiley presents a case on mindfulness practice in her population of older adults (ages 70–100). Wiley argues that while many current treatments, like Life Review, are standard practice for folks living out the last stage of the cycle, mindfulness keeps the elderly present rather than stuck in the past or worried about the future.

Chapters 9 and 10 close the book with chapters that integrate yoga and Reiki into mental health practice. Joan Ordille, in "The Asana of Being with Living and Dying: Reflections from a Day of Hospice Social Work," discusses how the tenants of Eastern contemplative practice and philosophy, which view living and dying on the same continuum, complement the hospice philosophy of care while providing a holistic and integrated, body-mind-spirit approach to clinical practice. In Lynda Fabbo's chapter, she finds a shared spiritual energy among early psychoanalytic practice and modern alternative therapies, specifically reiki. Fabbo's case describes a personal spiritual awakening, something like my own, which leads her from evidence-based psychotherapy practices into her certification as a reiki provider.

★ ★ ★

This collection of cases builds off of traditional work on spirituality in mental health practice in order to expand the definition of spirituality in and beyond its relationship with religion. As editors, we know that the narratives printed here serve as evidence that compels readers to consider their assumptions about what constitutes spirituality for clients and clinicians. However, the podcasts that Widian Nicola has produced to accompany these chapters open the door to our pedagogy of active listening, or "close hearing," a form of close reading that promotes radical empathy. When one hears the actual voices of professionals involved in our pursuit—without the distraction of their visages on the screen—one engages in the kind of deep, active listening that is necessary to begin new, sometimes uncomfortable, and even scary conversations. We believe that conversations bring about change not only through one's sharing of experience or opinion, but through listening "to" rather than listening "for." In other words, we hope that the connections between the podcasts and the chapters in this volume elicit respect for our topic rather than the immediate defense mechanism of looking for "crazy" in relation to the spiritual. To that end, I lead you to Nicola's introduction to the pedagogy of this book, which features questions that relate the readings to the podcasts. The podcasts are available on the *E-Resources page* for personal use and use in the classroom.

References

Emba, C. (2019, October 27). Why millennials are skipping church and not going back. *The Washington Post*. https://www.washingtonpost.com/opinions/why-millennials-are-skipping-church-and-not-going-back/2019/10/27/0d35b972-f777-11e9-8cf0-4cc99f74d127_story.html

Freeman, M. (2019, October). Time use of millennials and nonmillennials. *The Bureau of Labor Statistics*. https://www.bls.gov/opub/mlr/2019/article/time-use-of-millennials-and-nonmillennials.htm

Pew Research Center. (2019, October 17). In U.S., decline of Christianity continues at rapid pace: An update on America's changing religious landscape. Washington, DC. https://www.pewforum.org/2019/10/17/in-u-s-decline-of-christianity-continues-at-rapid-pace/

INTRODUCTION

Making the Case for Podcasts

Widian Nicola

Social work is guided by a few simple notions: that people are built for connection, that every person matters, that we have a responsibility to uphold the dignity of all those we meet, and that attentive, empathic listening is the gateway to real, personal, and social change. Creatively teaching social work students the importance of this *embodied* identity, particularly listening, is essential. If psychotherapy, and by extension social work, is "good communication *within* and *between* people," as Carl Rogers (1992) suggests, then the latter is also true: "empathic understanding – understanding *with* a person, not *about* her" is a key distinction in how we relate to those with whom we work (p. 106). In other words, while listening is often associated with passivity or, conversely, the need to quickly "fix" the issues being presented, in the field of social work, listening is a fundamentally relational, engaged process that moves beyond evaluation and assessment. Instead, listening, particularly with intentional therapeutic attention, esteems connection. This connection, which is central to social work, can lead to individual and systemic change.

While diverse fields of study have offered a plethora of considerations on the mechanics of listening (Haley et al., 2017; Halone, Cunconan, Coakley, & Wolvin, 1998; Rogers & Welch, 2009), others have offered theoretical reflections (and implications) related to listening (Lipari, 2010; McRae, 2015; Palmer-Mehta, 2016). As Palmer-Mehta (2016) notes in her examination of the discourses of the US radical lesbian feminist Andrea Dworkin, "failing to listen enables oppressive structures to reproduce" (p. 4177). Thus, multi-dimensional instruction that emphasizes both the mechanical process *and* the theoretical social significance of listening is necessary in effective social work pedagogy. A case study, for example, reveals the clinical complexities of a client's lived experience. Likewise, that same case study can also reveal the way in which larger social systems impact the client. Further, that same case study invites the reader to participate in the intersubjective nature of meaning-making and the call to action. Through reflexivity and the "empathic work of understanding" (Hollan, 2008, p. 487) the experience of another, students can learn to listen and integrate the nuanced aspects of a client's lived experience and be inspired to connect more deeply and act more effectively. Ultimately, as Palmer-Mehta (2016) highlights, "personal stories have the potential to provide concrete knowledge that may serve as the basis of challenging social structures and motivating collective action" (p. 4178) that go well beyond the case study or social work interview.

Lipari (2010) takes a similar ethical social stance and contends that "*listening being...* can reveal the ethical possibilities that arise when listening begins not from a speaking, but from the emptiness of awareness itself — a place from which human beings can both *be* and *become*" (p. 348). While Palmer-Mehta (2016) suggests a theoretical approach to listening, Lipari (2010) suggests a philosophical, "utopian" view whereby listening is an *embodied* experience and is a "dwelling place from where we offer our ethical response, our hospitality, to the other and the world" (p. 350). Thus, listening as a process of knowing and learning (McRae, 2015) about others also requires a willingness on the part of the listener to be changed by the message, as well as the messenger. Given the fundamental social nature of the profession, it must be the goal of social work educators to creatively train students in the mechanics of listening (Haley et al., 2017), as well on listening systemically, relationally (Halone et al., 1998; Jones, 2011), multi-dimensionally (Halone et al., 1998), and multi-culturally (Grant & Bolin, 2016).

Podcasts as a Teaching Tool

Various multimedia tools have shown to enrich the learning experience for social work students (Grant & Bolin, 2016; Lenette, Cox, & Brough, 2015; Loya & Klemm, 2016; Walsh, Shier, Sitter, & Sieppert, 2010). Although a relatively new instructive modality, podcasts are being used more frequently in classrooms due to their pedagogical efficacy. For example, Hill, Nelson, France, and Woodland (2012) found that podcasts are perceived as an effective tool in supporting learning, largely by offering a flexible and portable learning experience. Likewise, Merhi (2015) examined student podcast adoption with survey data collected from 352 students in a higher education institution and found that podcasting provides students the ability to build their knowledge and learn individually in a unique way. Additionally, Fernandez, Simo, and Sallan (2009) conducted a study that consisted of the creation and broadcast of 13 podcasts over 4 months in which 90 distance students took part. The study revealed that podcasting is a powerful tool as a complement to traditional course resources, but "not regardless of them" (p. 391). Not surprisingly, with the increased demand in higher education to incorporate multimedia into the classroom, podcasts are becoming a means by which this demand can be met (Evans, 2008).

As with social work, a podcast is a medium built on the power of connection, specifically through conversation. Defined, a "podcast (an amalgam of the word broadcast and the iPod digital audio player) is essentially a broadcast of digital audio files on the web that users can listen to on their computer or digital audio player (e.g., iPod)" (Swan & Hofer, 2009, p. 95). Beyond the classroom, these conveniently accessed and consumed digital audio files are increasingly becoming an effective instrument for disseminating and gaining new knowledge for general audiences. Not unlike written case studies used to illustrate the profound complexities of client experiences, digital case studies (also referred to as oral histories or digital narratives) delivered in audio form have the capability to reflect the same complexity when used in social work classrooms. Additionally, the platform challenges the listener to engage with the content and critically listen in context.

Similar to the use of movies (Hudock & Warden, 2001) or Technology, Education, and Design (TED) talks (Loya & Klemm, 2016) in education, digital narratives/oral histories can develop listening skills in social work students as well as have the potential to empower them (Merhi, 2015). While instructors may find some challenges in the use of this relatively new technology, the benefits have been shown to favor student learning. For example, a study conducted by Brown et al. (2009) highlighted the usefulness of podcast among 11 faculty members at Southeastern University in which students reported a "much greater sense of social (online) presence based on the podcasting" (p. 367), as well as an increase in the sense of "social presence that creates a strong argument for making use of podcasting technology to provide through voice and image a more intimate, human experience for distant learners" (p. 370). Furthermore, the use of instructor-generated podcasts in nursing education has also shown to be effective in "sparking student learning and critical thinking" (Hargett, 2018, p. 55).

While there are countless genres of podcasts available for consumption, this book provides directly linked podcast interviews to supplement and complement each chapter. Various experts within the field of social work provide insights and enhanced considerations of each chapter's themes, while other contributors provide personal narratives of their lived experiences.

One such expert is Adam Powell, Junior Research Fellow in the Department of Theology and Religion at Durham University. His interview offers an expansive overview of his research in the Hearing the Voice interdisciplinary study of voice hearing. In addition to shedding light on the relations between hearing voices and everyday processes of sensory perception, memory, language, and creativity, the Hearing the Voice team "explores why it is that some voices (and not others) are experienced as distressing, how they can change across the life course, and the ways in which voices can act as important social, cultural and political forces" (https://hearingthevoice.org). As such, Dr. Powell introduces us to his research with spiritualists who designate their voice-hearing experiences as a form of clairaudience, as well as the lived experience of other voice hearers, specifically those who have received a diagnosis of schizophrenia or some other psychosis. He offers listeners an array of considerations regarding the way in which we can understand voice hearing both objectively and esteem for the connective sense of identity of those who hear voices.

In another audio, listeners are invited into an intimate illustration of the life of a woman in recovery from substance abuse. While extensive interdisciplinary literature has offered us vast insights regarding the epistemological, cultural, historical, and epigenetic bases for addictions, in this audio, the narrator details the personal and fundamental aspects of her lived experience of alienation, connection, and desperation in her experience of substance use and recovery. A more nuanced experience, the personal position the narrator takes is paradoxically singular, yet is arguably a generalized aspect of the human journey of healing.

Although most humans are acquainted with grief, loss and suffering are particularly painful and difficult to comprehend at early stages of development. In a moving and powerful account, a child specialist clarifies the ways in which, through her work, she has used play to help children understand and communicate their interior experiences of the external world, particularly in healthcare settings. Making sense of the frailty of their bodies, the potential and looming possibility of death, as well as discussions about the afterlife, the narrator conveys the vulnerable and deeply emotional experiences of children on the verge of death.

In yet another audio, we hear the confident and grounded voice of a seasoned social worker who outlines and illuminates the fascinating and curious journey of how she chose – and continues to choose – the inspired life of social work. As a woman, and particularly as someone who identifies as being divinely inspired to action, the narrator gives listeners a glimpse into a realm of possibility in living out "the call" in the social work profession, one that is engaged, reflective, and collaborative. And, while the narrator's experience is both nuanced and singular, the listener is invited to connect to the themes that bridge differences and, thus, resonate on deeper levels.

As a social worker and rabbi, one narrator points readers to enter into the deeply perplexing, complicated, and forgiving crossroads of life and death, particularly related to pregnancy loss. While Rabbi S introduces the parameters of how miscarriage can be understood in Judaism, she emphasizes the cultural distinctions within the faith tradition. While religious rituals do not exist for miscarriages, she reveals the healing power of the community's religious response to loss. Rabbi S also points to the various understandings of when the soul enters the body and when life begins, but esteems the direct obligation by the community to comfort a mourning parent in their process of bereavement no matter the philosophical or religious interpretation of the law.

We also feature a psychic medium and Reiki practitioner, Karen, and her long-time student, Lynda Fabbo, invite listeners into an intimate conversation about the healing properties of Reiki. The two discuss the exchange between the healer and the person in need of healing, one that is both passive (client) and spiritually accessible (practitioner). The two elaborate, as well as illuminate the captivating aspects of the connection between the spirit world and the physical world, highlighting the essential embodied posture of the healer as merely a conduit of a Universal energy that ultimately bestows the healing.

Lastly, social work clinician Michael Garbe confronts the difficult question of suffering considered throughout human history. As someone who has experienced a kundalini awakening, Dr. Garbe expresses the centrality of the work of a social worker: to provide a space whereby clients can freely and openly express their spiritual experiences, particularly within predominantly medically based models of suffering and illness. The narrator attests to the centrality of spiritual work with clients, particularly those who have experienced trauma. It is in this work of touching suffering that clients can experience a spiritual emergence and spiritual awakening.

Finally, in order to enhance the close listening experience of the listener, a reflexive methodology adopted from Jaffe, Floersch, Longhofer, and Winograd (2018), which allows students to cultivate a richer listening practice that is relational, multi-dimensional, and multicultural, is provided for each podcast interview.

Privileging Narrative Podcasts in Social Work Education

Narratives are a lot like icebergs: what is shared is what can be seen above the surface of the water. As the metaphor suggests, though, the multiplicity and multi-dimensionality of a person's story and lived experience: their emotions, perceptions, expectations, and the need for connection lie undiscovered on deeper levels. Hence, a story told in first person is a sacred disclosure of sorts, whereby hidden details lurk deep beneath.

In many helping professions, narratives are often questioned or pathologized. As physicians Good et al. (1982) contend, "the term story seems to imply a fictional quality lacking the urgency to be accurate in representing diseases and responding… [thus] physicians learn to distrust patients' stories as inaccurate by purpose or by accident. They learn to 'edit' patients' account" (pp. 66–67). Yet, while the term "story" may imply a fictional quality to some practitioners, it is no less telling of the universal truths of the human experience. Narratives often reveal what is on the surface, and conversely, what has yet to be explored. More recently, Greenfield et al. (2015) also recognize the value in the use of narrative as a valuable pedagogical tool in the medical field – in this case, for physical therapist students, residents, and clinicians to develop skills of reflection and reflexivity in clinical practice. They contend that narrative enhances the learner's reflective and interpretive practice, and, ultimately, the clinical care provided by the learner or practitioner. Thus, "the aim of reflection," they contend, "is designed to be transformative—aiming for new levels of understanding, meaning, and insights about clinical care" (p. 925). Ultimately, the sharing of the story is the story itself and hence articulates the human desire to move from the shallow to the deep; it is neither diagnosis nor craft, but rather a process. Educating social work students to be curious about what is below the surface – meaning, intention, desire – in addition to what is overtly said, is essential to good social work practice.

The narrative exchange process between the storyteller and the listener is fundamentally relational. For social work students, cultivating an embodied listening posture is a critical element of engaging in the narrative exchange. Given the extensive research that has been done on the positive impact of the therapeutic alliance (Horvath & Symonds, 1991; Martin, Garske, & Davis, 2000; Safran, Muran, & Proskurov, 2009), or the "something more" (Tronick, 2007, p. 420) that accounts for positive client outcomes, teaching effective, supportive, and therapeutic listening skills – beyond the mechanics – is vital to long-term positive client outcomes. In my experience of working with students, the persistent practice of embodied listening has shown to produce higher levels of empathy. Some research also suggests that hearing narrative (or stories) can improve learning and recall, as well as increase students' interest (Glonek & King, 2014). This recall is important, particularly as students are learning and cultivating the practice of double listening (Guilfoyle, 2015), identifying themes and patterns, and building ongoing rapport with clients. As many seasoned social work practitioners and educators can attest, the mechanics of listening is only part of the exchange process. An embodied listening posture that includes curiosity, humility, imagination, and a desire to participate in the narrative collaboratively completes the process. Perhaps that is why narratives are memorable: they are embedded as more than just stories, but resonant connections.

The resonant qualities of an active, empathic exchange are not only relational but also favorable to the parts of our experiences that are mechanical in nature. "Narratives serve as mnemonic devices in a number of ways," Lenette et al. (2015) contend, "creating a compelling motivation for the listener, invoking historical memory, and uniquely suited for the employment of metaphor" (p. 32). The benefit of increased motivation is priceless, particularly when those narratives highlight the plight of vulnerable populations. As Grant and Bolin (2016) discovered in their use of digital storytelling, "diversity awareness and cultural competency, as related to education as well as professional work, is crucial to communication, advocacy, building relationships and communities, reducing prejudice and stereotyping, transforming conflict, and developing leadership" (p. 46). Further, they discovered this form of narrative distribution to deepen understanding and empathy of community inequities and diverse human experiences (p. 47). As such, first-person narratives are a means by which the listener can enter into the experience of the storyteller. This is significant for social work students who, by virtue of their educational placement, are, as practitioners in training, learning the "centrality and privilege of storytelling" in their future practice with their clients (Charon, 2005, p. 261).

In the listening, students are likely to discover that what is above the surface in a narrative is not always congruent with what is below. In other words, a practice of critical listening fosters students' ability to hear beyond and beneath what is said, enhancing the use of the "third ear" for later practice (Reik, 1948), placing the client's experience at the center of the narrative, rather than the practitioner's assumptions and biases. As Good et al. (1982) reveal,

> in the evolution of their medical training, not unlike social work, students witness client narratives that become practitioner-centered, whereby the practitioner is in control, dictates what is said and omitted, and offers a conclusion through technical interventions articulated by the practitioner.
>
> *(p. 58)*

This arbitrary nature prevents the social worker, as well as the client, from fully experiencing and expressing the deeper, client-defined reality taking place below the surface. Thus, what makes listening to narrative storytelling effective for social work students is multifold.

A "close hearing" of the narrative (or oral history) allows students to explore and define the components of a critical listening practice that cannot be achieved in text-only form. While it can also be a means by which students learn about current events and the contexts in which the storyteller resides, this form allows students to "listen to" as well as "listen for" a variety of explanations within an experience. In other words, paying attention to contextual surround sound, a unique perspective to social work, allows students to "listen to" the storyteller, as well as "listen for" the systems of influence of which the storyteller is a part. This multi-dimensional listening is a key ingredient in enhancing student competency and connection for later practice. In a more ideological way, the power of narrative decongests the expectations and tendencies social work students have toward the need to neatly package client problems and solutions or be robotic in their role as social worker. Narratives can often invite new social workers into a place of uncertainty, non-doing, and unknowing, whereby they are challenged to pay attention and listen critically, *then* become inspired to action. Further, the hearing of a narrative can both illuminate the client's expert role in his or her life, and highlight the students' needs to expand his or her understanding of clients' unique experiences as well as empathic capacity that requires an ongoing intersubjective process (Hollan, 2008). Finally, a relational, multi-dimensional, and multi-cultural listening practice is an ethical responsibility in the process of challenging systems of oppression, expanding perceptions, and demonstrating a commitment to cultural competence, diversity, and social justice.

Reflexive Methodology in the Use of Podcasts

Personal reflection is an integral part of learning. It heightens self-awareness and improves critical thinking (Wain, 2017), as well as facilitates meaning-making (Costa & Kallick, 2009). By definition, reflection involves "taking the unprocessed, raw material of experience and engaging with it as a way to make sense of what has occurred. It involves exploring often messy and confused events and focusing on the thoughts and emotions that accompany them" (Boud, 2001, p. 10). For social work educators, reflection is a pedagogical tool that allows students to decrease the distance between theory and practice. Further, it allows students to explore their subjective experiences, attitudes, and biases toward that which they are exposed to: diverse ideas, lifestyle choices, decisions, and value systems that clients hold (Greenfield et al., 2015). Ultimately, reflection is a means by which students can identify their connection to the narrative – on a micro level, and especially on a macro level. Reflexivity coupled with narrative, then, is a means by which social work students can gain knowledge and skill through a broader epistemological basis for thoughtful, intentional clinical practice.

Structure of Assignment

"Close hearing" is directly linked to "close reading," now being used more intentionally in social work education by Jaffe (2018). Jaffe (2018) defines "close reading" as:

> The careful, sustained interpretation of a text. Such a reading places great emphasis on the particular over the general and pays close attention to syntax, tone, rhetorical devices, the order in which sentences and ideas unfold as they are read, and individual vocabulary words in relation to their context. This requires the definition of key terms and phrases as well as the reader's *response* to them as a method to promote the discovery of purpose, different levels of meaning, and connective thinking.
>
> *(p. 8)*

A parallel process to "close reading," a pedagogical approach to enhance student learning and ultimately, practice, "close hearing" can be defined as the careful, sustained interpretation of a narrative. While the listener pays close attention to tone, contextual surround sound, affect, word choice, and deeper meaning, "close hearing" requires a reflexive, critical, and connective component, that is, the bridge that translates what is said in the narrative into social work practice skills. As a result, this intentional form of *embodied* listening is best cultivated and enhanced through a reflexive methodology.

The following reflexive methodology or formula can be adapted to the supplemental audio narratives for this text, as well as any narrative podcast or audio of the educator's choosing. Borrowed from Jaffe et al. (2018) and adapted to audio form, the complementary assignments permit students to demonstrate the skill of close hearing, critical/connective thinking, as well as cultivate a richer listening practice that is relational, multi-dimensional, and multicultural.

1. Pre-listening. Designed by the instructor, pre-listening questions introduce general social work topics and help students to assess their own theoretical assumptions about those topics. As prompts for class discussion and/or quick writing exercises, the first set of questions is designed to reveal what students want to learn from the story they are going to listen to: what they know and what they do not know. The questions ask students to define key terms and to think about how their own experiences will inform their listening before they even start. Students are encouraged to identify their preconceived notions and to track how their thinking changes through the act of listening to the narrative podcast.

2. Close-listening. Close-listening questions offer a framework to discuss, with attention to specific sets of words, the details in the story that drive the conceptual argument. Initially, the questions ask for some summary as a way to test the students' more basic understanding of the content. But the secondary close hearing questions encourage students to explore the storyteller's motivations for including certain details of the story.

3. Connective thinking. Connective thinking questions privilege the student's voice. Students have been well trained to regurgitate the right answers, but this section puts a variety of answers into conversation with each other. These questions often pair narratives with other narratives and research articles so that students can evaluate how one set of ideas sits in relation to another set of ideas. These pairings often call for the student to make connections between several narratives. Students are asked to generate their own ideas about what the story and its theoretical frameworks can teach them about important elements of their own practice.

Assignments can be completed in essay form or through in-class discussions. Most importantly, educators are encouraged to preserve the reflective nature of the learning process. The above-provided reflexive methodology emphasizes students' connections to the stories they will hear and the participatory nature of being in conversation with the message delivered by the storyteller.

Conclusion

Finding creative ways to engage students in the learning process can be a challenge. And it can also be exciting. Of particular interest to social work educators is a call to action to educate on micro and macro levels of service. On that note, it is imperative that educators continue to train and equip students to be critical, reflective thinkers who are connected with clients and causes in the office and beyond. And, "as social work education prepares for the next generation of social work students," Ahmedani, Harold, Fitton, and Shifflet contend (2011), "the current method of teaching must also be influenced by technology" (p. 842). On that note, social work education must continue to evolve to meet the growing need of an ever-evolving student body. Given the pedagogical efficacy of podcast use in the classroom, educators can expand the means by which they facilitate the adoption of an embodied listener identity among students. Through the use of an adapted reflexive methodology, students can cultivate a richer listening practice that is relational, multi-dimensional, and multicultural.

References

Ahmedani, B. K., Harold, R. D., Fitton, V. A., & Shifflet Gibson, E. D. (2011). What adolescent can tell us: Technology and the future of social work education. *Social Work Education, 30*(7), 830.

Boud, D. (2001). Using journal writing to enhance reflective practice. *New Directions for Adult & Continuing Education, 2001*(90), 9.

Brown, A., Brown, C., Fine, B., Luterbach, K., Sugar, W., & Vinciguerra, D. C. (2009). Instructional uses of podcasting in online learning environments: A cooperative inquiry Study. *Journal of Educational Technology Systems, 37*(4), 351–371.

Charon, R. (2005). Narrative medicine: Attention, representation, affiliation. *Narrative, 13*(3), 261.

Costa, A. L., & Kallick, B. (2009). Learning and leading with habits of mind: 16 essential characteristics for success. *Adolescence, 44*(173), 245.

Evans, C. (2008). The effectiveness of m-learning in the form of podcast revision lectures in higher education. *Computers and Education, 50*(2), 491–498.

Fernandez, V., Simo, P., & Sallan, J. M. (2009). Podcasting: A new technological tool to facilitate good practice in higher education. *Computers & Education, 5*(3), 385–392.

Glonek, K. L., & King, P. E. (2014). Listening to narratives: An experimental examination of storytelling in the classroom. *International Journal of Listening, 28*(1), 32–46.

Good, B., Herrera, H., Delvecchio Good, M., Cooper, J., Good, B. J., Herrera, H., & Cooper, J. (1982). Reflexivity and countertransference in a psychiatric cultural consultation clinic. *Culture, Medicine & Psychiatry, 6*(3), 281.

Grant, N. S., & Bolin, B. L. (2016). Digital storytelling: A method for engaging students and increasing cultural competency. *Journal of Effective Teaching, 16*(3), 44–61.

Greenfield, B. H., Jensen, G. M., Delany, C. M., Mostrom, E., Knab, M., & Jampel, A. (2015). Power and promise of narrative for advancing physical therapist education and practice. *Physical Therapy, 95*(6), 924–933.

Guilfoyle, M. (2015). Listening in narrative therapy: Double listening and empathic positioning. *South African Journal of Psychology, 45*(1), 36–49.

Haley, B., Heo, S., Wright, P., Barone, C., Rao Rettiganti, M., & Anders, M. (2017). Relationships among active listening, self-awareness, empathy, and patient-centered care in associate and baccalaureate degree nursing students. *Nursing Plus, 3,* 11–16.

Halone, K. K., Cunconan, T. M., Coakley, C. G., & Wolvin, A. D. (1998). Toward the establishment of general dimensions underlying the listening process. *International Journal of Listening, 12*(1), 12–28.

Hargett, J. L. (2018). Podcasting in nursing education: Using commercially prepared podcasts to spark learning. *Teaching & Learning in Nursing, 13*(1), 55–57.

Hearing the Voice. Retrieved from www.hearingthevoice.com

Hill, J., Nelson, A., France, D., & Woodland, W. (2012). Integrating podcast technology effectively into student learning: A reflexive examination. *Journal of Geography in Higher Education, 36*(3), 437–454.

Hollan, D. (2008). Being there: On the imaginative aspects of understanding others and being understood. *Ethos, 36*(4), 475–489.

Horvath, A. O., & Symonds, B. D. (1991). Relation between working alliance and outcome in psychotherapy: A meta-anaysis. *Journal of Counseling Psychology, 38*(2), 139–149.

Hudock, A. J., & Warden, S. G. (2001). Using movies to teach family systems concepts. *The Family Journal, 9*(2), 116–121.

Jaffe, M. (2018). *The "practice" of close reading and writing in social work education.* Unpublished manuscript.

Jaffe, M., Floersch, J., Longhofer, J., & Winograd, W. (2018). *The social work and k-12 schools casebook: Phenomenological perspectives.* New York, NY: Routledge.

Jones, S. M. (2011). Supportive listening. *International Journal of Listening, 25*(1/2), 85–103.

Lenette, C., Cox, L., & Brough, M. (2015). Digital storytelling as a social work tool: Learning from ethnographic research with women from refugee backgrounds. *British Journal of Social Work, 45*(3), 988.

Lipari, L. (2010). Listening, thinking, being. *Communication Theory, 20*(3), 348–362.

Loya, M. A., & Klemm, T. (2016). Teaching note—Using TED talks in the social work classroom: Encouraging student engagement and discourse. *Journal of Social Work Education, 52*(4), 518–523.

Martin, D., Garske, J., & Davis, M. (2000). Relation of the therapeutic alliance with other outcome and other variables: A meta-analytic review. *Journal of Consulting and Clinical Psychology, 68,* 438–450.

McRae, C. (2015). *Performative listening: Hearing others in qualitative research.* New York, NY: Peter Lang.

Merhi, M. I. (2015). Factors influencing higher education students to adopt podcast: An empirical study. *Computers & Education, 8*(3), 32–43.

Palmer-Mehta, V. (2016). Theorizing listening as a tool for social change: Andrea Dworkin's discourses on listening. *International Journal of Communication* (Online), *10,* 4176–4192.

Reik, T. (1948). *Listening with the third ear: The inner experience of a psychoanalyst.* New York, NY: Grove.

Rogers, A., & Welch, B. (2009). Using standardized clients in the classroom: An evaluation of a training module to teach active listening skills to social work students. *Journal of Teaching Social Work, 29*(2), 153–168.

Rogers, C. R. (1992). The necessary and sufficient conditions of therapeutic personality change. *Journal of Counseling and Clinical Psychology, 60*(6), 827–832.

Safran, J. D., Muran, J. C., & Proskurov, B. (2009). Alliance, negotiation, and rupture resolution. In R. Levy & S. J. Ablon (Eds.), *Handbook of evidence based psychodynamic psychotherapy* (pp. 201–205). New York, NY: Humana Press.

Swan, K. O., & Hofer, M. (2009). Trend alert: A history teacher's guide to using podcasts in the classroom. *Social Education, 73*(2), 95–102.

Tronick, E. (2007). Chapter 31: Noninterpretive mechanism in psychoanalytic therapy: The "something more" than interpretation. In *The neurobehavioral and social-emotional development of infants and children* (pp. 418–438). New York, NY: W.W. Norton & Co.

Wain, A. (2017). Learning through reflection. *British Journal of Midwifery, 25*(10), 662–666.

Walsh, C. A., Shier, M. L., Sitter, K. C., & Sieppert, J. D. (2010). Applied methods of teaching about oppression and diversity to graduate social work students: A case example of digital stories. *Canadian Journal for the Scholarship of Teaching and Learning, 1*(2).

PODCAST PAIRINGS WITH CHAPTERS AND CLOSE HEARING QUESTIONS

For more questions that relate the podcasts to chapters, please see the "Prompts for Thinking and Writing" at the end of each chapter.

Narratives are a lot like icebergs: what is shared is what can be seen above the surface of the water. As the metaphor suggests, though, the multiplicity and multi-dimensionality of a person's story and lived experience: their emotions, perceptions, expectations, and the need for connection lie undiscovered on deeper levels. Hence, a story told in first person is a sacred disclosure of sorts, whereby hidden details lurk deep beneath.

By tuning in to this audio, you are invited into a sacred disclosure of sorts. Here, you will hear a reflection of the themes presented in the corresponding chapter. In order to hear beyond and beneath what is said, by paying close attention to tone, contextual surround sound, affect, word choice, and deeper meaning, you are encouraged to place the storyteller's experience at the center of the narrative. This careful, sustained attention gives way to an embodied listening experience, a posture that creates real, personal, and social change. After all, this is what social work is all about.

Podcasts:

Addiction and Spirituality

As you enter into this unique narrative, please consider the following pre-listening questions:

This podcast can be productively paired with a chapter by Ruisard.

1. The complex etiology of addiction is reflected in the historical tensions between contrasting attitudes still deliberated today: whether or not addiction is a matter of will power, morality, biology, or social pressures. How do you understand the phenomenology of addiction as you listen to this unique narrative?
2. While there are a number of treatment options available to those who suffer from addiction, how might we understand the reasons why some individuals are successful in treating their addiction while others are not?
3. Many individuals, particularly those who consider themselves members of Alcoholics Anonymous, turn to a "God of my own understanding," in their attempts to maintain sobriety. How might we understand the power of this spiritual element for those in recovery?

The Spirituality of Grief and Loss in Children

★*This podcast can be productively paired with chapters authored by Wiley and Ordille.*
    As you enter into this unique narrative, please consider the following pre-listening questions:

1. Although most humans are acquainted with grief, loss and suffering are particularly painful and difficult to comprehend at early stages of development. How might we understand the grief and loss process through the lens of early childhood development?
2. Making sense of the frailty of their bodies, the potential and looming possibility of death, as well as discussions about the afterlife, children are drawn to and have a strong propensity for that which is spiritual. How might the narrative help you understand the reasons why?
3. Do you recall your spiritual experiences at a young age? If so, how might those resonant memories be translated into what you hear here?

Spiritual Awakening

★*This podcast can be productively paired with a chapter by Garbe.*
    As you enter into this unique narrative, please consider the following pre-listening questions:

1. Can you remember a time in your life when you experienced a transcendental awakening or healing? If so, how do you understand that experience today?
2. While spiritual healings have been a transformative reality for people throughout history, how might we reconcile those experiences with our understanding of neuroplasticity and what we know about the life-long process of development and change?

3. The centrality of the work of a social worker is to provide a space whereby clients can freely and openly express their spiritual experiences, particularly within predominantly medically based models of suffering and illness. What do you see as the primary benefits of this type of allowance in the healing process of our clients?

Reiki as a Healing Spiritual Practice

★This podcast can be productively paired with chapters by Fabbo and Blasoni.
  As you enter into this unique narrative, please consider the following pre-listening questions:

1. The spiritual practice of Reiki is believed to connect the physical world to the spiritual world by a channeling of energy to restore balance and bring healing. How might we understand healing in light of medical explanations about the body/spirit dualism?
2. What is the relationship between the healer and the person in need of healing? How does this differ, if at all, from the role of a social work practitioner?

The Spiritual Call to Social Work

★This podcast can be productively paired with chapters by Nicotera and Okuda.
  As you enter into this unique narrative, please consider the following pre-listening questions:

1. Many social workers claim to be in the profession because they are "called" by a Higher Power. How might that description resonate for you, or not?
2. Social work is fundamentally relational and has the capacity to heal relational ruptures. What lens do you use in the way in which you approach your clients or understand your work?

Voice Hearing

★This podcast can be productively paired with Jaffe's preface and a chapter by Blasoni.
  As you enter into this unique narrative, please consider the following pre-listening questions:

1. How do I understand the experience of a voice hearer?
2. The experience of hearing voices continues to be stigmatizing. How might we understand the phenomenon more objectively from the narrative you are about to hear?
3. Given what I've heard, what is my primary take-away about this unique and nuanced phenomenon?

Miscarriage and Judaism

★This podcast can be productively paired with the preface by Jaffe and a chapter by Ramos-Channer.

As you enter into this unique narrative, please consider the following pre-listening questions:

1. Debates about when life "begins" can often create a barrier to entering into the lived experience of a woman who has miscarried, distracting us from being still in the process of grief. How do we make sense of the relational aspects of life in and outside the womb?
2. Many women experience miscarriage a traumatic event that can be painful and enduring. Prayer, maintaining a connection to the child in the spiritual realm, as well as a ritual to honor the life of the child can be important aspects of healing for those who have experienced miscarriages. How might spiritual expression and/or religion play a role in meaning-making in regard to death, grief, and loss?

1

A HISTORY OF SPIRITUALITY, RELIGION, AND SOCIAL WORK

Using the "Circle of Insight" to Challenge, Question, and Create a Framework for Spiritually Sensitive Practice

Anthony Nicotera

Pre-Reading Questions

1. What do you make of the ethical requirement to extend our curiosity about our clients' spiritualities? Is there a distinction between "spirituality" and "spiritualities"?
2. What do you believe is the minimum amount of training in "spirituality" that a mental health practitioner should acquire? What is the ideal amount of training? What is your own level of training?
3. How would you define the differences and connections between "religion" and "spirituality"?

Understanding Spirituality and Religion

A vital step in addressing the tensions, questions, and complexities inherent in spiritually sensitive social work pedagogy and practice includes more fully exploring the epistemological challenges of what we mean by spirituality and religion. Generally, spirituality is understood to be a universal and fundamental human quality consisting of the search for a sense of meaning, purpose, morality, well-being, and profundity in relationships with ourselves, others, and ultimate reality. Religion, however, involves an institutionalized, systematic pattern of values, beliefs, symbols, behaviors, and experiences oriented toward spiritual concerns, shared by a community, and transmitted over time in traditions, often relying on a set of scriptures, teachings, or moral code of conduct and rituals (Canda, Furman, & Canda, 2020; Dudley, 2016; Koenig, 2008;

Oxhandler, & Pargament, 2014). Careful examination of these terms, as well as conversations among scholars and students, and practitioners and clients, about their respective theoretical and practical understanding of these concepts, provides an important foundation for spiritually sensitive social work practice and pedagogy. As Dudley (2016) asserts, "a consensus on a specific definition of spirituality may be less important to provide to others than encouragement for them to define spirituality for themselves" (p. 8). Arguably, for social workers engaging in spiritually sensitive social work practice, it is as important to understand how a person or group understands and actualizes the concepts of spirituality and religion as it is to understand more formal, scholarly definitions of these terms, if not more so.

Additionally, in light of the nuanced, complex, often ambiguous, and subjective nature of these concepts and distinctions, many researchers have asserted that a single definition of spirituality is not realistic (Belcher, & Sarmiento Mellinger, 2016; Corry, Lewis, & Mallett, 2014). For example, some argue that spirituality reduced to mere meaning-making does not distinguish it from moral or ethical inquiry. Thus, words like divine, god, higher power, and even mystery, they assert, should be used explicitly when discussing and defining spirituality. Others argue that using terms like divine and mystery, because they carry religious overtones, potentially exclude those who might consider themselves spiritual but not religious. These terms also exclude those who consider themselves to be atheist or agnostic. Senreich (2013) suggests that we use the less religiously charged word unknown, as opposed to divine, sacred, transcendent, or mystery, when speaking of the spiritual aspect of the person. He argues that using the term unknown honors all people, for "the spiritual component of a bio-psycho-social-spiritual model for social work practice needs to capture each client's relationship to what cannot be known in a way that fully honors that person's belief system and does not exclude any individual's way of perceiving the nature of existence" (Senreich, 2013, p. 553). Using the term unknown avoids conflicts and concerns that people who are spiritual but not religious may have with words such as god, divine, ultimate, or higher power. Senreich's careful contemplation of terminology reminds us too that as important as it is to take the time to examine, describe, and understand common aspects of, and distinctions between, spirituality and religion, it is equally important, maybe more so, to understand how people with a particular viewpoint might uniquely define and react to these terms.

Pew research (2015) affirms that a growing number of people, especially young people, consider themselves to be spiritual but not religious. Others are uncomfortable with spiritual language but affiliate with a particular institutionalized religious tradition. Some are less comfortable with spiritual language but acknowledge mystery and the unknown in life. Some do not pray but will meditate or practice mindfulness. There are many diverse ways in which clients define and practice spirituality and religion. This diversity raises an important creative tension that must be held and maintained. As a counterpoint to Senreich's suggestion, it is quite possible that at least some people who consider themselves religious, or who believe in god, may feel that using the word unknown is not sacred or spiritual enough, or that it objectifies or somehow sanitizes the concept of spirituality, making it less than what it is. While some, like Senreich, may like the word unknown precisely because it does not use god language but still resonates as spiritual in relation to that which is not rationally knowable, others may believe the word unknown to be inadequate. These linguistic challenges remind us of four key considerations that provide context for the complex, multifaceted study and practice of spiritually sensitive social work: language is critically important; language will almost always fall short, be somehow inadequate, or at best incomplete; spirituality and religion are incredibly intimate and always, at some level, personal and subjective; and thus, when engaging in spiritually sensitive social work practice, we must listen first, meeting the client where they are, exploring the nuances and complexities of an individual or group's understanding of these terms as they relate, dialectically, in creative tension, to current research and scholarship.

In addition to studying and investigating key concepts, as defined by both scholars and clients, another related, arguably central, aspect of spiritually sensitive social work practice is what Dudley (2016) refers to as affirming one's own spirituality. He proclaims, "Let's begin a spiritual exploration, not with our clients, but with ourselves" (p. 25). We are invited to do the work required to further examine and define our own spirituality and understanding of faith and religion as a central component of accompanying and counseling clients. Just as doing our own work, engaging in therapy ourselves, contributes to our capacity to be available to clients clinically, so too does exploring critical questions about our own beliefs and spiritual practice contribute to spiritually sensitive social work practice. There is a need to empower and ethically train social workers to effectively engage, assess, practice, and evaluate in a spirituality sensitive way, and this includes their effort to understand and explore their own beliefs about religion and spirituality (Canda et al., 2020; Crisp, 2010; Dudley, 2016; Oxhandler & Pargament, 2014; Sheridan, 2014). Thus, the symphony that is spiritually sensitive social work practice necessarily embraces at least three fundamental movements: how scholars define concepts of religion and spirituality; how these concepts are defined and understood by individuals, groups, organizations, institutions, and society; and how we as social workers seek to understand who we are as spiritual selves.

This chapter provides an overview of some of the creative tensions and critical questions at play in inviting and implementing spiritually sensitive social work pedagogy and practice in the United States, and suggests topics for further research. It also presents an overview of the historical context in which these tensions and questions exist. Finally, it invites application of the "See, Reflect,

Act" Circle of Insight framework (Nicotera, 2018, 2019) to guide contemporary spiritually sensitive social work pedagogy and practice in the context of our ethical code and accreditation standards.

Integrating Spirituality and Religion into Social Work Pedagogy and Practice

While a Jesuit in Jesuit spiritual formation and also an MSW student at a faith-based institution in the mid-1990s, I found it ironic and deeply troubling that there was no course focused on spirituality and social work. In fact, discussing spirituality in social work classes was discouraged. Most often it was simply ignored. If the subjects of religion, faith, or spirituality were raised in the classroom, the most common recommendation was that we not bring them up with clients. This perspective predominated for various reasons. Some professors suggested that spirituality was not our domain, or not relevant to the therapeutic alliance and process, or not supported by research or science, not evidence-based. Well-meaning mentors and educators taught us that engaging in spiritual conversation with clients was beyond our area of expertise. They also told us that addressing spirituality and religion in social work practice could be construed as proselytizing, imposing our views on the client, which would be unethical.

Those of us interested in studying and discussing spirituality in the context of social work pedagogy and practice met in the catacombs of our social work building. There we would talk about our own spiritual lives, the role spirituality, faith, and religion played in meaning-making and identity development, and our understanding of the influence of religion and spirituality on the evolution of social work values, our profession, and the mission of our institution. We talked about what it would mean to practice in a way that respected the spiritual nature of the human person as well as our social work ethical code. As a result of our conversations and meetings, we formed a spirituality and social work student organization and openly asked why social workers were so reluctant to consider the spiritual and religious roots of the social work profession. We wondered together why we were not taught to assess and address a person's spiritual understanding of self. We questioned the ethics of not doing so. We posited that the absence of a bio-psycho-social-spiritual approach to social work compromised our professional ethical commitment to social justice and duty to affirm the inherent human dignity of all people. We postulated that just, ethical social work practice included spiritual and religious assessment, engagement, and reflection personally, and with clients and communities. We advocated for classroom and practice opportunities to integrate spiritual and religious scholarship, and evidence-based practice tools and techniques.

However, despite professional and pedagogical movement toward greater acceptance and inclusion of spiritually sensitive social work practice since my time as a graduate student, spirituality still is not included in most social work curricula, and the majority of social workers, when surveyed, report that they have not been well educated, if at all, about spirituality sensitive social work pedagogy or practice (Canda et al., 2020; Dudley, 2016; Sheridan, 2014). My experience teaching spirituality, social justice, multifaith leadership, and social work courses, and my work as a clinical social worker, pastoral counselor, and chaplain, as well as my conversations with hundreds of students and colleagues over the past 20 years, support these research findings. In light of our profession's commitment to a holistic person-in-environment perspective, this void is cause for concern. This case is my response to that concern.

I have come to believe that it is an ethical and professional failure to forego studying and integrating spirituality and religion as it impacts clients and social work practice. In classrooms, presentations, and at conferences, participants and students continue to ask why there is not a casebook focused on spirituality and social work. I have asked the same question. Whether at the micro, mezzo, or macro level, spirituality and questions of faith, mystery, religion, and the unknown profoundly influence people and environments. Thus, our failure to explore this confluence, in the classroom and in practice, is not only a pedagogical and professional failure but also an ethical failure. Our ethical obligation requires that we meet people as they are, where they are, as people with religious and spiritual lives and beliefs that affect their well-being.

In my current role as director of a spirituality and social work post master's certificate program at a university continuing education program in the northeast United States, I continue to address the lack of education in spiritually sensitive social work practice. Most students affirm that spirituality and religion were not discussed in any detail, if at all, in their undergraduate or graduate social work classes. In fact, like me and my fellow students who met surreptitiously, underground, in the caverns of our social work building over 20 years ago, my students express a similar frustration, even anger at the fact social work accreditation and ethical standards are not clearer in their call for competence in spirituality and social work (Canda et al., 2020), and there have not been more substantive or significant efforts to integrate the spiritual into the bio-psycho-social person-in-environment perspective. Many students interested in discussing spirituality or religion in the classroom continue to be dismissed, or looked upon with suspicion, even labeled as overly zealous. I remain concerned that I am having the same conversations with my students today that I had with my fellow students and colleagues in the mid-1990s.

Though I am pleased to learn that the third edition of *Spiritual Diversity in Social Work Practice: The Heart of Helping* (Canda et al., 2020) doubles the number of cases included in their seminal text, I remain concerned about the paucity of casebooks providing practical examples of spiritually sensitive social work practice. Mental health practitioners seek concrete stories, strategies, and tools to encourage and assist our profession in its attempt to more fully realize its stated desire to teach and practice in a way that honors and engages the spiritual, mysterious, unknown, and unknowable nature of the human person.

A mentor of mine often said that to be human is to hold in creative tension disparate ideas without allowing them to devolve into destructive polarities. This captures well the challenge of integrating spirituality and social work, and the invitation this integration presents to embrace the both/and nature of a phenomenological, spiritually sensitive social work practice. Social workers accompany and attend to people and the environments in which they live and love, suffer and struggle. We meet persons in their respective environments as they are, where they are, acknowledging and lifting up their inherent human dignity, and their capacity to heal and hope in the context of spiritual and religious beliefs and practices. Simultaneously, we shine a light, and invite critical reflection, on the power people possess to harm and hurt, even devastate and destroy in the name of God and religion.

The profession of social work has struggled with these creative tensions over the years as it has evolved from a profession rooted in religious and spiritual principles dedicated to promoting social justice and the common good, consistent with Judeo-Christian values, to a more secular, scientific, professionalized practice committed to individual, personal well-being less concerned with structural justice or spiritual precepts. In recent years, there seems to have been a return to the spiritual, faith-doing-justice foundations of social work, but from a less dogmatic or strictly religious perspective, more analogous to the spirit of poet William Blake's movement from innocence to experience to organized innocence. Tensions remain and yet research and the evolution of our profession affirm that there is a renewed openness to addressing more holistically the bio-psycho-social-spiritual person. Past concerns and fears continue to give way to a more organized innocence, a willingness to return to our professional roots, and yet to do so having lived through the experience of understanding that there is also an ethical consequence to not understanding the importance and place of a person's spiritual sense of self.

Canda and Furman (2010) outlined several important dichotomies that have often been held in creative tension and debated when making arguments for and against studying religion and spirituality in social work. Challenges and concerns include claims about: the inherent deficiencies of religion and spirituality, such as the limited, dogmatic, and rigid nature of many religious perspectives; religion as an expression of psychopathology; spirituality being overly individualistic at the expense of concerns about macro social justice practice; and broad concerns about professional boundaries (e.g. social work, like the government, should not mix with religion or spirituality). They also identified value conflicts, e.g. certain religious or spiritual values that are inconsistent with social work values. They called attention to spiritually sensitive social work research and definitional problems, like the fact that efforts to combine social work practice and religion and spirituality are not adequately researched or developed, and spirituality and religion are not clear concepts easily defined. There are several reasons that educators and social workers have been suspicious of spiritually sensitive social work practice, believing that studying the spiritual aspects and experiences of the human person is unnecessary, or detrimental and counterproductive, or risks compromising ethical practice principles. Some assert that spiritually sensitive social work practice jeopardizes client self-determination and opens the door to preaching, manipulation, and the imposition of worker values on the client. Others assert that spirituality and religion are pseudo-science or beyond the scope of the discipline of social work. Additionally, Sheridan (2009), in a two-volume issue of *The Journal of Religion & Spirituality in Social Work: Social Thought*, entitled "Controversial issues in Religion, Spirituality, and Social Work," identifies four categories where there have been tensions between spirituality, religion, and social work pedagogy and practice: conceptual and theoretical, practice and policy, educational, and research. These categories affirm challenges and concerns between spiritual, religious, theist, and sacred principles, values, and assertions, and secular, reasoned, humanist, scientific, rational, and material principles, values, and assertions.

All of these conflicting categories and concerns present our profession with significant challenges and obstacles to engaging in spiritually sensitive social work practice. The Council on Social Work Education (CSWE) and National Association of Social Workers (NASW) now affirm that spiritually sensitive social work practice and competency, understanding and addressing holistically the bio-psycho-social-spiritual person, is essential to ethical practice (CSWE, 2015; Dudley, 2016; NASW, 2017). Therefore, inasmuch as our ethical and accreditation standards require us to integrate spirituality into social work practice and pedagogy, I assert that social workers are now being invited to embrace the fact that although conflicts exist between religion and spirituality and science, they also can and do coexist, and even complement one another. Scholars who advocate for spiritually sensitive social work agree (Canda & Furman, 2010; Canda et al., 2020; Dudley, 2016). Thus, inasmuch as the human person is both matter and mystery, secular and spiritual, known and unknown, spiritually sensitive social work pedagogy and practice is invited to more critically reflect on, engage, and wrestle with the both/and nature of these tensions.

Sadly, for the majority of social workers, this critical reflection is not being invited. Despite this hunger and desire for spiritually sensitive education and training, studies have found that nearly 65% of social workers receive no content on spirituality or religion in their social work education. Though discouraging, there is some movement in a positive direction. In 1997 the number of social workers who reported no religious or spiritual education content was 73%. For social workers to feel more competent to practice in a spiritually sensitive way – a way that implements spiritual and religious engagement, assessment, intervention, and evaluation – more education is required. It is also worth mentioning that the desire for additional training and education with respect to the integration of religion and spirituality, and practice has been explicitly expressed by other helping professionals as well, such as nurses, marriage and family therapists, and psychologists (Canda et al., 2020; Crook-Lyon et al., 2012; Dudley, 2016; Prest et al., 1999). Despite the tensions and challenges, it is important that we respond to these desires; and inasmuch as social workers account for almost half of mental health personnel (Oxhandler & Pargament, 2014), there is arguably a responsibility for our profession to lead the way in providing the training and preparation necessary to more fully address the spiritual or religious aspects of the human person.

Avoiding Harm in Spiritually Sensitive Practice

As the complex creative tensions presented above remind us, spirituality and religion can also be used to oppress and harm (Belcher & Sarmiento Mellinger, 2016; Canda et al., 2020; Dudley, 2016; Webb, Hirsch, Visser, & Brewer, 2013). Thus, creative tensions necessarily invite critical questions that must be examined and considered again and again as we develop both personal and professional skills for spiritually sensitive social work pedagogy and practice. I present here some of those questions that case studies help us further and more deeply examine and consider. They are also questions that invite ongoing research, reflection, and response.

To what degree is it necessary for social workers to explore their own understanding of religion and spirituality in order to engage in spirituality sensitive social work practice?

How do varying definitions of spirituality and religion, i.e. client, social worker, scholarly, influence how we understand and approach social work practice?

What is the difference between exploring concepts and questions pertaining to meaning-making, values, and ethics, as opposed to the divine, God, mystery, and the unknown?

What does spiritually sensitive social work competency look like? What criteria can be used to gauge a social worker's spiritually sensitive practice competency?

How might concepts of cultural and spiritual humility serve to balance expert-driven and positivistic ideas of spiritually sensitive social work competence?

What is our ethical obligation with respect to the pedagogy and practice of spiritually sensitive social work? How does this obligation translate into courses and competencies?

What connections exist between a person's spirituality and religious expression and her or his intersectional identity, i.e. race, culture, ethnicity, gender, and sexual orientation?

What are perceived and real barriers to integrating religion and spirituality into practice, i.e. agency policies, ethical conflicts, institutional support, time constraints, training?

When does spiritually sensitive social work practice become preaching or proselytizing?

What should social workers do if a client or an agency's spiritual, religious beliefs or practices conflict with their own, or with our profession's ethics and values?

When should we refer clients to faith-based experts or religious leaders?

Why do many social workers express the belief that spiritual and religious interventions are appropriate and important, and yet fail to engage in these interventions?

What can social workers in the United States learn about spiritually sensitive practice from international social work practice and research?

These questions and others must continue to be critically reflected upon today, in the present, as we consider the future of ethical and just spiritually sensitive social work practice. In this regard, case studies provide an important complement to quantitative analysis and research. So too does understanding our past. In order to fully appreciate and examine these questions as they impact how we move forward as a profession, it is also imperative that we understand our past, and the central role religion and spirituality has played in the evolution of social work.

A Brief History of Religion and Spirituality in the Evolution of Social Work

From charity organization societies to the settlement house movement, religion and spirituality have played a central role in the history and evolution of the profession of social work. However, over the years, despite being rooted in religious values and principles, social work has distanced itself from religion, in part as a result of: its movement toward professionalism, evidence-based practice, and societal acceptance; concerns regarding Christian teachings; the evolution of scientific knowledge; the growing diversity of religious traditions, in particular among immigrants; concerns about proselytization; and issues regarding separation of church and state, especially as more social workers were employed in government agencies (Canda, 2002; Dudley 2016; Ellor, Netting, & Thibault, 1999; Loewenberg, 1988; Sheridan, 2012).

Citing 19 scholars and 13 published works (Axin & Levin, 1982; Brower, 1984; Bullis, 1996; Cnaan, Wineburg, & Boddie, 1999; Garland, 1992; Gelman, Andon, & Schnall, 2008; Kreutziger, 1998; Leiby, 1985; Loewenberg, 1988; Marty, 1980; Niebuhr, 1932; Reid & Popple, 1992; Van Hook, 1997), Canda and Furman (2010) traced the early history of the connection between spirituality and social work in the United States, detailing movement from colonial voluntary social services and governmental social welfare policies rooted in Judeo Christian notions of charity and community responsibility, to the professionalization of social work. They explained that "as social work professionalized in competition with… medicine and law, secular humanistic and scientific perspectives, such as socialism, social functionalism, Freudianism, and behaviorism became more influential than theology" (p. 112). This evolution contributed to social work's movement away from its spiritual and religious roots. Some considered this professionalization important in advancing social work's place in society, while others believed it to be an abandonment of social work's roots, and a compromising of its core values and ethical principles. Tracing further social work's relationship with spirituality and religion, Canda and Furman (2010) described the profession's resurgence of interest in spirituality in the late 20th century, which "expanded on the ecumenical, interreligious, and nonsectarian spiritual undercurrents that existed in the profession from its beginning" (p. 112). Again, like Blake's organized innocence, this evolution of social work reflects a rediscovery and renewed understanding of its roots, having moved through the experience of professionalization and medical, healthcare, and scientific advances. Finally, Canda and Furman (2010) found that currently social work is in a phase that they call transcending boundaries: "The distinguishing features of this period are the formal recognition of spirituality in the U.S. social work education standards and the movement among scholars and practitioners 'to transcend boundaries between spiritual perspectives, academic disciplines, nations, governmental and religious institutions, and between humans and nature' (Canda, 2005a, p. 99)" (p. 113). This phase and our current professional reality call for spiritually sensitive social work pedagogy and practice that "seeks to nurture persons' full potentials through relationships based on respectful, empathic, knowledgeable, and skillful regard for their spiritual perspectives, whether religious or nonreligious. It promotes peace and justice for all people and all beings. (Canda, 2008d, pp. x–xi)" (p. 5). The challenge, however, rests in how we actualize this nurturing, respectful, empathetic spiritually sensitive practice – how to make manifest a spiritually sensitive practice that transcends boundaries and promotes peace and justice.

Despite advances in acknowledging and reconnecting and holding in creative tension mind, body, and spirit as essential to contemporary spiritually sensitive social work practice, the influence, understanding, and role of religion and spirituality in social work remain complex. For example, given the Judeo-Christian roots of social work and the current 900 plus Christian denominations in the United States, it is important not to assume clients have particular religious beliefs or practices, even as Christians. Also, as most social workers in the United States are influenced by Christianity, it remains important to be aware of the potential of imposing our religious assumptions on clients, and to be sensitive to the needs of non-Christians, who are likely to experience much greater religious oppression and injustice (Canda & Furman, 2010).

In light of these tensions and complexities, social workers struggle with how to integrate religion and spirituality into curricula and practice (Belcher & Sarmiento Mellinger, 2016; Carrington, 2013; Dessel, Woddfrord, & Gutierrez,

2012; Dwyer, 2010), and research continues to affirm that they have been poorly prepared for spiritually sensitive social work practice (Barker, 2007; Canda et al., 2020; Carrington, 2013). This struggle to confront the questions and complexities of integrating spirituality and religion into social work pedagogy and practice can be engaged by applying the Circle of Insight framework (Nicotera, 2018, 2019).

Circle of Insight: A Framework for Spiritually Sensitive Social Work

The three-phase See, Reflect, Act Circle of Insight framework (Nicotera, 2018, 2019) can help us embrace the beauty and power of the symphony that is spiritually sensitive social work practice in its scientific and artistic fullness. It can help us take the personal and professional steps necessary to deepen our commitment to understanding and integrating spirituality, religion, and social work. The first step of the Circle requires that we explore, examine carefully, and listen deeply to, like an investigator or reporter, how scholars, persons-in-environments, clients, and social work practitioners define, understand, and practice spirituality and religion. The next step invites critical reflection. Social work values are applied to what has been investigated, examined, and seen. This phase requires that we ask critical questions about definitions, research, clients, values, and beliefs as they relate to the observed reality of spirituality, religion, and social work in practice. It challenges us to ask what social work's commitment to bio-psycho-social-spiritual practice requires of us. It beckons us to examine our own beliefs and spirituality in light of various understandings of spirituality and religion, social work ethical values, and its commitment to meeting people as spiritual beings, where they are, as they are. The third step is to act, to discern with scholars, researchers, and clients, and in light of our own spiritual awareness, appropriate individual and collective action.

This action involves the two levels of the Circle, the internal and the external. Internal action exists at the level of social worker self-examination as well as the social work profession's internal consideration of appropriate practical steps to concretize its ethical values and accreditation standards. External action exists at the level of social worker engagement with clients, at the micro, mezzo, and macro levels of practice, and the social work profession's engagement in and with the world to build what Martin Luther King, Jr. called the beloved community (King, 1967).

The Circle is one continual process, comprised of central characteristics; it is dialectical, open, purposeful, and enlightening (Nicotera, 2018, 2019). As it continues, it invites lyrical movement toward ever deeper authenticity, insight, and liberation. It uses the chords of our core NASW values: service, social justice, dignity and worth of the person, importance of human relationships, integrity, and competence (NASW, 2017) to harmonize and heal, to reconcile and reveal, to invite the personal and collective singing of our song in the world, the song that sings our social work commitment to spiritually sensitive pedagogy and practice.

I had the privilege of working with Vietnamese Zen Master Thich Nhat Hanh, nominated for the Nobel Peace Prize by the Reverend Dr. Martin Luther King, Jr. Nhat Hanh considers himself a social worker and is the father of what is referred to as socially engaged Buddhism, a form of spiritually sensitive social work, helping victims of violence and oppression heal and become their deepest, truest selves. In the spirit of the first phase of the Circle of Insight, Nhat Hanh invites us to look deeply, to see, to absorb with all of one's senses, to be fully aware in the present moment, to pay attention to the spiritual stories and nature of our fellow beings. In so doing, Nhat Hanh asserts that our stories challenge us to see ourselves as inextricably connected. He refers to this as interbeing (Nhat Hanh, 2003). Interbeing is the ability to look deeply at the other, and see my sister, my brother, myself. This truth is also understood scientifically in the law of conservation of mass – that matter is neither lost nor gained, that we are all composed of the same substance. It is captured in the fact, the insight, that the flower and the soil are one. The flower needs the soil and when it dies the flower becomes one with the soil and nurtures and nourishes the rebirth of the flower. They depend on each other. Nhat Hanh (2014) succinctly says it this way, "No mud, no lotus" (p. 12). Both are part of the mystery and the matter, the science and the art of life. Both are required for organic growth and transformation.

The Circle of Insight process applied to spirituality and social work case studies also invites us to understand this work as a labor of love. This is not the love of *eros*, erotic or romantic love, though there is nothing wrong with this form of love. In fact, it should be celebrated. This is not the love of *philia* or *storge*, friendship or the love of family, though there is nothing wrong with these forms of love. They too should be celebrated. This labor of love at the heart of the social work profession and spiritually sensitive social work practice is the love of *agape*, selfless love. This love loves not because one is worthy of love, but simply because one is human. Social workers affirm the inherent human dignity of the other, and promote the common good, the building of the beloved community. This is the work of selfless love, *agape*, that embodies the creative tension that in losing one's self, one finds oneself, in dying to oneself, one finds life. Spiritually sensitive social work practice invites and models *agape* and interbeing. In South Africa, indigenous peoples use the term *ubuntu* to express our interconnectedness and common humanity. Archbishop Desmond Tutu (1999), who headed South Africa's Truth and Reconciliation Commission post-Apartheid, describes the concept this way, "*Ubuntu* is very difficult to render into a Western language. It speaks of the very essence of being human.... It is to say, 'My humanity is caught up, is inextricably bound up, in yours'" (p. 31). The Circle of Insight offers a framework, a process, that moves us as spiritually sensitive social work practitioners more fully into the heart of healing and justice, reconciliation and love, belonging and belief, interbeing and insight. Case studies - real life stories that are sacred and profane, messy and multidimensional, mysterious and pregnant with meaning - animate the Circle and provide us with poignant, palpable, and powerful substance, matter and material, that propels deeper learning, and holds open the possibility of liberation and transformation.

The Circle of Insight's framework applied to a clinical story from one of my former students in our Post-Master's Certificate Program in Spirituality and Social Work exemplifies this love, and spiritually sensitive social work practice, in action. This former student and practitioner, who I will call the clinician, shared that in working with a young seven-year-old, who I will call the child, the Circle of Insight and our class helped foster deeper engagement in spiritually sensitive social work practice. Looking deeply at and investigating the child's reality, the clinician identified critical facts – evidence of fracture in care, love, and well-being. The child's mother was largely absent, and the child's father was an active alcoholic with serious narcissistic traits. The child presented with very poor impulse control and was struggling academically. The child had an active imagination and enjoyed action figures and superheroes. In one session, the child wanted to draw action figures and asked the clinician to do so as well. As the child began to draw, the child described the action figure as dark, with weapons and sinister powers. The clinician explored with the child why the figure was dark. The child responded that the action figure had been bullied as a child. As the child continued to draw, the clinician started following an intuitive thought, inspired in part by spiritual notions of light and dark, hope and despair. The clinician drew a figure full of light and peace, colorful with golden beams of light emanating from its body. The child inquired as to what the clinician's action figure's superpowers were. The clinician responded that love was its only power.

The clinician reported that this response did not come from an intellectual place, but rather a deeply spiritual one. The child was initially confused. Each time the child engaged the clinician in battle by unleashing the child's action figure's "dark powers," the clinician responded by wielding the power of light, simply saying "I love you." This happened repeatedly and each time the child became confused, and then giddy and ultimately calmer. Eventually the child put the "dark" action figure down, deciding it might be more fun to sit next to the clinician and have the clinician read to the child. What was revealed to the clinician in this interaction was the profound lack of love and acceptance the child felt. The clinician surmised in fact that this lack of love and acceptance lies at the root of the child's acting out behaviors.

Applying the Circle of Insight's second phase, reflecting critically on the child and clinician's behavior and story, in light of the invitation to spiritually sensitive social work practice, a few important insights surface. It is important to note that the child does not come from a religious background, and given the child's age, the child is not capable of engaging in advanced discussions about the spiritual life per se. Instead the child's understanding of larger forces and power comes from the child's passion for Pokémon and other action figures. The clinician uses a more mature understanding of power, morality, and what the clinician refers to as an understanding of "good and evil," to begin to affect an emotional shift in the child. The clinician believes that this shift occurred, in part, due to the clinician's awareness of and openness to a loving and accepting Higher Power (the clinician uses capital letters).

In this encounter, spiritually sensitive social work practice did not require the clinician to explain the clinician's spiritual beliefs to the child; however, it was imperative that the clinician acted in a way consistent with the child's understanding of reality and spirituality, in light of critical reflection on social work values (the third phase of the Circle of Insight). This action phase included both the clinician's personal work, to wrestle with spiritual notions of Higher Power, mystery, and love, and the clinician's clinical work, to integrate creative tensions conveyed in these spiritual concepts into concrete love in action, seeking to make manifest *agape*, *ubuntu*, and interbeing in a way that appreciates and honors social work values and spiritual insights. This involved an application of scientific inquiry, evidence, and process, as well as an artistic acceptance of mystery and the unknown – the self as knowable and unknown, matter and mystery.

After working with the child, the clinician offered the following key learnings. The Circle of Insight and spiritually sensitive social work practice require that practitioners: (1) ask the questions that hold open the possibility of surfacing spiritual conversations and sharing. Do not shy away from including spirituality in the initial assessment and as an ongoing discussion in treatment; (2) respect the client's spiritual place and autonomy. Use their language, their worldview, and their religious and cultural understanding of spirituality to guide and inform the discussion; and (3) engage in spiritual critical self-reflection as a social worker, counselor, and human being. Be keenly aware of who you are as a spiritual person: what role spirituality plays in your life; how and when it informs your work; and how it differs from your client's spiritual beliefs and perspective. Finally, the clinician added that this area of social work requires further research and exploration. In particular, the clinician hopes that this vignette sparks further research and additional case studies that in turn help other social workers more deeply and effectively engage in spiritually sensitive practice with children. The clinician also added that further exploration of spiritually sensitive social work practice, including case study research, with those who might be resistant to exploring issues of spirituality and religion would be helpful.

I share this case and these insights from one of my post-master's program students not only to provide an illustration of the Circle of Insight applied to spirituality sensitive social work, but also to invite others, as I do my students, to share their own spiritually sensitive social work case studies. Researchers agree that a critically important aspect of developing competency in spirituality and social work involves being exposed to teaching methods and tools that integrate spirituality and practice (Belcher & Sarmiento Mellinger, 2016; Seitz, 2014). My hope is that this chapter will serve as a tool and resource for educators and practitioners alike and make a helpful contribution to the evolution and development of this much needed research and competency. I seek to encourage and inspire practitioners to build upon and apply lessons learned and tools presented in this phenomenological casebook. As Oxhandler and Pargament (2014) point out, though there is a growing amount of research that clearly states that social workers agree that integrating spirituality and religion into practice is appropriate, even important, further case studies and research are needed to assess why it is that the majority of practitioners do not engage with clients in specific religious or spiritual helping activities, such as those detailed in the Spiritually Derived Intervention Checklist (SDIC) (Canda et al., 2020). Clearly, social workers need additional education, support, and guidance with respect to how to implement these spiritually sensitive social work practices and interventions. In my experience, they are hungry for it. This chapter and text attempt to help satisfy that hunger, to provide nourishment and sustenance for personal and professional growth in spiritually sensitive social work practice. I hope too that the Circle of Insight, in particular, will provide a useful pedagogical and practice tool and frame for considering spiritually sensitive case studies.

Arguably, if we do not acquire competence in spirituality and social work: we jeopardize our commitment to holistic, ethical practice; we fail to meet persons-in-environments where they are; we miss the opportunity to fully assess, understand, and invite deeper insight into the self; and we abdicate our responsibility, let alone our opportunity, to explore individual and community sources of pain, tension, suffering and grief, as well as reservoirs and wellsprings of strength, hope, healing, and joy. In my work over the years teaching and practicing spiritually sensitive social work, and living and working with spiritual leaders from various traditions, such as Buddhist Zen Master Thich Nhat Hanh and Roman Catholic Saint Mother Teresa, I have learned the importance of critically examining and studying stories of spiritual practice; spending regular time in silence and critical reflection; and, as Mother Teresa often said, attempting to do not the great things, but rather the little things with great love. My clinical and teaching experience and my time with Mother Teresa and Thich Nhat Hanh affirm and support what many researchers have found, that integrating spirituality and social work can be vitally important to promote the holistic healing and well-being of human people. Whether practicing spiritually oneself, or inviting clients to share stories pertaining to their spiritual and religious practices, or, in appropriate situations, inviting them to engage in a spiritual or religious practice as part of treatment and healing, research and scholarship affirm that these practices can bring calm and peace, and reduction in stress (Belcher & Sarmiento Mellinger, 2016). This calm, in turn, can support the body's immune system in its effort to prevent and fight infection and disease, and help the body heal and stay well.

Of course, this healing requires people to participate in their own well-being. It requires holding in creative tension our right to self-determination as well as our need for support, connection, and community. In my experience, neither Thich Nhat Hanh nor Mother Teresa attempted to convert people to Buddhism or Catholicism respectively. They reverenced each individual's unique belief system, each individual's faith tradition, and spiritual or religious experience, including atheism and agnostic convictions. They listened deeply to people as they shared and often wrestled with spirituality, God, religion, and belief. In my experience of both Thich Nhat Hanh and Mother Teresa, they never proselytized or imposed their beliefs on others. They did, however, invite people to engage in spiritual conversation and discernment. They did encourage people to explore more deeply their own beliefs, values, and spiritual traditions, and invited them to engage in spiritual or religious practices that made sense for them. They did invite and model healthy, healing personal and communal spiritual practices. I believe this is why so many people with varying spiritual practices, and none at all, were so drawn to both of them, as social workers and spiritual leaders. They invited a profound respect for the beauty, awe, and mystery of life, and the power of beloved community, sharing humbly their belief in God without ever imposing or inflicting it. They also modeled the maxim taken from the Jesuit founder St. Ignatius of Loyola's *Spiritual Exercises*, that love is manifest more in deed than word (Ganss, 1992). They lived the Circle of Insight process in a way that summoned solemn and sacred, as well as disciplined and determined movement toward spiritual sensitivity, insight, healing, and wholeness.

As spiritually sensitive social workers, we too must not shy away from seeking to understand the place and prominence of spirituality and religion in the human experience. We must listen well to our own spiritual story and reflect critically on our own effort to grapple with mystery and all that is unknown in life. We must invite, and listen well to, the sacred stories of clients and communities, their sorrows and their celebrations. We must not shy away from more courageously confronting the need to invite deeper, more reflective exploration of the confluence of spirituality, religion, and social work. We must not shy away from spiritually sensitive social work practice. We must dare to delve into the depths of this phenomenological exploration of the simultaneously sacred and secular, holy and all-too-human, spiritual and material person.

Only then will we, together, as bio-psycho-social-spiritual beings, be able to cultivate and care for, nurture and nourish, transformative, liberating, life-giving seeds of insight – socially engaged insight that is crucial, even central, to holistic healing, health, hope, and well-being.

Close Reading Questions

1. Summarize Nicotera's "Circle of Insight." How does it promote spiritually sensitive practice?
2. In the spirituality education of mental health training, what has changed in the time between when Nicotera was a student and now? What more needs to change?
3. When Nicotera uses the word "tension," does he use the word positively or negatively?

Prompts for Thinking and Writing

1. Listen to the podcast about the spiritual call to social work, featured on the E-Resources page. Cite what you have learned from connecting the podcast to Nicotera's invitation to the social work profession to deepen its commitment to spiritually sensitive social work pedagogy and practice.
2. Read Okuda's chapter on job crafting, meaning-making, and spiritually guided supervision. How does her chapter exemplify Nicotera's hopes for the profession?
3. Which elements of "spiritually sensitive practice" are most important in the realm of mental health practice? How does one acquire these elements?

References

Axin, J., & Levin, H. (1982). *Social welfare: A history of the American response to need* (2nd ed.). New York, NY: Harper & Row.

Barker, S. L. (2007). The integration of spirituality and religion content in social work education: Where we've been, where we're going. *Social Work & Christianity, 34,* 146–166.

Belcher, J. R., & Sarmiento Mellinger, M. (2016). Integrating spirituality with practice and social justice: The challenge for social work. *Journal of Religion & Spirituality in Social Work: Social Thought, 35*(4), 377–394.

Brower, I. C. (1984). The 4th year of the spiritual-sensitive social worker. Union for Experimenting Colleges and Universities. Ann Arbor, MI: University Microfilms International, 8500785.

Bullis, R. K. (1996). *Spirituality in social work practice*. Washington, DC: Taylor & Francis.

Canda, E. R. (2002). A world wide view on spirituality and social work: Reflections from the USA experience and suggestions for internationalization. *Currents: New Scholarship in the Human Services, 1*(1), 1–6.

Canda, E. R., & Furman, L. D. (2010). *Spiritual diversity in social work practice* (2nd ed.). New York, NY: Oxford University Press.

Canda, E. R., Furman, L. D., & Canda, H-J. (2020). *Spiritual diversity in social work practice* (3rd ed.). New York, NY: Oxford University Press.

Carrington, A. M. (2013). An integrated spiritual practice framework for use within social work. *Journal of Religion & Spirituality in Social Work, 32*, 287–312.

Cnaan, R. A., Wineburg, R. J., & Boddie, S. C. (1999). *The newer deal: Social work and religion in partnership*. New York, NY: Columbia University Press.

Corry, D. A., Lewis, C. A., & Mallett, J. (2014). Harnessing the mental health benefits of the creativity-spirituality construct: Introducing the theory of transformative coping. *Journal of Spirituality in Mental Health, 16*, 89–110.

Crisp, B. R. (2010). *Contemporary social work studies: Spirituality and social work*. New York, NY: Routledge.

Crook-Lyon, R. E., O'Grady, K. A., Smith, T. B., Jensen, D. R., Golightly, T., & Potkar, K. (2012). Addressing religious and spiritual diversity in graduate training and multicultural education for professional psychologists. *Psychology of Religion and Spirituality, 4*, 169–181.

CSWE (Council on Social Work Education). (2015). *2015 Educational policy and accreditation standards for baccalaureate and master's social work programs*. Educational Policy approved by the CSWE Board of Directors on March 20, 2015; Accreditation Standards approved by the CSWE Commission on Accreditation on June 11, 2015. Alexandria, VA; Author.

Dessel, A. B., Woddfrord, M. R., & Gutierrez, L. (2012). Social work faculty's attitudes toward marginalized groups: Exploring the role of religion. *Journal of Religion & Spirituality in Social Work: Social Thought, 31*, 244–262.

Dudley, J. R. (2016). *Spirituality matters in social work: Connecting spirituality, religion, and practice*. New York, NY: Routledge.

Dwyer, M. M. (2010). Religion, spirituality, and social work: A quantitative and qualitative study on the behaviors of social workers in conducting individual therapy. *Smith College Studies in Social Work, 80*, 139–158.

Ellor, J. W., Netting, F. E., & Thibault, J. M. (1999). *Religious and spiritual aspects of human service practice*. Columbia, SC: University of South Carolina Press.

Ganss, S. J., G. E. (1992). *The spiritual exercises of St. Ignatius: A translation and commentary*. Chicago, IL: Loyola Press.

Garland, D. R. (Ed.). (1992). *Church social work: Helping the whole person in the context of the church*. St. Davids, PA: North American Association of Christians in Social Work.

Gelman, S. R., Andon, S., & Schnall, D. J. (2008). Jewish communal services. In T. Mizrahi & L. E. Davis (Eds.), *Encyclopedia of social work* (e-reference edition). Oxford University Press. University of Kansas. Retrieved August 12, 2008, from http://www.oxford-naswsocialwork.com/entry?entry=t203.e213.

King, Jr., M. L. (1967). *Where do we go from here: Chaos or community?* Boston, MA: Beacon Press.

Koenig, H. G. (2008). Concerns about measuring "spirituality" in research. *Journal of Nervous and Mental Disease, 196*(5), 349–355.

Kreutziger, S. S. (1998). Social work's legacy: The Methodist settlement movement. In B. Hugen (Ed.), *Christianity and social work: Readings on the integration of Christian faith and social work practice* (pp. 27–40). Botsford, CT: North American Association of Christians in Social Work.

Leiby, J. (1985). Moral foundations of social welfare and social work: A historical view. *Social Work, 30*(4), 323–330.

Loewenberg, F. M. (1988). *Religion and social work practice in contemporary American society.* New York, NY: Columbia University Press.

Marty, M. E. (1980). Social service: Godly and godless. *Social Service Review, 54*(4), 4463–4481.

NASW (National Association of Social Workers). (2017). *Code of ethics of the national association of social workers.* Washington, DC: National Association of Social Workers. Approved by the 1996 NASW Delegate Assembly and revised by the 2017 NASW Delegate Assembly. Retrieved from https://www.socialworkers.org/about/ethics/code-of-ethics/code-of-ethics-english.

Nhat Hanh, T. (2003). *Interbeing: Fourteen guidelines for engaged Buddhism.* New Delhi, India: Full Circle.

Nhat Hanh, T. (2014). *No mud, no lotus: The art of transforming suffering.* Berkeley, CA: Parallax, Press.

Nicotera, A. (2018). Teaching note—circle of insight: A paradigm and pedagogy for liberation social justice social work education. *Journal of Social Work Education, 54*(2), 384–391.

Nicotera, A. (2019). Social justice and social work, a fierce urgency: Recommendations for social work social justice pedagogy. *Journal of Social Work Education.* doi:10.1080/10437797.2019.1600443.

Niebuhr, R. (1932). *The contribution of religion to social work.* New York, NY: Columbia University Press.

Oxhandler, H. K., & Pargament, K. I. (2014). Social work practitioners' integration of clients' religion and spirituality in practice: A literature review. *Social Work, 59*(3), 271–279.

Pew Research Center, Religion and Public Life. (2015). America's changing religious landscape. Pew Research Center, Religion and Public Life, Washington, DC, May 12, 2015. Retrieved from http://www.pewforum.org/2015/05/12/americas-changing-religious-landscape.

Prest, L. A., Russel, R., & D'Souza, H. (1999). Spirituality and religion in training, practice and personal development. *Journal of Family Therapy, 21*, 60–77.

Reid, P. N., & Popple, P. R. (Eds.). (1992). *The moral purposes of social work: The character and intentions of a profession.* Chicago, IL: Nelson-Hall Publishers.

Seitz, C. R. (2014). Utilizing a spiritual disciplines framework for faith integration in social work: A competency-based model. *Social Work & Christianity, 41*, 334–354.

Senreich, E. (2013). An inclusive definition of spirituality for social work education and practice. *Journal of Social Work Education, 49*(4), 548–563.

Sheridan, M. (Eds.). (2009). Controversial issues in religion, spirituality, and social work identify. *Journal of Religion and Spirituality in Social Work: Social Thought, 28*(1/2), 1–4.

Sheridan, M. (2012). Spiritual activism: Grounding ourselves in the spirit. *Journal of Religion and Spirituality in Social Work: Social Thought, 31*(1–2), 193–208.

Sheridan, M. (Ed.). (2014). *Connecting spirituality and social justice: Conceptualizations and applications in macro social work practice.* New York, NY: Routledge.

Tutu, D. (1999). *No future without forgiveness.* New York, NY: Doubleday.

Van Hook, M. P. (1997). Christian social work. In R. L. Edwards (Ed.), *Encyclopedia of social work* (19th ed., 1997 Supplement, pp. 68–77). Washington, DC: National Association of Social Workers.

Webb, J. R., Hirsch, J. K., Visser, P. L., & Brewer, K. G. (2013). Forgiveness and health: Assessing the mediating effect of health behavior, social support, and interpersonal functioning. *Journal of Psychology, 147,* 391–414.

2

THE SPIRITUAL CALL TO HELPING PROFESSIONS

Job Crafting, Meaning Making, and Field Work as Spiritual Experience

Kanako Okuda

Pre-Reading Questions

1. What do you know, or what are your assumptions, about Zen Buddhism? What is a Shinto shrine?
2. How might mental health field work and supervision be considered a spiritual practice?
3. What do you think causes a person to choose a helping profession?

Introduction

Many people choose to work as mental health practitioners because they want to help others, but what made them choose this path? My view is that mental health "helpers" engage with spirituality as a form of making meaning in their work. One way to make meaning in work is to conceptualize work through job crafting (Wrzesniewski, LoBuglio, Dutton, & Berg, 2013). Job crafting can play an essential role in people finding a purpose in their lives (Park, 2010; Park 2016). In mental health field education, finding meaning in work helps students arouse their intrinsic motivation to serve while learning (Okuda, 2018a). Spirituality may play an integral role in transforming students into professional social workers. Spirituality is important because it allows for what students experience in the field: human suffering, perspectives of hope, and a reach beyond what has been known before (Sermabeikian, 1994).

Field learning is where students develop their professional identities by evaluating their values and life experiences. Through assignments and supervision, field learning is designed to foster students' reflections. Field learning is where students' own beliefs, values, and assumptions are challenged so that they begin cultivating their professional values and identity. Field learning encompasses more than achieving task competencies; it is designed to require students to connect to their tasks with their intrinsic meaning of helping, serving, and learning through their assignments. "Job crafting" encourages students to reflect on and reframe their work. Job crafting looks at how workers come to find personal meaning in their work by reinterpreting what they are doing, though focusing on aspects of their work that are particularly meaningful, by relating their practice to personal history and values, and other aspects of work that are under the control of the worker.

I offer a personal narrative about my spiritual journey from Japan to the United States, and from Buddhism to New Age spirituality, as the backdrop to the work I do as a social work field educator training future practitioners because I believe that to successfully answer the call to help others, one must engage in continuous meaning making and job crafting, two skills deeply enmeshed with one's spiritual identity and spiritual journey.

Personal Background

Spirituality has been the one force that has felt consistent throughout my life. My sense of spirituality has always guided my path, although my attention to it has fluctuated at times. I was born and raised in Japan. My immediate and extended family all shared the same cultural-spiritual values of a Zen Buddhist sect. We went to a Shinto shrine for every New Year to pray for health, good luck, and prosperity. It was also common for my family members to get married in a church as some of them attended Catholic schools. My family believed in spirit energy because it was a part of their folk beliefs. Mythology and folklore were passed down from older generations to teach children basic morals and values. When I was born, my grandparents visited a fortune teller and asked for a prediction of my life. A fortune teller told them that I would be strong-willed, should not marry young, would "cross the ocean," and would live apart from her parents. It was very hard for my mother to accept the prediction because she wanted her only daughter to be close to her.

When I was in middle school, I practiced Kendo, the Japanese traditional martial art of sword fighting. Meditation was part of every practice, and Zen Buddhism, a way of the Samurai, was part of its practice. My instructors taught me the art of sword fighting through these teachings, and its approach was philosophical. In contrary to a popular image that I heard about martial arts as self-defense, Kendo was a form of discipline through understanding a way of being. Most of what I was taught was through oral tradition. As a child, I trusted what I told and made meaning out of what I thought I understood. I recognize that the way I experienced spirituality through Kendo practice has formed the way I approach my life journey.

Living in the United States had been my dream since my teen years because I felt as though I would find a new identity and live in a value system that gives me the freedom to be me. It was a frigid day in January when I arrived in New York for the first time. I felt as though I was leaving a chapter of my life. I attended a dance school while managing several odd jobs from cleaning homes, pet sitting, to selling designer handbags in Midtown stores. While I was having a difficult time adjusting to life in New York City, my dancer friends introduced me to a New Age spirituality they were practicing, and I found it comforting and healing. Through friends, I learned about this "New Age" spirituality with various methods of healing and self-discovery. Simultaneously, I realized that I was landing in a community that was deeply affected by the AIDS epidemic.

Spirituality helped me to cope with the loss of close friends. My friends' deaths also meant death in part of me. Spirituality helped me shape the meaning of death as a loss, ending, and rebirth, yet the process was very difficult. Spiritual practice is not easy. During that time, I became particularly interested in a spiritual psychotherapy method, and I attended lectures and study groups regularly to deepen my understanding. Positive affirmations, breathing, and exercises based on these teachings helped me so much more than the few psychotherapy sessions I had tried back then. In understanding this method, I made sense out of my Western experiences through my Eastern lenses; I thought joining the seminary would deepen my understanding of the relationships between myself and others. I began developing an interest in spiritual counseling and decided to pursue a career in a helping profession. I thought the social work profession embodied my personal values and ideals, so I thought it was the career I could grow as a spiritual practice.

My uncle passed away around the time I became a social worker. Before he died, I met him briefly, and the words he shared with me are still fresh in my mind. He said that he had led a very selfish life. He wanted to be supportive of my becoming a social worker so that he would, although indirectly, be able to help people whom he had never ever have the chance to meet. This would make his life meaningful. Sincerely, I didn't know how to take his comment. I did not see anything I was doing as work was worth such attention or aid.

Literature Review

Social work students choose their career as a way to seek a purpose in life (Okuda, 2018b). Career choice serves as an expression of their values. Humans have an innate need to understand the meaning of their experiences, and meaning gives people life purpose and transcends their experiences (Park, 2010). When people's motivation and purpose is well connected, they are more likely to have fulfilling lives (Stager, 2009). Job crafting is a way to address this problem because people can draw from the intrinsic meaning of their work and make the work their own instead of performing tasks as prescribed (Wrzesniewski et al., 2013). Meaning making helps people better understand their relationships with others; moreover, motivation derives from the meaning people make in their lives, and the purpose that is consistent with their motivations is more likely to make their work feel rewarding (Steger, 2009). Meaning making can transform people's motivation for their career choice as well as the way they approach the purpose of the work and its reward to them.

Social work practice can be a transformative experience (Canda & Furman, 2010). Social work field education experiences encourage students to transform from informal helpers to professional helpers. In the process, many students learn the meaning of their serving and learning as they bear witness to the lives of their clients and the communities they serve. Mezirow (1991) suggested that people integrate their previous frame of reference and make new ideas through meaning making. Students integrate their personal values, professional training experiences, and the knowledge they acquire in the classroom to practice (Bogo, 2018). Field education assignments and their setting offer professional socialization as beginning social workers (Pierce, 2016). Many students enter field education with a set idea of what their field placement experience would feel like (D'Aprix, Dunlap, Abel, & Edwards, 2004). During their learning processes in field education, their views and ideas toward the social work profession are supposed to change (Buck, Bradley, Robb, & Kirzner, 2012; Zeff, Kaersvang, & Raskin, 2016). The transformation of students to social workers is often fostered by their identification to the professional values (Brill, 1997; Pierce, 2016; Shulman,, 1997).

Humans have an innate need to understand the meaning of their experiences (Park, 2010). Studies suggest that many social workers reported experiencing some family problems in their childhoods (Black, Jeffreys, & Hartley, 1993; Lackie, 1983; Rompf & Royse, 1994; Russel, Gill, Coyne, & Woody, 1993; Sellers & Hunter, 2005). By choosing social work, many people attempt to resolve unfinished family issues (Lackie, 1983). With students' personal values and experiences transformed through their life purpose, students transform into empathic, curious, and understanding social workers. Social work field educators often assist students to find meaning in their field learning experiences so that students can transform their past personal experiences into the tools in which they help and serve others (Okuda, 2018a).

Case Illustration

Helping people one at a time is meaningful to me, and sharing what I learn through teaching is even more meaningful. I still remember the first day when I met my student Stephanie (pseudonym). During our first supervision session, she appeared anxious and asked me many questions. Stephanie and I worked closely together as a field instructor and a student managing a caseload of clients, yet I knew that her inspiration could not be replaced by words of encouragement or hours of teaching. On the last day of Stephanie's internship, I asked her to tell me about the most memorable moments in her field learning experiences. She said that when she realized that she was able to do the tasks on her own and trusted that everything will work itself out. While learning to help, Stephanie thought that her ability causes the outcome of her work. She then learned that there are many other elements in her clients' lives that are beyond their control. She told me that she tried her best and worked hard and let go of control for what she cannot control. Stephanie continued by saying that was when she felt like she was becoming a social worker because something within her shifted and her anxiety transformed into the fuel in which she served her clients. This feeling resonated with me because learning to let go of my own expectations of the process and the outcome was a spiritual experience.

Teaching students this fundamental type of spiritual experience has been very challenging for me: "Why do bad things happen to good people?" In such situations, making meaning through spirituality can be challenging because there is no meaning that ameliorates the discomfort the question brings us. I worked with a social work student, Morgan (pseudonym), in pediatric hematology and oncology. Morgan said she wanted to work with children with cancer because of her future career aspiration. She said that she had a strong spiritual belief and was confident that she would be able to cope with any outcome of her patients' medical treatment. I was very impressed by her commitment to serve this population, so I accepted the proposition to be her field instructor.

Although many children completed treatments and did well, there were some who died in our care. Addressing psychosocial challenges of the children and their families, Morgan often shared with me that she felt helpless and had difficulty seeing how she was being helpful. Morgan worked with Mrs. Gray (pseudonym), the mother of a two-year-old boy, Michael (pseudonym), with leukemia. Morgan connected with Mrs. Gary and adored her son. Mrs. Gray was very religious and identified as a Christian. Morgan made sure that pastoral service visited Mrs. Gray as often as they could for spiritual support. When Michael's condition declined, Morgan took the news very hard. Morgan was helping Mrs. Gray with her hope for her son being cured, but it became very unlikely. Every time Mrs. Gray talked about her hope and Morgan listened, she felt as though she was not being sincere. I explained to Morgan that as social workers, we need to support our clients by meeting them where they are.

Michael passed away while Morgan was on a break. She had asked me to let me know should anything would happen to Michael while she was away. I called her and let her know about Michael's passing, and I was there to support her with the loss. Morgan returned after the break, but I felt as though something has changed. Morgan experienced difficulty focusing, sleeping, and her attendance became sporadic. I sat down with Morgan and discussed what was happening to her. She said that she had difficulty understanding why Michael had to die, that she was having trouble with her spiritual sensibility. Intellectually, it was no one's fault that Michael had leukemia, and Mrs. Gray, a wonderful, loving mother who did everything she could, had to lose her only son. I thought Morgan's grief was complicated because she was away when Michael passed. She acknowledged that her absence might have contributed to her feelings. However, she said that she was having an existential question about why Michael's death landed on someone so faithful and good, like Mrs. Gray. As a field instructor, I tried my best to support her and help her process her grief. At some point, I had to accept that it may have been more than I could do as a field instructor. In her process recordings, she wrote that she was angry with God. The very foundation of what she used to believe in was shaken given Michael's death.

I had very little information about Morgan's religiosity or practice. In retrospect, I wish I did. Spirituality can serve as the fuel for our service to others, but the very same fuel can potentially burn us, too. Morgan was burned out. Morgan continued with her field placement until she graduated. I did my best to teach and guide Morgan however I could: I listened without rushing her to get over it. She said that she had learned from this experience. However, I am uncertain how she overcame the spiritual question. Through this experience, I learned that experiences may come our way, and it is our job to catch the lessons that are given to us and do our best to learn from it. But not all spiritual experiences are resolved in the time period during which we want them to be.

I had never thought of how learning, teaching, and serving are connected until found what it means to be a social work field educator. Doing work as a social worker was fulfilling. Certainly, I felt as though I was making a difference in my clients' lives. What I thought was even more fulfilling was to share my skills and knowledge with social work students who are about to enter into the field.

Discussion

A field educator in an academic setting is responsible for training many students; this humbling experience changed the way I understand service. Searching for meaning in what I do as a social work field educator set me beyond my own goals and needs, shifting the way I related to my work. I began paying more attention to how I would best serve using everything about me. It was no longer about what I wanted to gain from my career. Instead, my focus was on how to use myself in the best possible way so that I could serve others effectively. For me, being a social work field educator is a spiritual act because I feel as though I am fulfilling a purpose that is given to me. Seeing myself as a vehicle for a force that is something larger and beyond myself gives me comfort. Teaching social work students inspires me because the process allows me to see students transforming to professionals while they make meaning in their work. The meanings they make cause their learning and their experiences to be uniquely theirs, and this spirituality—the sum total of the past that brought one into a helping role—becomes the foundation of their professional identity.

There are many ways to make meaning out of life experiences, and I notice that my meaning making is deeply influenced by my spirituality. Spirituality allows me to contemplate how I can be the best service while considering what I want as a person. It is comforting to realize that instead of my thinking that I have to control everything about me and my life, something bigger than me is leading me to the path that may be beyond what I can "plan" or fathom. In other words, it is not what "I" am serving. Instead, "I" am being allowed to be and serve by the forces that are bigger than me. Sometimes, I wonder if I am in alignment with my purpose. My spiritual practice has always led me to return to "me," setting me free from what weighs me down.

Spirituality liberates me from regret, guilt, and things that I want to let go of. Forgiveness is a concept that I have mulled over and has fostered my growth. To me, forgiveness is letting go of my own shortcomings, struggles, and expectations and release it to the power that is bigger/higher than me (Foundation for Inner Peace, 2007). As field director, the notion of forgiveness saved my mental and spiritual health. In this role, the work feels like a constant catch-up. I am always on the alert for something going wrong. Various stakeholders have their own perspectives, and it can be difficult to please everyone sometimes (Shaffer, 2013; Zeff et al., 2016). Dealing with thorny issues can cause me to feel defeated. Forgiving self and others allows me to relax and accepts things the way they are. Practicing forgiveness allowed me to leave work every day knowing that the work I did was enough for the day and trust that I did the best I could. Practicing forgiveness is a way to approach self-care. It is not about something that I have to get externally. Self-care is a way we approach our work (Cox & Steiner, 2013).

In working with students, I think of a Zen Buddhist concept, a "beginner's mind." To remember the beginner's mind, "Shoshin," is to remember what is like to approach a situation for the very first time by letting go of any preconceived notions or expectations so that one will be open to many possibilities (Suzuki, 2010). Each action is sacred; therefore, approaching with reverence allows us to be connected to the "wholeness of life itself" (Tanahashi & Levitt, 2013, p. 19). Field instructors guiding students to become social workers involve a balance of being there for the students and letting go (Hendricks, Finch, & Franks, 2013). Some may say that students will learn what to do by observing my actions. Field instructors play the role of teacher and mentor (Vinton & Wilke, 2011). If students see how I approach my work and how I make meaning out of my work, then this aligns with my Zen Buddhist modeling; I want students to notice the knowledge within themselves (Suzuki, 2010). During supervision, students often ask me about

my interpretation of situations. I have learned that teaching through meaning making is an effective way of field instruction because it draws students'
intrinsic motivation for serving and make meaning out of their assignments
(Okuda, 2018a). If helping and serving are spiritual acts, teaching to serve is
a spiritual experience in and of itself.

Conclusion

People choose social work with various motivations, and the process of social
work field education may create the foundation of the way in which people
transform the meaning of their work as they grow into their professional
lives. My own path to social work field education and the challenges that
came with the path helped me grow as a person. In the process, having
my spirituality as a guide has carried me through and allowed me to make
meaning of each experience so that I understand every experience is a lesson
that I am meant to learn from. I attest that my helping profession is a spiritual experience because it is a way to affirm people's struggles and transform
through meaning making.

Close Reading Questions

1. Okuda paraphrases that "Mezirow (1991) suggested that people integrate their previous frame of reference and make new ideas through
   meaning making." How did Okauda's previous frame of reference help
   her to achieve meaning making?
2. What do you make of Morgan's experience of loss, and how did it affect
   her spiritual underpinning during field work?
3. What does it mean for life to be bigger than the "I"? Is that idea idealistic
   or actually possible?

Prompts for Thinking and Writing

1. How might a Zen Buddhist meditative approach serve in one self-care
   and in one's service to others?
2. Nicotera, Okuda, Wiley, Fabbo, and Ordille write about Eastern practices. How do Eastern practices balance Western ones in mental health
   practice?

References

Black, P. N., Jeffreys, D., & Hartley, E. K. (1993). Personal history of psychosocial trauma in the early life of social work and business students. *Journal of Social Work Education, 29*(2), 171–180.

Bogo, M. (2018). *Social work practice: Integrating concepts, process, and skills* (2nd ed.). New York, NY: Columbia University Press.

Brill, N. I. (1997). *Working with people: The helping process* (6th ed.). New York, NY: Longman.

Buck, P. W., Bradley J., Robb, L., & Kirzner, R. S. (2012). Complex and competing demands in field education: A qualitative study of field directors' experiences. *Field Educator, 2*(2), 1–17.

Canda, E. R., & Furman, L. D. (2010). *Spiritual diversity in social work practice: The heart of helping.* New York, NY: Oxford University Press.

Cox, K., & Steiner, S. (2013). *Self-care in social work. A guide for practitioners, supervisors, and administrators.* Washington, DC: NASW Press.

D'Aprix, A. S., Dunlap, K. M., Abel, E., & Edwards, R. L. (2004). Goodness of fit: Career goals of MSW students and the aims of the social work profession in the United States. *Social Work Education, 23*(3), 265–280.

Foundation for Inner Peace. (Ed.). (2007). *A course in miracles: Combined volume.* Mill Valley, CA: Foundation for Inner Peace.

Hendricks, C. O., Finch, J. B., & Franks, C. L. (2013). *Learning to teach, teaching to learn: A guide for social work field education.* Washington, DC: CSWE Press.

Lackie, B. (1983). The families of origin of social workers. *Clinical Social Work Journal, 11*(4), 309–322.

Mezirow, J. (1991). *Transformative dimensions of adult learning.* San Francisco, CA: Jossey-Bass.

Okuda, K. (2018a). Learning through meaning making: Applying job crafting in field learning. *Journal of Teaching in Social Work, 38*(5), 470–485.

Okuda, K. (2018b). Kintsugi: Choosing a path of transformation in social work. Manuscript in preparation.

Park, C. L. (2010). Making sense of the meaning literature: An integrative review of meaning making and its effects on adjustment to stressful life events. *Psychological Bulletin, 136*(2), 257–301.

Park, C. L. (2016). Distinctions to promote an integrated perspective on meaning: Global meaning and meaning-making process. *Journal of Constructivist Psychology, 30*(1), 1–6.

Pierce. D. (2016). History, standards, and signature pedagogy. In C. A Hunter, J. K. Moen, & M. S. Raskin (Eds.), *Social work field directors* (pp. 5–22). Chicago, IL: Lyceum Books.

Rompf, E. L., & Royse, D. (1994). Choice of social work as a career: Possible influences. *Journal of Social Work Education, 30*(2), 163–171.

Russel, R., Gill, P., Coyne, A., & Woody, J. (1993). Dysfunction in the family of origin of MSW and other graduate students. *Journal of Social Work Education, 29*(1), 121–129.

Sellers, S. L., & Hunter, A. G. (2005). Private pain, public choices: Influence of problems in the family of origin on career choices among a cohort of MSW students. *Social Work Education, 24*(8), 869–881.

Sermabeikian, P. (1994). Our clients, ourselves: The spiritual perspective and social work practice. *Social Work, 39*(2), 178–183.

Shaffer, G. L. (2013). Social work education: Field work. In T. Mizrahi & L. E. Davis (Eds.), *Encyclopedia of social work* (Vol. 5, 20th ed., pp. 120–124). [Adobe Digital Editions version]. Washington DC: NASW Press and Oxford University Press.

Shulman, L. (1997). *The skills of helping: Individuals, families, and groups* (3rd ed.). Itasca, IL: F.E. Peacock Publishers, Inc.

Shulman, L. S. (2005). Signature pedagogies in the profession. *Daedalus, 134*(3), 52–59.

Steger, M. F. (2009). Meaning in life. In S. J. Lopez & C. R. Snyder (Eds.), *Oxford handbook of positive psychology* (2nd ed., pp. 679–687). [Adobe Digital Editions version]. New York, NY: Oxford University Press.

Suzuki, S. (2010). *Zen mind, beginner's mind: Informal talks on Zen meditation and practice.* Boston, MA: Shambhala Publications.

Tanahashi, K., & Levitt, P. (Eds.). (2013). *The essential Dogen: Writings of the great Zen master.* Boston, MA: Shambhala Publications.

Vinton, L., & Wilke, D. J. (2011). Leniency bias in evaluating clinical social work student interns. *Clinical Social Work Journal, 39*(3), 288–295.

Wrzesniewski, A., LoBuglio, N., Dutton, J. E., & Berg, J. M. (2013). Job crafting and cultivating positive meaning and identity in work. In A. B. Bakker (Ed.), *Advances in positive organizational psychology* (pp. 281–302). Bungley, England: Emerald Group Publishing Limited.

Zeff, R., Kaersvang, L., & Raskin, M. (2016). Placing students. In C. A. Hunter, J. K. Moen, & M. S. Raskin (Eds.), *Social work field directors* (pp. 83–104). Chicago, IL: Lyceum Brooks.

3

SPIRITUAL EMERGENCE AND SPIRITUAL EMERGENCY

Michael Garbe

Pre-Reading Questions

1. Have you previously heard the terms mentioned in Garbe's title? What do you think they mean?
2. Try answering the following question with total honesty: if a sober client with a history of substance addiction told you that he was currently experiencing visions and spikes of energy tingling throughout his body, what is the first thing you would think, and what is the first thing you would do?
3. Have you ever had a spiritual experience that would be difficult to disclose? Would you fear misunderstanding or rejection?

A survey conducted by the Pew Research Center shows that approximately 50% of Americans say that they have had a religious or mystical experience, defined as a moment of religious or spiritual awakening (Pew Research Center, 2009). This figure is even higher among certain populations. For example, a study of 180 long-term Alcoholics Anonymous members demonstrated that 89% have had a spiritual awakening, including feeling God's presence or experiencing God as real, having an intense positive feeling of great happiness, hearing or physically feeling something extraordinary, or experiencing white light (Galanter, Dermatis, & Sampson, 2014). Despite the evidence that reveals a large percentage of individuals have reported a spiritual experience, Canda (2002) stated that social workers lack the competence to deal with spiritual issues in treatment. Furthermore, discussion of specific types of spiritual phenomena is also lacking in the social work research and literature. The terms "spiritual emergence" and "spiritual emergency," which were coined by psychiatrist Stanislav Grof and Grof (1992), are defined as:

The movement of an individual to a more expanded way of being that involves enhanced emotional and psychosomatic health, greater freedom of personal choices, and a sense of deeper connection with other people, nature, and the cosmos. An important part of this development is an increasing awareness of the spiritual dimension in one's life and in the universal scheme of things ... when spiritual emergence is very rapid and dramatic, however, the natural process can become a crisis, and spiritual emergence becomes spiritual emergency. People who are in such a crisis are bombarded with inner experiences that abruptly challenge their old ways of existing, and their relationship with reality shifts very rapidly. Suddenly they feel uncomfortable in the formerly familiar world and may find it difficult to meet the demands of everyday life. (pp. 34–35)

My name is Michael Garbe. I am a licensed clinical social worker. In 2010, after years of intense spiritual practice, including a daily yoga practice, meditation, fasting, and emersion in Hindu-Vedantist literature, all of which could be considered my spiritual emergence, I also experienced my own spiritual emergency. This spiritual emergency came in the form of a Kundalini Awakening, which is only one category of spiritual emergence that will be discussed in the following literature. The most important piece of this self-disclosure, and what made this experience an emergency, is that I did not know what was happening to me at the time. I was scared. I sought help from the helping professions, and there was no help to be found. I went to doctors, neurologists, therapists, and nutritionists, looking for some kind of explanation as to why I was feeling energies shooting throughout my body, why my sense of self and my interaction with the world around me felt so surreal, as if I was walking around in a dream or alternate reality; of course, I never self-disclosed having "visions," which I knew would be translated into "hallucinations." What I encountered, regardless, from the helping professions, was confusion, misunderstanding, and worst of all, misdiagnosis. With no scientific explanations or answers, the final suggestion for me would be psychotropic medication, which I would ultimately refuse. I am not adamantly opposed to medication for certain ailments; I just knew, intuitively, that this was not the solution for me at the time.

What would ensue was years of having to figure it out on my own. I was fortunate to find literature from other individuals who had shared of their own spiritual emergence, and emergency, experiences. One book in particular, "Living with Kundalani," by the author Gopi Krishna, I credit with saving my life. It affirmed for me that what I was experiencing was real and that I was not crazy. Most importantly, it helped me realize that I was not alone, that there were other people out there who had experienced similar phenomena and survived. The writings of Gopi Krishna have a direct correlation to why I write on this topic today, and I am forever grateful that he had the courage to share from his experience, especially when there were few others who had at that time.

My spiritual experiences have changed my life. I feel more spiritually connected, while at the same time feeling more grounded, stronger, and more purposeful than I had ever felt in my life prior. This purpose includes having had to work through the fear of being judged when sharing of my experiences. All the while, I was guided by faith in my belief that by not sharing my story I would be leaving other individuals, experiencing spiritual emergence and spiritual emergencies in the same predicament: alone, lost, and afraid. Since coming out, so to speak, I have assisted many individuals who also felt they had nowhere to turn out of fear of being perceived as crazy by other helping professionals. Through my research, I have also connected to a large group of doctors, social workers, psychologists, and helping professionals, that I never knew existed, who have had spiritual experiences of their own and are interested in assisting individuals struggling with their own spiritual journeys. There is much work to be done, to increase spiritual competence within the helping professions, and this case study is my effort to do so. I hope that this study opens minds and connects readers to the possibilities of their own continuing spiritual emergence, or at least allows for a helping professional to not jump so quickly to the conclusion of pathology, when dealing with a phenomenon that was previously unknown. If the clinician reading this study is not comfortable with the topic that is okay, and I provide referral resources to increase either competence or use for referral purposes when encountering clients who may be experiencing spiritual emergence or emergency.

Senreich (2013) stated that it is important for social workers to learn to accept clients' reported mystical and psychic experiences as valid, rather than quickly attempting to interpret such phenomena according to a psychological or pathological perspective (p. 560). Studies have repeatedly shown that many clients want to have their spirituality integrated into the therapeutic enterprise (Arnold, Avants, Margolin, & Marcotte, 2002; Dermatis, Guschwan, Galanter, & Bunt, 2004; Hodge & Horvath 2011; Rose, Westefeld, & Ansley, 2008); however, data suggest that clients perceive low levels of spiritual competence among helping professionals (Hodge, 2007). The NASW code of ethics requires services that address spirituality to be culturally competent (NASW, 2017, Ethical Responsibilities to Clients) and that social workers should examine and keep current with emerging knowledge relevant to social work (NASW, 2017, Ethical Responsibilities as Professionals). These standards raise ethical dilemmas if social workers are not properly trained to work with clients experiencing spiritual emergencies. Thus, the purpose of this study is to further educate social workers on the topic of spiritual emergence and spiritual emergency. This chapter begins with a literature review summarizing the context of spirituality within social work. The review aims to identify gaps in the literature regarding working with clients experiencing spiritual emergence and spiritual emergency. I then present a case depicting an individual who sought services for a spiritual emergency and the therapeutic work conducted to assist him.

Literature Review

The social work literature on spirituality touches on many topics: most saliently on the need for spiritual competence within the profession (Canda, 1988; Canda & Furman, 2010; Carrington, 2017; Cascio, 1998; Gotterer, 2001; Hodge, 2016; Hodge & Bushfield, 2007; Holloway & Moss, 2010; Sermabeikian, 1994), as well as the need for the social work profession to include spirituality in social work education (Ai, 2002; Barker, 2007; Hodge, 2005; Rothman, 2009; Russel, 1998), and the importance of receiving competent supervision in regard to spiritual issues (Berkel, Constantine, & Olson, 2007; Gilham, 2012). A review of studies by Sheridan (2009) showed that although there is a widespread interest in the area of spirituality, social workers frequently reported having received minimal training on this subject matter. Although this seems to be the case, Canda (2002) pointed out that some progress has been made to address these issues. An increasing number of social work programs are now offering elective courses related to spirituality (Canda, 2005). Additionally, spiritual assessment (Hodge, 2007, 2011, 2013, 2015; Hunt, 2014), and spiritual intervention (Alawiyah, Bell, Pyles, & Runnels, 2011; Hodge, 2008, 2011b, 2013) have been discussed in the social work literature, to work toward meeting the needs of clients who wish to have spirituality integrated into therapy.

Furthermore, the social work literature has discussed the intersection of spirituality when working with African Americans (Alawiyah et al., 2011; Boyd-Franklin, 2010), Native Americans (Limb & Hodge, 2007, 2008), LGBTQ clients (Buser, Goodrich, Luke, & Buser, 2011), substance abusing clients (Hodge, 2011; Kissman & Maurer, 2002; Lietz & Hodge, 2013), the elderly (Hodge, Bonifas, & Chou, 2010), hospice clients (Callahan, 2009, 2015; Duncan-Daston, Foster, & Bowden, 2016), chronically ill and disabled clients (Higashida, 2016; Stoltzfus & Green, 2013), clients with mental health issues (Sullivan, 2009), veterans with PTSD (Wade, 2016), natural disaster survivors (Jang & LaMendola, 2007), and social justice issues (Prior & Quinn, 2012); however, there has been minimal discussion of issues related to working with clients experiencing spiritual emergence or spiritual emergency.

To demonstrate the importance and need for health professionals to have a knowledge of working with clients experiencing spiritual emergencies and given the importance of spiritual issues to clients, Religious or Spiritual Problem (V62.89) was added as diagnostic category into the DSM-IV (American Psychiatric Association, 2000). Lukoff, Lu, and Turner (1998), doctors within the field of transpersonal psychology in which there is an abundant and ongoing discussion pertaining to the topic of spiritual emergence and spiritual emergency, spearheaded the movement to have this category added, to address issues where the "initial focus was on spiritual emergencies – forms of distress associated with spiritual practices and experiences" (p. 1). The proposal for the new diagnostic category was specifically aimed to increase the competence and sensitivity of mental health professional to such spiritual issues, based on the high prevalence of religious and spiritual problems reported by the public, the lack of training of clinicians in religious or spiritual issues, and an ethical mandate for institutions to provide training in social and cultural factors that may affect assessment and treatment pertaining to these issues. There is a continued need for proper assessment, assistance, and cultural competence in regard to spiritually related issues. This is evidenced by a recent study by Lindahl, Fisher, Cooper, Rosen, and Britton (2017), which demonstrated a phenomenon of underreported meditation-related experiences, described as challenging, distressing, difficult, functionally impairing, and requiring additional support. The article further inferred the connection between an increase in the popularity of the use of mindfulness techniques with these reported negative experiences. Interestingly, Kornfield (1989) discussed the case of a karate student on retreat who, contrary to instructions, sat in meditation for two days straight and experienced a meditation-induced psychosis; this psychosis was resolved through the cessation of meditative practice and the engagement in physical exercise to bring him back into his body. The author stated that the spiritual opening was not brought about in a natural and balanced way, and therefore could not be integrated. Experiences such as these, as well as the recent study by Lindahl et al., suggest that the previous addition of the diagnostic category of Religious or Spiritual Problem into the DSM-IV still carries weight, as the phenomenon of spiritual emergence and spiritual emergency continues and makes great the need for ongoing and increasing competence within the professional helping community. Religious or Spiritual Problem (V62.89) has been included in the DSM-V.

To increase the knowledge regarding spiritual emergence and spiritual emergency, Canda and Furman (2010) discussed this topic in their seminal social work text *Spiritual diversity in social work practice*. As defined through the social work lens, spiritual emergence facilitates a gradual transpersonal awareness, which allows for a smoother transition into new ways of experiencing the world. Spiritual emergency, however, involves a sudden opening to transpersonal awareness, flooding an individual with mind-blowing insights, visions, sensations, and feelings, which can be a shock to the ego. Examples of spiritual emergence as listed by Canda and Furman (2010) include: identifying and merging with other people, plants, animals, and other beings of nature; communicating with ancestral spirits, deceased loved ones, and spirit powers associated with nature; communicating with angels, spirit guides, and God; feeling a oneness with the universe and ultimate reality; remembering of past incarnations; remembering of a past cosmic evolution; distress caused by harmful spirits or psychic attack; out-of-body travel; near-death experience; insight into universal and symbolic meanings; extrasensory perceptions such as telepathy, telekinesis, and precognition; and the awareness of subtle energies in the body. Chi is Chinese culture or Kund-alini in Yogic-Hindu culture are some examples of this subtle energy. It is important for social workers to have an understanding of these phenomenological categories in order to conduct culturally competent assessments, when encountering indi-viduals who may seek services presenting with these spiritually oriented concerns.

When working with individuals seeking services for spiritual emergence and spiritual emergency, it is important to be able to distinguish between these phe-nomena and pathology such as psychosis. Sermabeikian (1994) stated that spiri-tuality is a human need that is too important to be misunderstood or viewed as neurotic or pathological in nature, and the practitioner must acknowledge that spirituality in a person's life can be a constructive way of facing life's difficulties. However, Gotterer (2001) stated, what clients often see as a strength, their spir-ituality, is often pathologized and that clients frequently cannot discuss their beliefs in therapy, out of fear of being judged as crazy. Assessment and treatment protocols have been discussed in the transpersonal psychology literature and can be used by social workers to differentiate between spiritual emergence and pathology; Lukoff (2007) offered criteria based on published research to differ-entiate between the two. For a spiritual emergency, the criteria should include an absence of a medical illness including drug intoxication. One should look for a phenomenological overlap of client's presenting symptoms with previously stated categories of spiritual emergence as discussed by Canda and Furman (2010). There should be prognostic signs indicative of a positive outcome, in-cluding: good pre-episode functioning, an acute onset of symptoms during a period of three months or less, a stressful precipitant, a positive exploratory atti-tude toward the experience, an absence of conceptual disorganization and con-fusion, and no significant risk for homicidal or suicidal behavior (pp. 637–638). Furthermore, in order to identify and assist individuals experiencing a genuine spiritual emergency, Grof and Grof (1990) suggested to rule out medical criteria such as physical disease that may impair psychological functioning as well as to assess for no serious psychiatric history, including no: disorganization, inco-herence, loosening of associations, hostile delusions of persecution, or acoustic hallucinations of enemies with very unpleasant content. Additionally, the client should have the awareness of the intra-psychic nature of the process and be able to distinguish between inner and outer worlds, in order to internalize the process rather than project, blame, and act out. Lastly, in regard to personality, Grof and Grof (1990) suggested assessing for the evidence of good interpersonal skills and the ability to relate and cooperate, even during episodes of dramatic experiences. There should be no history of serious difficulties in interpersonal relationships since childhood, poor social adjustment, autistic withdrawal, and aggressive, manipulative, or controlling behavior, which make therapeutic en-gagement and cooperation difficult. Destructive and self-destructive behavior should be ruled out as well.

Treatment protocols discussed by Lukoff (2007) include normalizing the experience, through providing a positive context and sufficient information regarding the process which clients are going through. Clinicians should create a therapeutic container, to empathize, appreciate, and facilitate the process rather than attempting to halt or interfere with it; assist the client to reduce environmental and interpersonal stress; have the client temporarily discontinue spiritual practices until they are more stable; encourage the client to participate in calming physical activities to bring attention back to the body; encourage the use of expressive arts in psychotherapy and at home; and lastly refer the client for a psychiatric evaluation for medicine if necessary, to titrate some of the most distressing symptoms and to allow the client to better assimilate the experience (pp. 639–640). Canda (1998) stated that social workers are in an especially appropriate position to assist people in their transpersonal exploration and reflect on the interplay between their spiritual growth and societal responsibilities, given our person-in-environment focus. Additionally, due to our client-centered, strength-based, and systems theory approach, I suggest that social workers who utilize a bio-psycho-social-spiritual assessment, to determine factors that are contributing to client stress, are in an excellent position to assist clients to multi-systemically interpret and integrate their spiritual experiences.

Lastly, as stated in the NASW code of ethics, "social workers should refer clients to other professionals when the other professionals' specialized knowledge or expertise is needed to serve clients fully or when social workers believe that they are not being effective or making reasonable progress with clients and that other services are required" (NASW, 2017, Ethical Responsibilities to Clients). Organizations such as the American Center for the Integration of Spiritually Transformative Experiences (ACISTE) offer online referral services for clients which can be used by clinicians, to refer to professionals who have expertise in working with clients experiencing spiritual emergence and spiritual emergencies; these professionals include social workers, such as myself. ACISTE also offers trainings, national certification, and ongoing supervision for helping professionals who wish to increase competence in this area of work. David Lukoff's Spiritual Competency Resource Center (www.spiritualcompetency.com) is another useful resource.

Following is a case presentation, depicting a client who contacted me via a website I created to assist individuals seeking assistance with spiritual emergence and spiritual emergency. Symptomology, assessment, and treatment protocol are portrayed and then discussed.

The Case

John is a 51-year-old white male who contacted me via a website that I had created to assist individuals experiencing challenges with spiritual emergence and spiritual emergencies. The creation of this website was my way to pay it forward, inspired and helped by the writings of Gopi Krishna. In what I defined as my "coming out" narrative, this website was also a way for me to move past fear and self-judgment and to share of myself to those who could benefit from hearing of my experiences. Soon after launching the website, I started to receive emails and phone calls, not only from within the United States but from other countries as well, from individuals who stated that they were experiencing difficulties with their spiritual emergence process and felt they had nowhere to turn. In working with this population and beginning to conduct research in this area, I also discovered the organization ACISTE. I completed a training, receiving national certification with them. The trainings offered by ACISTE are available to all helping professionals who are interested in increasing their competency in spiritual matters. I currently continue to see clients privately, as well as present my research at conferences, geared toward this area of interest. In fully accepting myself, as a helping professional who is spiritually oriented, I bridged a gap between myself and many clients who have been seeking spiritual therapeutic support. When I ask my clients how they have found me, they usually state something along the lines of, "I searched on the internet for spirituality and therapy, and you were the only one who popped up." My hope is that more and more helping professionals pop up in the near future.

One of the individuals who sought me out was John. John stated that he was scared, that he had just recently been discharged from a three-day psychiatric observation from a local hospital, and that he believed he was experiencing a "dark night of the soul" which is spiritual terminology used to describe extreme difficulties and the "darkest" moments experienced on a spiritual path. John stated that he was experiencing challenging emotional states which were connected to what he described as "divine energies." Similar to what I had experienced, these energies manifested as buzzing sensations throughout his body, visions including seeing lights, and lucid dreams. During a recent hospitalization, which was his second in a two-week period, he stated to the hospital staff that he felt extremely high, like he was having an out-of-body experience. He was observed for three days and then released with a prescription for Trazadone, which he stated that he took for two weeks before stopping; they did not make him feel well, and he did not believe that they would help. John could not provide me with a diagnosis for which he was treated for during his hospital stay. After his discharge from the hospital, John returned to his normal routines, consisting of work and family duties, although he stated that he had stopped all spiritual practice because he was scared to continue. John, seeking assistance for what he defined as a spiritual awakening, contacted me via my website at this time. Sessions were conducted online for a period of approximately three months.

During my initial meeting with John, I assessed for any current or prior mental health issues. John did not present with any prior history of mental health problems and did not present with any current psychotic symptoms. He was assessed for and did not present with any history of suicidal or homicidal ideation. John did present with an extensive history of alcohol abuse, which led to his engaging with AA at the age of 46. This coincided with the start of an intensive daily meditation practice. John stated that he has been sober for five years and that his spiritual growth process has paralleled his sobriety. He was a highly successful athlete throughout his childhood and young adulthood, and he is currently a successful business owner and is married with one daughter. John stated experiencing positive and healthy relationships within his family system, as well as experiencing positive and healthy interpersonal relationships in his social systems.

John described a history of spiritual occurrences that began at a young age: a near-death drowning experience at the age of nine, having visions of white light, paranormal experiences of seeing orbs since the age of 13, being struck by lightning at age 17, and continued experiences of visual and auditory phenomena throughout his adulthood. At the age of 51 years, John stated he experienced more "difficult" symptomatology, when "Kundalini energy" was reported to shoot up his spine. Kundalini is defined in Hindu culture as an energy that resides dormant at the base of the spine and, when awakened, rises up the spinal column to the top of the head; this process removes physical and psychological blocks stored in the body, thus, the process of Kundalini Awakening can be seen as a purification process (Grof & Grof, 1989). Following his Kundalini Awakening, John stated experiencing "love, unity, kindness, and bliss" for three weeks, although accompanied by a feeling of leaving his body and being high at all times, which "freaked him out," prompting him to go the hospital. He was observed overnight and released as stable. He returned home and for five days he continued to meditate which exacerbated his symptoms, including the onset of sensations of energy that surged throughout his body. John stated that the energy moving through his body was so powerful that it shot his arms up into the air. At this time, he returned to the hospital, was observed, prescribed medication, and released again, prior to him contacting me.

Due to the high levels of anxiety connected to his spiritual emergency, the initial therapeutic work done was to normalize John's experience and reduce his fear, which was facilitated by empathizing with him and assuring him that I was aware of, and had a knowledge of, what he was experiencing. I also connected John to resources such as literature on spiritual emergency, so that he knew that he is not alone in his experience. A major concern expressed by John was the fear that he was crazy, and a very important aspect of treatment was to normalize his experience for him to be assured that he was not. Utilizing a client-centered and strength-based approach, rooted in competence of spiritually related issues, John's history of spiritual occurrences from a young age was accepted, validated, and viewed as special and extraordinary, rather than pathological. In finding an outlet to discuss his spiritual experiences and having them normalized, a majority of John's anxiety related to his spiritual emergency diminished.

Due to John's history of compulsive behaviors, I explored with John his self-described excessive use of meditation which had taken on a compulsive quality and was linked by John to the increased intensity of the "divine energies." John was asked to discontinue his spiritual practices, which John stated that he had already done, due to him having made a connection between his practice and the exacerbation of his symptoms. Utilizing a psychodynamic and systems theory approach and conducting a full bio-psycho-social-spiritual assessment, I continued by exploring with John the underlying stressors contributing to his use of compulsive behaviors as a maladaptive coping mechanism.

Through my own self work, and working with clients experiencing spiritual emergencies, an important aspect of assisting individuals experiencing a spiritual emergency is highlighted, which is the need to ground the process, through exploring and identifying underlying "real world" issues that have contributed to the emergency. Through therapeutic exploration, we discover a history of trauma which John had used his compulsive behaviors to avoid. John stated that daily alcohol and marijuana abuse began between the ages of 15 and 16. Underlying traumas include emotional childhood abuse from his "tough" father who was described as a "functioning alcoholic." John stated that he grew up, from the ages of five to ten years, in a dangerous neighborhood filled with racial tension, having to fight everyday at school and remembering his need to have to plan a safe route home from school on a daily basis to avoid danger. John stated remembering being scared everyday. In exploring his traumas, John identified his use of alcohol and drugs as a compulsive behavior, and with this awareness he also identified his use of meditation as a new compulsion, "like a new drug." This compulsive use of intensive meditation was identified to have contributed to his spiritual emergency, for which he was seeking help. Further exploration with John revealed feelings of inadequacy, of being a husband and father, stemming from feelings of inadequacy of being a son in the eyes of his father. John described feeling the need to have to prove himself on the basketball court, as a star athlete, and always feeling that he had not lived up to the high expectations of his tough father. Throughout treatment, John expressed his desire to be a good man, and through a strength-based approach I assisted John in exploring all the ways that he was a good father, and good husband, and a good man. A cathartic moment in treatment came when John verbalized that he was a good boy and is a good man.

By assisting John to work through "real world" trauma, he grounded his process and, along with the cessation of intense meditative practice, began to feel less high and less out of his body. Healthy family and social activities were identified, that John could engage with, including: enjoying time with his wife, daughter, and grandchildren, as well as exercising, and increasing his attendance at local AA meetings where John stated that he had been supportive of others in recovery. Through Johns' use of psychotherapy as an avenue to express himself, his anxiety diminished and he felt more connected to himself, his family, his business, and his life. As of today, John continues to experience "divine energies" and states that he has days that are more sensationally and emotionally difficult; however, he feels that he now understands the process better, has passed through his dark night of the soul, and is aware that this process is making him a better man.

Discussion

The most critical aspect of assisting an individual seeking help, for issues related to spiritual emergence or a spiritual emergency, is through competence of spiritually related issues and spiritual phenomena, normalizing the experience in order to reduce the high levels of anxiety and stress that the client may be experiencing. The creation of a welcoming, warm, empathetic therapeutic container is critical in facilitating the client's needed expression of his or her experience. Clients experiencing spiritual phenomena often have not had an opportunity to discuss their experiences, out of fear of being judged and labeled as "crazy." Using a client-centered and strength-based approach, it is important to validate and encourage the client's spiritual meaning-making process, rather than pathologizing it. An assessment to differentiate between a genuine spiritual emergency and pathology, such as psychosis, should be conducted in order to determine the appropriate avenue of care.

Using a systems theory approach, it is important to see the client as a whole and not merely as the symptomology of their spiritual emergence process. It is helpful to ground the process, which can be facilitated by encouraging the client to explore all areas of their life that may be contributing to the spiritual emergency. In the case of John, as I have seen in many cases of spiritual emergency, it is often the use of spiritual practices compulsively, to avoid "real-life" issues, that results in the emergency. When compulsive and excessive spiritual practice is reduced or halted, the most extreme aspects of the spiritual emergency desist. It is then important to explore with the client the underlying causes that have contributed to the use of these compulsive behaviors as a maladaptive coping mechanism; these underlying causes are often unexplored trauma. As in the case of John's self-described Kundalini Awakening, defined as a spiritual process that assists in the purging and cleansing of psychological blocks, a clinician should have the cultural competence to assist the client in utilizing his or her spiritual meaning making, to assist in this process; this cultural competence is not only vital, in assisting an increasing number of individuals reporting and seeking services for spiritually related issues, but is also a social work ethical mandate which should be professionally honored.

Conclusion

This case study is one depiction of an individual experiencing a self-reported spiritual emergency, the symptomology that he experienced during his process, and the work done to assist him. It is limited to the specific phenomena described in this study; however, it calls for more research and competence building, on spiritual topics, and spiritually oriented interpretation and meaning making, across multi-cultural populations. With the increasing popularity of spiritual practices, in and out of the treatment environment, and due to recent studies depicting an increasing number of individuals experiencing meditation-related difficulties described as distressing, functionally impairing, and requiring additional support, further research into these difficulties is warranted. The use of spiritual practice as a compulsive behavior, as depicted in this case study, is an additional area of interest.

A major dynamic in the process of spiritual emergence is how an individual, having been changed by his experiences, can then integrate these experiences within himself and then himself back into society. It is the social work profession's emphasis on systems that makes the profession so well equipped to work with this population; however, first, from the strengths-based perspective, social workers must meet the clients where they are at. This can only be accomplished through understanding, sensitivity, and (spiritual) cultural competence. The integration of my experiences also coincided with by re-integration back into society, which began with engaging in a social work masters, working as a social worker, and has culminated in being able to express my spiritual ideas, through a social work doctorate and the writing of this chapter. I will admit that I was also scared, to expose and share of myself, wondering if the social work field would accept me; it has. With gratitude, I hope that the values we social workers hold so dear continue to bridge the gap between us and our clients, as well as, spiritually, bridge the gap between us and ourselves. Namaste.

Close Reading Questions

1. What do you make of the use of psychotropic drugs to treat clients' Kundalini-related experiences?
2. What treatment protocols did you learn from Garbe's chapter?
3. Paraphrase the concepts of spiritual emergence and spirituality emergency in your own words.

Prompts for Thinking and Writing

1. Imagine that John was your client. Write a creative narrative that describes the way you would work with him.
2. Tune in to the podcast featuring Garbe on the E-Resources page. What is it like to hear the voice and personal contemplations of the person who wrote this chapter?
3. What do you make of the connection between folks with spiritual experiences, like Kundalini Awakenings, and folks with histories of trauma?

References

Ai, A. L. (2002). Integrating spirituality into professional education: A challenging but feasible task. *Journal of Teaching in Social Work, 22*(1–2), 103–130.

Alawiyah, T., Bell, H., Pyles, L., & Runnels, R. C. (2011). Spirituality and faith-based interventions: Pathways to disaster resilience for African American Hurricane Katrina survivors. *Journal of Religion & Spirituality in Social Work: Social Thought, 30*(3), 294–319.

American Psychiatric Association. (2000). *Diagnostic and statistical manual of mental disorders: DSM-IV-TR*. Washington, DC: American Psychiatric Association.

American Psychiatric Association (2013). *Diagnostic and statistical manual of mental disorders:* Fifth Edition. Arlington, VA: American Psychiatric Association.

Arnold, R. M., Avants, s. K., Margolin, A. M., & Marcotte, D. (2002). Patient attitudes concerning the inclusion of spirituality into addiction treatment. *Journal of Substance Abuse Treatment, 23*, 319–326.

Barker, S. L. (2007). The integration of spirituality and religion content in social work education: Where we've been, where we're going. *Social Work & Christianity, 34*(2), 146–166.

Berkel, L. A., Constantine, M. G., & Olson, E. A. (2007). Supervisor multicultural competence: Addressing religious and spiritual issues with counseling students in supervision. *The Clinical Supervisor, 26*(1–2), 3–15.

Boyd-Franklin, N. (2010). Incorporating spirituality and religion into the treatment of African American clients. *The Counseling Psychologist, 38*(7), 976–1000.

Buser, J. K., Goodrich, K. M., Luke, M., & Buser, T. J. (2011). A narratology of lesbian, gay, bisexual, and transgender clients' experiences addressing religious and spiritual issues in counseling. *Journal of LGBT Issues in Counseling, 5*(3–4), 282–303.

Callahan, A. M. (2009). Spiritually-sensitive care in hospice social work. *Journal of Social Work in End-of-Life & Palliative Care, 5*(3–4), 169–185.

Callahan, A. M. (2015). Key concepts in spiritual care for hospice social workers: How an interdisciplinary perspective can inform spiritual competence. *Social Work and Christianity, 42*(1), 43.

Canda, E. R. (1988). Spirituality, religious diversity, and social work practice. *Social Casework: The Journal of Contemporary Social Work, 69*(4), 238–247.

Canda. E. R. (1998). Afterword: Linking spirituality and social work: Five themes for innovation. *Social Thought, 18*(2), 97–106.

Canda, E. R. (2002). A world wide view on spirituality and social work: Reflections from the USA experience and suggestions for internationalization. *Currents: New Scholarship for the Human Services, 1*(1), 11.

Canda, E. R. (2005). Integrating religion and social work in dual degree programs. *Journal of Religion and Spirituality in Social Work, 24*(1/2), 79–91.

Canda, R. E., & Furman, D. L. (2010). *The heart of helping: Spiritual diversity in social work practice*. New York, NY: Oxford.

Cascio, T. (1998). Incorporating spirituality into social work practice: A review of what to do. *Families in Society, 79*(5), 523–532.

Carrington, A. M. (2017). A spiritual approach to social work practice. In B. R. Crisp (Ed.), *The Routledge handbook of religion, spirituality and social work* (pp. 291–299). New York, NY: Routledge.

Dermatis, H., Guschwan, M. T., Galanter, M., & Bunt, G. (2004). Orientation toward spirituality and self-help approaches in the therapeutic community. *Journal of Addictive Diseases, 23*, 39–54.

Duncan-Daston, R., Foster, S., & Bowden, H. (2016). A look into spirituality in social work practice within the hospice setting. *Journal of Religion & Spirituality in Social Work: Social Thought, 35*(3), 157–178.

Galanter, M., Dermatis, H., & Sampson, C. (2014). Spiritual awakening in alcoholics anonymous: Empirical findings. *Alcoholism Treatment Quarterly, 32*(2–3), 319–334.

Gilham, J. J. M. (2012). The ethical use of supervision to facilitate the integration of spirituality in social work practice. *Social Work and Christianity, 39*(3), 255.

Gotterer, R. (2001). The spiritual dimension in clinical social work practice: A client perspective. *Families in Society, 82*(2), 187–193.

Grof, C., & Grof, S. (1989). *Spiritual emergency: When personal transformation becomes a crisis*. New York, NY: Jeremy P. Tarcher/Putnam.

Grof, C., & Grof, S. (1990). *The stormy search for the self*. New York, NY: Jeremy P. Tarcher/Putnam.

Higashida, M. (2016). Integration of religion and spirituality with social work practice in disability issues: Participant observation in a rural area of Sri Lanka. *SAGE Open, 6*(1), 1–8. doi:10.1177/2158244015627672

Hodge, D. R. (2005). Spirituality in social work education: A development and discussion of goals that flow from the profession's ethical mandates. *Social Work Education, 24*(1), 37–55.

Hodge, D. R. (2007). The spiritual competence scale: A new instrument for assessing spiritual competence at the programmatic level. *Research on Social Work Practice, 17*(2), 287–294.

Hodge, D. R. (2008). Constructing spiritually modified interventions: Cognitive therapy with diverse populations. *International Social Work, 51*(2), 178–192.

Hodge, D. R. (2011a). Alcohol treatment and cognitive-behavioral therapy: Enhancing effectiveness by incorporating spirituality and religion. *Social Work, 56*(1), 21–31.

Hodge, D. R. (2011b). Using spiritual interventions in practice: Developing some guidelines from evidence-based practice. *Social Work, 56*(2), 149–158.

Hodge, D. R. (2013). Implicit spiritual assessment: An alternative approach for assessing client spirituality. *Social Work, 58*(3), 223–230.

Hodge, D. R. (2015). *Spiritual assessment in social work and mental health practice.* Chichester, West Sussex, England, New York, NY: Columbia University Press.

Hodge, D. R. (2016). Spiritual competence: What it is, why it is necessary, and how to develop it. *Journal of Ethnic & Cultural Diversity in Social Work,* 1–16. doi:10.1080/15 313204.2016.1228093

Hodge, D. R., Bonifas, R. P., & Chou, R. J. A. (2010). Spirituality and older adults: Ethical guidelines to enhance service provision. *Advances in Social Work, 11*(1), 1–16.

Hodge, D. R., & Bushfield, S. (2007). Developing spiritual competence in practice. *Journal of Ethnic and Cultural Diversity in Social Work, 15*(3–4), 101–127.

Hodge, D. R., & Horvath, V. E. (2011). Spiritual needs in health care settings: A qualitative meta-synthesis of clients' perspectives. *Social Work, 56*(4), 306–316.

Holloway, M., & Moss, B. (2010). *Spirituality and social work.* New York, NY: Palgrave Macmillan.

Hunt, J. (2014). Bio-psycho-social-spiritual assessment? Teaching the skill of spiritual assessment. *Social Work and Christianity, 41*(4), 373.

Jang, L. J., & LaMendola, W. F. (2007). Social work in natural disasters: The case of spirituality and post-traumatic growth. *Advances in Social Work, 8*(2), 305–316.

Kissman, K., & Maurer, L. (2002). East meets West: Therapeutic aspects of spirituality in health, mental health and addiction recovery. *International Social Work, 45*(1), 35–43.

Kornfield, J. (1989). Obstacles and vicissitudes in spiritual practice. In Grof & Grof (Eds.), *Spiritual emergency: When personal transformation becomes a crisis* (pp. 137–169). New York, NY: Jeremy P. Tarcher/Putnam.

Lietz, C. A., & Hodge, D. R. (2013). Incorporating spirituality into substance abuse counseling: Examining the perspectives of service recipients and providers. *Journal of Social Service Research, 39*(4), 498–510.

Limb, G. E., & Hodge, D. R. (2007). Developing spiritual life maps as a culture-centered pictorial instrument for spiritual assessments with Native American clients. *Research in Social Work Practice, 17*(2), 296–304.

Limb, G., & Hodge, D. (2008). Developing spiritual competency with Native Americans: Promoting wellness through balance and harmony. *Families in Society: The Journal of Contemporary Social Services, 89*(4), 615–622.

Lindahl, J. R., Fisher, N. E., Cooper, D. J., Rosen, R. K., & Britton, W. B. (2017). The varieties of contemplative experience: A mixed-methods study of meditation-related challenges in Western Buddhists. *PLoS ONE, 12*(5), e0176239. doi:10.1371/journal. pone.0176239

Lukoff, D. (2007). Visionary spiritual experiences. *Southern Medical Journal, 100*(6), 635–641.

National Association of Social Workers. (2017). *Code of ethics of the national association of social workers.* Washington, DC: NASW Press.

Lukoff, D., Lu, F., & Turner, R. (1998). From spiritual emergency to spiritual problem: The transpersonal roots of the new DSM-IV category. *Journal of Humanistic Psychology, 38*(2), 21–50.

Pew Research Center: Religious and Public Life. (2009). *Many Americans mix multiple faiths.* Retrieved from http://pewrsr.ch/WnouQI

Prior, M. K., & Quinn, A. S. (2012). The relationship between spirituality and social justice advocacy: Attitudes of social work students. *Journal of Religion & Spirituality in Social Work: Social Thought, 31*(1–2), 172–192.

Rose, E. M., Westefeld, J. S., & Ansley, T. N. (2008). Spiritual issues in counseling: Clients' beliefs and preferences. *Psychology of Religion and Spirituality, Special Volume,* 18–33.

Rothman, J. (2009). Spirituality: What we can teach and how we can teach it. *Journal of Religion & Spirituality in Social Work: Social Thought, 28*(1–2), 161–184.

Russel, R. (1998). Spirituality and religion in graduate social work education. *Social Thought, 18*(2), 15–29.

Senreich, E. (2013). An inclusive definition of spirituality for social work education and practice. *Journal of Social Work Education, 49*(4), 548–563.

Sermabeikian, P. (1994). Our clients, ourselves: The spiritual perspective and social work practice. *Social Work, 39*(2), 178–183.

Sheridan, M. (2009). Ethical issues in the use of spiritually based interventions in social work practice: What are we doing and why. *Journal of Religion & Spirituality in Social Work: Social Thought, 28*(1–2), 99–126.

Stoltzfus, M. J., & Green, R. (2013). Spirituality, chronic illness, and healing: Unique challenges and opportunities. In M. Stoltzfus, R. Green, & D. Schumm (Eds.), *Chronic illness, spirituality, and healing* (pp. 15–45). New York, NY: Palgrave Macmillan.

Sullivan, W. P. (2009). Spirituality: A road to mental health or mental illness. *Journal of Religion & Spirituality in Social Work: Social Thought, 28*(1–2), 84–98.

Wade, N. R. (2016). Integrating cognitive processing therapy and spirituality for the treatment of post-traumatic stress disorder in the military. *Social Work and Christianity, 43*(3), 59.

4

RADICAL EMPATHY, THE THIN PLACE

Hearing Voices in Psycho-Spiritual Group Therapy

Cristina Blasoni

Pre-Reading Questions

1. What assumptions come to mind when you think of a dual diagnosis, mentally ill and chemically addicted, population?
2. What do you imagine hearing voices feels like? What energies do you think the voice hearer might sense?
3. What is empathy? What is radical empathy? What do you think is the key difference?

> Yet, the unseen region in question is not merely ideal, for it produces effects in this world. When we commune with it, work is actually done upon our finite personality, for we are turned into new men, and consequences in the way of conduct follow the natural world upon our regenerative charge. But that which produces effects within another reality must be termed reality itself, so I feel as if we had no philosophical excuse for calling the unseen or mystical world unreal.
>
> (William James, 1904, p. 516)

Introduction

During the 1980s, the pioneers of the Hearing Voices Movement (HVM), including the Dutch social psychiatrist Marius Romme, researcher Dr. Sandra Escher, and voice hearer Patsy Page, set out to redefine the phenomenon of hearing voices. By reframing the reductive biomedical approach, which numbs the voices heard and the voice hearer through medication, the voice hearers could now regain a sense of agency through acknowledgment and acceptance of their expertise and power. While the Hearing Voices Movement paved the way for the Psycho-Spiritual Group Therapy cases that I will discuss here, a long history of psychic voice hearing, which Freud and Jung discussed as the "Psi" factor. Freud wrote on the subject of a patient's telepathic communication: "If I had to live over again I should devote to psychical research rather than to psychoanalysis" (Rosenbaum, 2011, p. 59). But these ideas have been considered unsound, and as a result, mental health clinicians have no tools to take on these mysteries and apply them in practice. In response, I present how radical empathy allows for the "thin place," which serves as the theoretical basis for the way I conduct group therapy in the Hearing Voices Group that I run from the "Mentally Ill and Chemically Addicted" (MICA) unit at a local hospital.

COAL AIT, the "thin place," according to Gaelic mythology, is a site where the veil between the earthly and the heavenly is lifted. This site exists without chronological time and is virtually placeless because it exists in another realm, a realm made of memory and the spontaneous feeling of oneness with energy or energies otherwise sequestered. It is a space beyond judgment because there is nothing that one must control in this space. It is a space of being in awe of mystical states of consciousness. To be fully present in this space, the clinician might try to inhabit the thin space with a client experiencing psychic phenomenon.

In "Spiritual Transformation, Relation and Radical Empathy," Koss-Chioino (2006) describes spiritual transformation with an analogy to Zen Buddhism, "where the practice of meditation aims to slowly free the mind from materiality until illumination occurs" (p. 655); when clinicians can spiritually transform themselves in this way, they can achieve radical empathy, in which "individual differences are melded into one field of feeling and experience" (p. 656). As has been the tradition among many non-Western cultures, the healer, or clinician, becomes "an integral part of all Being in a timeless cosmic realm" and can commune in spirit-mediums (Koss-Chioino, 2006, p. 656). Koss-Chioino's work is the closest match I have found to the thin space in which I practice.

Finding the Thin Space in Group Therapy through Presence

Group therapy is a protected space where thoughts, emotions, ideas, and experiences can be safely uttered and understood in a subliminal/subconscious manner by all those witnessing and absorbing. The concept of having a forum where divergent realities come together in partnership of a universal consciousness of understanding and healing is powerful and authentic. The role of the facilitator is critical for the divergent realities to become a collective consciousness. Governed by the concept of *primum non nocere*, the clinician's state of presence allows for the enigma of the unknown to come to the forefront of consciousness.

To produce these same goals among group members, the clinician must emit an energy of unconditional positive regard to promote healing (Rogers, 1957). The clinician's energy of openness begins a synergetic healing bond among group members, perhaps formed by an intuitive notion that we are all linked by a higher and lower consciousness, masked and protected with overt behaviors to keep all pained people safe, sane, and secure. The clinician's respectful agàpe and universal loving kindness toward the pained person fosters a collective healing psi energy opening to non-ordinary, if not, mystical states of consciousness. Psychoanalyst Harold Searles, a specialist in the treatment of schizophrenia and other psi factors, expounded on the clinician's role to facilitate treatment with the pained person experiencing non-ordinary states of consciousness. Searles (1973) stated, "For the deepest levels of therapeutic interaction to be reached, both patient and therapist must experience a temporary breaching of the ego boundaries which demarcate each participant from the other. In this state there occurs…a temporary introjection, by the therapist, of the patient's pathogenic conflicts; the therapist thus deals with these at an intrapsychic, unconscious as well as conscious level, bringing to bear upon the capacity of his own relatively strong ego. Then, similarly by introjection, the patient benefits from this intrapsychic therapeutic work which has been accomplished in the therapist" (p. 158–159). Searles values the therapist's state of presence, specifically the clinician's own self-empowerment, shadow-self integration, and intuitive empathy.

In an ideal therapeutic experience, Miller and Baldwin (2000) explained the mechanism at work that creates the wounded-healer and pained person healing paradigm: "The conscious and direct support by the helper of the patient's inner healer is a positive interaction facilitating the integration and increased awareness of the inner healer of the patient" (p. 250). Similarly, Kreinheder (1980) elucidated the clinician's healing role: "If you are going to be a healer, then you have to get into a relationship. There is a person before you, and you and that person have to relate. That means touching each other, touching the places in each other that are close and tender where the sensitivity is, where the wounds are, and where the turmoil is. That's intimacy. When you get this close, there is love. And when love comes, the healing comes…When you touch each other intimately and with good will, then there is healing" (p. 17). Contrary to evidence-based practices (EBP) and the conventional discourse used in the current medical model, the clinician does not perceive the pained person through psychopathology, biases, DSM labeling, and diagnostic theories (Hycner & Jacobs, 1995); the clinician understands the pained person's unique existence at the present moment (Craig, 1986). The clinician's central focus is to assist the pained person to meet in the thin place, where radical empathy is most possible. Through this undertaking comes certain phenomenon inexplicable by natural laws.

The Psi Factor: A Primordial Taboo as the Building Block to Presence

Though phenomena inexplicable by natural laws has frequently been dismissed, many brave thinkers have continued to explore the topic and offer historical interpretations of why humanity, in general, is closed to the thin space, psi factors, or transient hypnotic states of mind. One probable, yet controversial hypothesis is in Julian Jaynes' "Bicameral Mind." Based on the study of ancient texts, Jaynes proposed that the development and power of language accounts for the evolutionary transition of a bicameral mind to a conscious one. This hypothesis suggests that consciousness arises from the use of words to form analogies and metaphors of the lived experience. Though the experience and reasoning of metaphors involving "me" and comparable models involving "I" allow self-examination and self-reflection, and self-responsibility, the individual is not operating on an automatic self-serving disposition, but rather on a higher-level abstract metaphor-induced mind-set which resembles the outer realm. According to Jaynes, before the acquisition of sophisticated meaningful language was procured all decisions were attributed to disembodied voices. In the Iliad, these voices came from the gods. Jaynes postulated that modern bicamerality is observed in hypnosis and with voice hearers (Cavanna, Trimble, Cinti, & Monaco, 2007; Jaynes, 1976). This does not portend Kaplan's and later Bleuler's coin term of schizophrenia. Even though the etymology of the word "schizophrenia" derives from the Greek roots schizo as "split" and phrene "mind" (Burton, 2017), their population consisted of young patients originally diagnosed with dementia praecox.

In another fraught moment for the psi factor, Freud was anxious about disclosing his attraction and experiences related to the subject. Though he stated that the likelihood of telepathy stemming from the unconscious mind was very strong, akin to dreams, and participated in many experiments on thought transference with Sandor Ferenczi (Rosenbaum, 2011), Jung writes in his book "Memories, Dreams, Reflections" that Freud's unease toward the paranormal was marginally histrionic. Jung stated, "I can still recall vividly how Freud said to me, 'My dear Jung, promise me never to abandon the sexual theory. This is the most essential thing of all. You see, we must make a dogma of it, an unshakable bulwark,"upon Jung asking bulwark against what, Freud answers, "Against the black tide of mud…of occultism" (Kerr, 1994, pp. 317–318). During this time period, psychiatry was trying to establish itself as a science compelled to divorce itself from what cannot be measured, reproduced, marred from epistemological value, and inconclusive, like the psi factor (Thurschwell,

1999). Regardless of establishing recognition and legitimacy, the quest for the psi factor in the human condition continues with other key contributors who are not inhibited by its ethereal and elusive nature.

Just as Freud was covertly interested in the psi factor and the occult, French educator, author, and translator Hippolyte Léon Denizard Rivail, who went under the pen name Allan Kardec as the founder of Spiritistism, argued on the validity of the psi factor. With a sort of valor, Kardec discussed the authenticity of the human spirit through his foundation, teachings, and books. In "The Book on Mediums," Kardec (2000) explained the reason for the system's rejection of spiritual and psi factors: "Before the causes were known, spiritual phenomena...might readily have passed for prodigies; but as the skeptics, the free-thinkers - that is, those who have exclusive privilege of reason and good sense - believe nothing possible which they cannot understand, all facts reputed wonderful are the object of their ridicule, and ...from thence to absolute skepticism is but a step" (pp. 30–31). Giving credence to Kardec's claim of ridiculing what cannot be measured, observed, or rationally understood, Carl Jung silently went through his own transcendental, if not, metaphysical experience, which eventually became known as the collective unconscious, the shadow self, archetypes, and the human spiritual side.

From around World War I until 1928, Jung compiled a series of notes, experiences, and bizarre rantings of his emotional, mental, and spiritual state, including thoughts, voices, and visions (Lucas, 2011). At the time, he shared his work with no one. Through the lens of a psychiatrist and rational thinker, Jung believed he was undergoing a psychotic break. Yet, by the virtue of his transmutation, Jung, along with Bragdon (1990), and Perry (1974), would redefine this experience as undergoing a *spiritual emergency*. Through this experience, Jung's controversial *Red Book* was created, only to be shared with others 50 years after his passing, sparing him from any collegial and public scrutiny and/or opprobrium. During this time, Jung experienced voices and visions, feelings of terror as the tension between what was rational and irrational grew thinner. Jung kept his experience silent, fearing the scrutiny of his peers. It was during this time of internal chaos that he became acquainted with his shadow self and discovered the collective unconscious. His fears and internal chaos ceased once he surrendered to his madness. Upon mindful surrendering, he was able to experience a spiritual, emotional, and cognitive awakening of his consciousness, creativity, and ability to be present (Lucas, 2011). During this ego shift, Jung continued seeing his private patients. Jung integrated his shadow self with his persona in a conscious effort to be objectively mindful of the shadow, ego, and persona's integrative manifestation. Through his own integration, he was able to feel the other in a way which bypassed any rational logical thought and stance. In other words, Jung treated his patients through his state of intuitive being bypassing the sententious pathologization of the pained person.

Long before the inception of modern technology to study the incidence of non-ordinary states of consciousness, Carl Jung, visionary and pioneer in his own right, established the quantum multidimensional interconnectedness that constitutes the human aspect. Jung postulated in his Analytical Psychology theorem that the part of our existence that we cannot see is a realm of reality consisting of non-material forms. These invisible forms are real and have the ability and capacity to enter in our minds and act upon them (Ponte & Schäfer, 2013). In his last writings, Jung elaborated on the expansion of the collective unconscious and the archetypes reaching beyond the human mind onto matter. Thus, coining unus mundi, as Linn Mackey (2007) explains, "He proposed that the unus mundi is the psychoid ground of both psyche and matter, and he saw the archetypes as patterning both" (p. 5). According to Jung (1960), "psychoid factor belongs, as it were, to the invisible, ultraviolet end of the psychic spectrum. It does not appear, in itself, to be capable of reaching consciousness" (p. 213). The images and concepts that arise in our minds are archetypical semblances from which they emanate. The reflections and conceptual forms we receive are analogous to the shadows perceived in Plato's Cave. However, the images are not impartially observed by the contemplator but are participatory in nature and construct. Physicist John Wheeler proposed that the role of consciousness and mind with the universe is not that of an observer, but one of the participator. According to Wheeler, humans cannot just observe something in the quantum reality without alternating it (Powell, 2009). Thus, in order to synergistically receive and emanate quantum energy in all of its manifestations, humans are naturally equipped on a neuro-cognitive-biological-spiritual stratum to interface with the universe and all the forms contained within (Powell, 2009). This idea is collaborated by Goodman (1988), who found that non-ordinary states of consciousness, such as trance or hypnagogic/hypnopompic states of mind, are natural and genetically endowed. While in ordinary waking mode (beta waves) perception can be metaphorically understood as a solid windowless building appearing that nothing exists beyond the solid walls. Goodman (1988) stated that this is just an illusion since in non-wake mode all humans slip into an alpha-theta state where the mind is freed to go anywhere in any realm. This may explain the notion that most individuals who see visions and hear voices have the proclivity of abstract thinking, absorbed with spiritual matters, or like Odysseus have a reciprocal communication with the gods and spirits.

Akin to this notion is the theosophical hypothesis of thoughtforms emmanting from the thinker onto the ether and the polydimensional universe. The pioneers studying and writing this phenomenon were Annie Besant and C.W. Leadbeater (1986). Similar to Jung's notion of the psychoid factor in the ultraviolet spectrum of the mind sphere, Bessant and Leadbeater postulated "that impressions were produced by the reflection of ultraviolet rays from objects not visible by the rays of the ordinary spectrum" (p. 2). That is, all those who can see these radiant vibrations are open minded, gifted, or in an altered state of consciousness. The authors go on to describe an experimental instrument to capture the impressions or thoughtforms from various subjects with much success. Other methodologies to capture thoughtforms may not be as sophisticated but just require a simple thought transference to a receiver through a simple deck of what J.B. Rhine called "Zener cards" (Algeo & Nicholson, 2001, p. 50).

What Jung, Freud, Bragdon, J.B. Rhine, Bessant, Leadbeater, and Kardec have in common is their first-hand experience with what science and social constructs deem as irrational and unsound behaviors. However, the phenomenological implication of a transcendental shift and the universal feeling of oneness confirmed that there is a guiding spiritual psi factor that led them through the *thin place*. Through the heuristic event that transformed their lives, each one, except for Freud, used their experience to rewrite what was once unexplainable, marginalized, and materialistic to transformative, spiritual, and empowering. Either by design or by direct experience, the quest for the psi factor is persistent. For example, Hans Berger, the inventor of the electroencephalogram, originally created this machine in 1924 as a means to study telepathy. His invention was based on receiving a telegram from his sister expressing her concern that something dreadful had happened to him. The timing of her communication was astonishing since earlier that day he almost got killed riding his horse. Berger hypothesized that there was some type of thought transmission or telepathy in the works, thus, the invention of the EEG. Even though he was not able to detect telepathy with the EEG, the device is still widely used today to measure brain waves (Powell, 2009). If this phenomenon is more common than science, social constructs, and materialists reckon, how can experiencers come together to bond and cope with a feared and out of bounds experience? The following case is an example.

Stacey's Experience of a Hearing Voices Group

I sit with 20 people with varying diagnoses in the cafeteria, the only space big enough in the unit for my group. From our chairs we can see the kitchen, an industrial-sized coffee maker, the cleaning staff, and lots of people going in and out of the broken accordion door, completing daily urinalysis and receiving medication from noisy nurses. I'm not judging the nurses; everyone has burnout around here. Most people who work here feel that they have to turn inward, toward themselves, to protect themselves from what they feel they cannot understand. Workers in MICA settings feel frustrated because making things better often feels hopeless, and expectations that things will run better often feel futile. But the spark that gets people into these settings meant for healing is something that never really goes out. Therefore, despite the business of the cafeteria, the space feels safe.

My presence in the room is palpable because I practice radical empathy. Radical empathy means to me that I empty myself of my energy, positive or negative, pertaining to myself and my beliefs. I breathe in the essence of people because I have made room for them. First, I open myself to Stan, who tells me about the Italian's president's plot to kill him. Then, we hear from Roberta, who admits that she recently lied to her brother: "I told him that space crafts don't exist in order to get my car back, but they do exist! That is why I went to tell the police!" I validate each experience along with the group. Stacey, new to the group, shyly raises her hand and shares her story.

My friend Jasmine has been with me since the age of nine. When my uncle would sexually abuse me, Jasmine would soothe me. Since I've been on Risperdal, I only hear "the mean one," and I don't hear Jasmine anymore. I miss her tremendously, so much that I can't live without her.

Stacey is in her mid-20s, and has a master's degree in the Culinary Arts. Stacey's suffering materialized at the age of nine when she started hearing the first voices. She became increasingly depressed, anxious, and aloof at school. Stacey remembers that the first voice identified itself as "the Mean One" and had a "demonic" demeanor. This voice embodied and communicated all of her fears, self-loathing, suicidal thoughts, and commanded her to carry out gruesome self-destructiveness. Amidst the darkness and despair that Stacey was feeling both within her internal and external realities came along another voice providing nurturance and hope named "Jasmine."

Stacey describes "Jasmine" as her confidant and protector to the group. Asomatous in nature, "Jasmine" communicates in a cryptesthetic way, which is comforting and soothing during Stacey's darkest moments. Since nine, Stacey knew she was different. Full of secrets, dirty, vile, and immoral. She has voices that verify her feelings. She feels alone and vulnerable, because or despite that she has an ethereal friend that no one else has.

Concerned or fearful about Stacey's extraneous behavior and isolation, her parents took her to the doctor only to be placed on Risperdal at the tender age of nine. This was the start of her recidivistic pattern of involvement with the mental health system. Even though she was able to complete her degree, the prepossessing voices and the medication halt her everyday living. Made sluggish by the neuroleptics and lonely without "Jasmine," Stacey stopped working and became solely dependent on her parents, which forced her to interact with her abuser. Both share the abhorrent secret in silence. Desperate to numb her reality, Stacey relies on psychotropic medication. As of yet, there are no real longitudinal studies on the effects of psychotropic medication on the developing brain. What is known is that the side effects are devastating: a flat affect, tiredness, fatigue, stiffness, and weight gain, contributors to her already existing poor sense of self.

During one particular Hearing Voices group, Stacey shares her encounters with the "Mean One" and how it makes her harm herself to the point of almost dying. Stacey claims that she is not suicidal per se, but influenced by the "Mean One's" narrative of who it believes her to be and protected on and off by "Jasmine." The paradoxical lived experience is excruciating at times, especially under the numbing influence of the psychotropic medication eradicating "Jasmine's" youthful presence from Stacey's reality. "Jasmine" is the only being who accompanied Stacey through time and pain. Indoctrinated and medicated from an early age, Stacey does not look into the cause or mechanics, just relief. Stacey said that she was afraid and upset that despite all the medication, she still hears the bad voices. Even with patient accounts and new evidence refuting the biochemical imbalance theory and damaging effects of medication, the medical model is the most prevalent in treating this experience (Whitaker, 2010).

Stacey explained her relationship with "Jasmine" since the age of nine during group: "I just don't understand why she is still nine years old. I grew but she didn't. But, she is still my best friend. She is the only one that encourages me." As the group discusses the various possibilities for this occurrence, something intriguing and powerful took place. I needed to talk to Stacey privately about this experience.

When I approach a patient with any statement or question, I am extremely mindful of the therapeutic value my communication and statement has. I knew at our brief meeting that this communication was to be of value for experiential validation. I started by stating that I had an unusual question and that she did not have to answer if she did not feel comfortable. Stacey agreed that I could. Thus, I describe Jasmine to her just the way I saw her when she was describing Jasmine in the group. Stacey's usual presentation is forlorn and flat; however, it drastically changed once she heard the description of her ethereal friend. Stacey looks at me and says, "Oh my God! You see her! Nobody has ever described her to me before! Thank you! How come you see her?"

"I don't know, but she seems real!" I do not tell Stacey that this experience is not new to me. I have been honored to have encountered and witness this phenomenon with many people. For the first time her lived experience was validated. Based on the empathetic synergy between myself and the pained person in front of me, I relied on the energetic manifestations and embodiments to understand the pained person to the fullest. I am thus left with the realization and confirmation that the current dualistic and materialistic discourse on experiencing voices and visions is inconclusive. More unorthodox research needs to be done to understand the quantum multimodal convergence of the lived experience.

For example, as the theosophical study of thoughtforms became more pronounced in the early 20th century, the examination of thoughtforms was prevalent in the pursuit of understanding consciousness (Bessant & Leadbeater, 1986). However, in their analysis of thoughtforms, Bessant and Leadbeater make no specific mention of embodied sentient thoughtforms, also known as Tulpas. It was not until 1929 Alexandra David-Neel a Belgian-French explorer wrote a publication titled "Magic and Mystery in Tibet" delineating her experience and creation of an embodied sentient thoughtform. According to traditional Tibetan Buddhism practices, Tulpas are created to empty fears, anger, or any other unpleasant human emotions from an advanced practitioner. According to Veissiere (2016), an anthropologist and researcher at McGill University, "Tulpas are understood as mental constructs that have achieved sentience" (p. 7). The Tulpas take any form the person deems it to be, an animal, an insect, a cartoon, or any other form. In David-Neel's case, she created a Tulpa similar to the image of Friar Tuck (Veissiere, 2016). In the chapter devoted to Tulpamancy, David-Neel describes that others are able to see and witness other creators' Tulpas. The interesting aspect of this manifestation is that Tulpas can be created as a result of mental concentration and/or generated impetuously (Juliani, n.d.). In Stacey's case, Jasmine, her childhood imaginary friend who never grew old, was originally created either by design or organically to assuage her loneliness, as well as to relieve her emotional and physical pain resulting from her sexual abuse. While thoughtform Jasmine was her companion and confidant, the demonic voices and visions are the embodied unconscious thoughtforms/Tulpa manifestations of psychic pain along with Jung's discovery of his own inner mindscape – the shadow self and the collective unconscious. The generation of thoughtforms and achieving plurality constitute a purpose for the host. Concentration, empathy, unconditional positive regard, and open mindedness are necessary for the clinician to transmute through the thin place into the realm of forms and timelessness.

As relevant thoughtforms, Tulpas, thought transference and the psi factor may be, much has not changed from Freud and Jung's time. The clinical conversation and narrative with other clinicians does not leave any space to communicate any other explanation regarding the human experience other than the reductionist and limited discourse presented and used at the time. Just as Freud who was fascinated with thought transference experiments and Jung's spiritual emergency had to be kept silent for so many years for fear of scrutiny, so happens at present. My clinical anecdotes with thoughtforms/Tulpas/psi factor are shared with few and never mentioned in the clinical presentation.

Hearing Voices

More research on aspects of hearing voices is slowly being disseminated in the scientific circle (Woods, 2013). New and perhaps controversial evidence opposes and refutes Big Pharma's claim of biochemical imbalance theory of mental illness (Whitaker, 2010). In reviewing the literature, the current biomedical discourse of utilizing evidence-based practices medicalizing and providing mechanical superficial clinical interventions is overlooking the implicit need of human bonding and healing. As one of my group members stated, "Just lock me up like they used for years! No one really cares! In five years no one will remember that I even existed!" This statement came after she confided in a group what the voices were telling her to do. Instead of validating, processing, and incorporating coping skills to deal with the voices, she was sent for two psychiatric evaluations and an ER visit.

Another incident transpired while I was giving a presentation on Hearing Voices. An attendee was describing his experience with voices and an attachment similar to a dark snake sucking his energy in his solar plexus region. Frank described that it drained, depressed, and exhausted him. Insomuch, he felt defeated and alone that no one believed that he was "possessed" as a result of it. While we were on break, I described to him the "attachment" he felt, and I confirmed that that was what he was seeing and feeling. Upon returning, I communicate to his mother that what Frank is feeling and seeing is real, and there are ways of dealing with it. His mother retorted that he didn't need me as a spiritual advisor.

Evidence-based medicine based on the oncological concept of hearing voices and seeing visions as the byproduct of a genetic disorder and chemical imbalance incapacitates the pained person to self-soothe. The psychiatric evidence-based interventions are devoid of the compassionate understanding of the pained other. Just by the nosological sterile classification of human behavior with the attached ignominy of the collective culture toward the experience establishes a subject/object relationship deficient of any emotional bond. In other words, the punative language used in systemic and collectivist culture makes the thin place an impossible destination. Insomuch, just by being labeled as sick, the identified patient is stripped of agency to feel any life contentment and self-empowerment.

But Stacey was lucky, I think. Through my state of presence and absolute open mindedness, Stacey's lived experience, which had been denied and questioned throughout her life and coined as a non-reality, a *psychotic hallucination*, became an observed reality. This reality was substantiated by my being able to understand Stacey's lived experience through the manifestation of "Jasmine." The thin place is a humbling venue because of the realization that the non-form has a name and a shape. It is a time of awe and contemplation that earth, the universe, and the heavens are connected. It is a time and place where one is present in all spheres. It is when the holistic ancient knowledge of integration converges to form wisdom and unity. It where healing becomes possible. This is radical empathy.

Conclusion

In closing, I want to say that being a social worker in the realm of mental health allowed me to have the privilege of meeting extraordinary individuals. Little did they know that it was not them being the student, but myself who learned from them the incredible feats that the human soul and psyche can accomplish to overcome the pain. Through the experience of just being, it is I who crossed the threshold to the thin place. For each meeting, each group, and each encounter, the awe of the human potential is both humbling and exhilarating to point of jubilant oneness. Barbara Taylor (2014) reminded us that it is the quality of the therapeutic relationship that allows the pained person to heal and not "a mechanistic, formulaic, depersonalized substitute for quality care" that the contemporary system offers (p. 262). Yet crossing over into the thin place comes with a responsibility, which is that clinicians have to be healing toward themselves first in order to witness and cross the threshold of the thin place. Once this crossing over into radical empathy is achieved, then one empowered human can lead the healing process. Perhaps it is the now that we as a society can learn to embrace our ancestral endowment and integrate our human potential and become whole.

Close Reading Questions

1. Blasoni's literature may sometimes feel dated, but the datedness has meaning. What political, social, and technological forces were at play during the 60s through the 80s, and how did those forces shift from the 90s through today? How do socially constructed worldviews affect what constitutes "evidence" and "science"?
2. What do you make of Blasoni's tone throughout the chapter? Would you call it reverent? Respectful? Gracious? Naive? What adjectives describe her writing style?
3. What is Plato's Cave?

Prompts for Thinking and Writing

1. Is "healer" another word for psychotherapist or mental health practitioner? Would you call yourself a healer?
2. Google the Hearing Voices Network. Describe your reaction to what you find. How does the Hearing Voices Network challenge your assumptions about schizophrenia?
3. Listen to the podcast, featured on the E-Resources page, that accompanies this chapter on hearing voices. How does Blasoni's text complement what you heard in the podcast?

References

Algeo, J., & Nicholson, S. (2001). *The power of thought*. Wheaton, IL: The Theosophical Publishing Company. ISBN: 0-8356-0797

Bessant A., & Leadbeater, C. W. (1986). *Thought-forms with 38 color, black and white illustrations*. Wheaton, IL: The Theosophical Publishing House. ISBN: 8356-0008-4

Bragdon, E. (1990). *The call of spiritual emergency: From personal crisis to personal transformation*. San Francisco, CA: Harper & Row.

Burton, N. (2017, September 11). A brief history of schizophrenia. Retrieved from https://www.psychologytoday.com/us/blog/hide-and-seek/201209/brief-history-schizophrenia

Cavanna, A. E., Trimble, M., Cinti, F., & Monaco, F. (2007). The "bicameral mind" 30 years on: A critical reappraisal of Julian Jaynes' hypothesis. *Functional Neurology, 22*(1), 11–15.

Craig, P. E. (1986). Sanctuary and presence: An existential view of the therapists contribution. *The Humanistic Psychologist, 14*(1), 22–28. doi:10.1080/08873267.1986.9976749

Goodman, F. D. (1988). *How about demons? Possession and exorcism in the modern world*. Bloomington, IN: Indiana University Press.

Hycner, R., & Jacobs, L. (1995). *The healing relationship in gestalt therapy: A dialogical/self psychology approach*. New York, NY: Gestalt Journal Press.

James, W. (1904). *The varieties of religious experiences: A study in human nature*. London, England: Longmans Green & Co.

Jaynes, J. (1976). *The origin of consciousness in the breakdown of the bicameral mind*. Boston, MA: Houghton Mifflin. ISBN: 0-395-20729-0

Juliani, A. (n.d.). On Tulpas – An analysis of imagined others. Retrieved July 27, 2019, from https://www.academia.edu/20174213/On_Tulpas_-_An_Analysis_of_Imagined_Other

Jung, C. G. (1960). *Structure and dynamics of the psyche, the collected works of C.G.Jung* (Vol. 8). London, England: Routledge.

Kardec, A. (2000). *The book on mediums: Guide for mediums and invocators*. York Beach, ME: Samuel Weiser.

Kerr, J. (1994). *A most dangerous method: The story of Jung, Freud, and Sabina Spielrein*. New York, NY: Vintage Books.

Koss-Chioino, J. D. (2006). Spiritual transformation, relational and radical empathy: Core components of the ritual healing process. *Transcultural Psychiatry, 43*(4), 652–670.

Kreinheder, A. (1980). The healing power of illness. *Psychological Perspectives, 11* (Spring 1), 9–18. doi:10.1080/00332928008410291

Lucas, C. G. (2011). *In case of spiritual emergency: Moving successfully through your awakening*. Forres, Scotland: Findhorn Press.

Mackey, J. L. (2007). The collective unconscious and the Akashic field. *Jung Journal, 1*(2), 2–15. doi:10.1525/jung.2007.1.2.2

Miller, G., & Baldwin, D. (2000). Implications of the wounded-healer paradigm for the use of self in therapy. In M. Baldwin (Ed.), *The use of self in therapy* (2nd ed., pp. 243–262). Binghampton, NY: Haworth Press.

Perry, J. W. (1974). *The far side of madness*. Englewood Cliffs, NJ: Prentice-Hall, Inc.

Ponte, D., & Schäfer, L. (2013). Carl Gustav Jung, quantum physics and the spiritual mind: A mystical vision of the twenty-first century. *Behavioral Sciences, 3*(4), 601–618. doi:10.3390/bs3040601

Powell, D. H. (2009). *The ESP enigma: The scientific case for psychic phenomena.* New York, NY: Walker.

Rogers, C. R. (1957). The necessary and sufficient conditions of therapeutic personality change. *Journal of Consulting Psychology, 21*(2), 97–103. doi:10.1037/h0045357

Rosenbaum, R. (2011). Exploring the other dark continent: Parallels between psi phenomena and the psychotherapeutic process. *The Psychoanalytic Review, 98*(1), 57–90. doi:10.1521/prev.2011.98.1.57

Searles, H. (1973). Concerning therapeutic symbiosis. *Annual of Psychoanalysis, 1,* 247–262.

Taylor, B. (2014). *The last asylum a memoir of madness in our times.* Toronto, Ontario Canada: Penguin Group.

Thurschwell, P. (1999). Ferenczis dangerous proximities: Telepathy, psychosis, and the real event. *Differences, 11*(1), 150–178. doi:10.1215/10407391-11-1-150

Veissiere, S. (2016). Varieties of Tulpa experiences: The hypnotic nature of human sociality, personhood, and interphenomenality. In A. Raz & M. Lifshitz (Eds.), *Hypnosis and meditation: Towards an integrative science of conscious planes* (pp. 1–28). Oxford, England: Oxford University Press.

Whitaker, R. (2010). *Anatomy of an epidemic.* New York, NY: Broadway.

Woods, A. (2013). The voice-hearer. *Journal of Mental Health, 22*(3), 263–270.

5

PULLING YOURSELF UP BY YOUR BOOTSTRAPS

Transcending the Stories of the Ego

Michael Jarrette-Kenny

Pre-Reading Questions

1. Is it possible to have spirituality in the absence of religious belief?
2. What are your assumptions about the use of hypnosis and trance in spiritually sensitive mental health practice?
3. What are the implications of meditation and the use of entheogens for the practice of social work and psychotherapy?

"I don't know who I am anymore," Felicia says, dropping her arms to her sides like a discarded marionette.

I have heard these words so frequently from clients over the years that it is hard to connect the many faces attached to them. The ancient dictum "know thyself" is perhaps the central reason psychotherapy exists in the first place. Most of the time, that desire to find out the answer is precipitated by considerable emotional pain.

"You're a mother," a well-meaning friend said to her earlier in the week, as she tried to tell her how fraudulent she feels.

"The middle-aged mother of two, nearly adult children, one in college the other one on the way. They won't need me soon and then what?"

I know better than to say a wife… to a husband who is barely home enough for the kids to remember his name. A stranger to fill the space next to her on the couch occasionally, a man really more married to his job than to her. She can hardly complain based on her own work tendencies, always at the job or obsessing about it in some way.

"I did everything I was supposed to do…"

A long pause follows. The silence contains a multitude of unnamed co-conspirators in her unhappiness: the parents and teachers she tried to please, the pop songs that lied to her about love, boyfriends who criticized and abused her, including the ones she ended up marrying. Her unfinished thought contains the seed of most of our discontent, the myth of the well-lived life and how it tyrannizes those who believe in it. We confuse what we are doing, the roles that we play, and the things that surround us for who we are. Follow this map to be happy, buy this car, take this drug, and, you too, will look like the bubbly, non-depressed cartoon character from the ad. Deviate from it, get sick, or be neglected, lose a job or relationship, be poor or an immigrant or minority, and you're on your own. Or maybe you're one of the few who have the incredible luck to get to adulthood relatively unscathed. Maybe you've done everything exactly as you were told to do and managed to pull it off, only to still feel empty and useless. It reminds me that we psychotherapists are collectors of these fragmented stories, told by unreliable narrators who have somehow wandered away from their storylines: the alcoholic relapsing after 20 years of sobriety, the woman who leaves the wrong man, only to find another wrong man, the honor student who gets busted for shoplifting, the loyal employee laid off after a lifetime of service. Who are we when we cease to recognize ourselves in our own narratives or are written out of the storyline against our will?

★ ★ ★

A brief disclaimer: what follows is also a kind of story, not just in the sense that I have changed details in order to protect the anonymity of the participants, but a story in that all explanations in some fundamental sense are a kind of story, pointing at some reality that is essentially elusive. More on that subject later.

★ ★ ★

"I'm trying so hard to get better," she concludes in a frustrated and angry, almost accusatory tone, reaching for the tissues on the table beside her.

It is a sentiment that involuntarily brings me back to notions of guilt and salvation from my time in Catholic grade school. It is the sinner who despite their good works fails to reach what can be achieved only by divine grace (or its modern healthcare equivalent; Prozac and cognitive behavioral therapy). The other image, stated somewhat enigmatically by the Korean Zen master Seung Sahn (1976), illustrates the tangled web of egoism involved in much spiritual aspiration; "The idea that you want to achieve something in Zen meditation is basically selfish. 'I want to get enlightened' means 'I want to get enlightened.' But aspiration is not for myself, it is not a merely individual desire, it transcends the idea of self. It is desire without attachment. If enlightenment comes, good. If enlightenment does not come, good. Actually, this is enlightenment.

(p. 91).The inimitable spiritual entertainer Alan Watts (1989) arrives at a parallel point, deriding the futility of trying to achieve enlightenment (or in the more prosaic realm of mental health, make oneself better) by some deliberate act of the will, as if "the ego can toss itself away by a tug at its own bootstraps" (p. 121). Go ahead and try if you dare. You'll see that this popular image of self-determination is in actuality an exercise in futility.

Similarly, in the realm of psychotherapy, the attempt to overcome emotional pain by our clients is often heightened by the very methods used in their healing, namely the reinforcement of a notion of self which, whether we choose to view it in its positive or negative manifestations, in some very real sense may lack existence, and, in either case, ultimately function as the source of our pain. At least this could be taken as the Buddhist position on human suffering or *dukka*.

The following chapter represents an attempt to come to terms with this notion of ego and the self (distinct but often entangled concepts), as it has arisen in my psychotherapeutic and meditation practice as well as the phenomenological and spiritual implications of these concepts.

Mindfulness and meditation practices have become integral tools within the psychotherapeutic toolbox, but have we trivialized the aims and methods of Buddhist and other meditative traditions for a strictly utilitarian purpose that is part of the problem it purports to solve? What are the implications of the use of plant medicines and other drugs as a means of inducing these enlightenment experiences on demand? Are these experiences merely a kind of self-delusion brought on by misinterpretations of our neurology, or do they reflect a more fundamental reality which eludes our everyday experience? The writer Aldous Huxley imagined in his final work, "Island," a society which has built the experience of moksha or spiritual awakening into the daily life of its citizens. Is it possible to build a bridge with these practices toward a kind of secular spirituality, an antidote to the excesses of neoliberalism consumer society, free of the dogmatic baggage associated with traditional religious practices?

I will attempt to explore the implications of some of these questions through the use of case material as well as contemporary popular accounts of mystical/enlightenment experiences. In addition, I will address the uses of traditional meditation practices within psychotherapy as well as the use of plant medicine (Ayahuasca and psilocybin in ceremonial and therapeutic context) on the functioning of the ego.

Defining the Ego

What is the nature of the ego? One has to state at the outset that a distinction must be made between ego in the Freudian sense (part of the three-part structural model of the mind whose function is "to represent reality and through the erection of defenses, to channel and control internal drive pressures in the face of reality," Mitchell & Black, 2016) and the spiritual concept of ego employed by writers like Eckhart Tolle. Tolle (2008) referred to the ego as "a false self created by unconscious identification with the mind" (p. 23), like the autobiographical, conceptual aspects of our experience reflected in our internal chatter and self-talk. Another way of describing the ego is the story that we tell ourselves about ourselves.

The "Story" of Felicia

Felicia sat across from me, the look of a wounded child drawing her gaze to some spot on the carpeting in front of my chair.

"I don't want you to be mad at me, I kept thinking about what a failure I have been. You must be tired of listening to me talk about the same things over and over again."

We had spent a considerable amount of time working through the ongoing struggles related to the extensive childhood abuse she had suffered at the hands of her physically abusive parents. From their repeated acts of violence, she had learned that she must be perfect at all times if she were to survive. Later in life, she had grown into an exemplary human being by any standard measurement of the concept. And yet each new accomplishment proved to be always short in one way or another from the mark. Her introduction to meditation practice had represented a similar struggle.

"I just can't seem to get it. I don't know what is wrong with me."

We talked about her experience of the voice in her head.

"It's my mother's voice; she's been dead for ten years, and I still hear her. 'What the fuck is wrong with you, what the fuck is wrong with you,' on this endless loop."

★ ★ ★

Early in my career, while undergoing training in Ericksonian hypnosis, the question of how to put someone into trance was quickly superseded by the awareness that myself and practically everyone I met was in a kind of trance already. As I stood with one of my classmates, a formidable, hyperintellectual psychiatrist with a thriving practice on New York's Upper East Side paying for our coffees in a 7–11, it struck me, watching her stand there at the checkout, her hand suspended for nearly a minute toward the cashier, despite the fact that her change was very visibly deposited in front of her. This anecdote is not meant to disparage my classmate but to illustrate a simple fact. Perhaps if you are like me, you find yourself entranced as you drive to work in the mornings. You notice the driver in the car next to you resembles an ex-partner. Shortly thereafter, you find yourself going over your last argument with them. Soon afterward, you begin to think of every romantic conflict of your early life and what you should have done differently. Over the course of five minutes, you have experienced a decade worth of frustration or humiliation and fought with a half a dozen people without having left the front seat of your car. My own experience and the excerpt from my session with Felicia are fairly typical examples of this egoic self described by Tolle.

The appeal of mindfulness lies in the insidious character of mindlessness, or rather in the propensity of the Default Mode Network (DMN), to weave stories and scenarios out of the traces of our past and potential futures. The DMN refers to areas of the brain consisting of "dorsal and ventral medial prefrontal cortices, medial and lateral parietal cortex, and parts of the medial and lateral temporal cortices," which are known to become more active when the individual is not actively engaged in some type of goal directed activity. It is "involved in the evaluation of potentially survival-salient information from the body and the world: perspective taking of the desires, beliefs, and intentions of others and in remembering the past as well as planning the future" (Sheline, Barch et al., 2009). It is the DMN which has been noted to be most affected by meditation practices and the use of psychedelic drugs, primarily related to our experience of the self. When active in a depressed or anxious person, the DMN acts upon us in ways far beyond the benign description.

Transcending the Trance

The focus of transcendence of the ego, *satori* or *samadhi* as it is referred to in the terminology of zen, has been the subject of some reflection and misapprehension at the dawn of Western psychotherapy, most notably in Freud's assessment of the infantile narcissistic impulse or oceanic experience. In "Civilization and Its Discontents" (1989), he dismisses the phenomena as some sort of regression to the prenatal Eden of the womb, forever pined over but lost irretrievably at birth (Epstein, 2013). His former acolyte, Carl Jung, was more appreciative of this mysterious state. In his forward to the Buddhist scholar D.T. Suzuki's "An Introduction to Zen" (1964), Jung acknowledges the similarities between the Buddhist conception of enlightenment and the Christian mystical conception of union with the divine, while simultaneously noting the essentially inscrutable nature of this type of spiritual awakening for the Western mind. (In a late interview, Jung appears to approach this ineffable experience when asked about his belief in God, stating, "I do not believe, I know.") In Jung's assessment some aspect of the Western character is incapable of the herculean effort involved in achieving *satori*. Perhaps this effort is a result of an excessive emphasis on rational means to attain an end that is beyond the merely cognitive.

The venerable Chinese sage Lao Tzu (a central influence on zen) noted in the opening stanzas of the *Tao Te Ching* that "The Tao that can be told is not the eternal Tao. The name that can be named is not the eternal name," meaning that in a certain sense, the ineffable nature of reality prohibits us from making any statements about it without creating misunderstanding. The very language that we use to speak, our means of conceptualizing experience, creating symbols in place of reality, is ultimately an act of separation between our experience of the world and the world itself. The nearest articulation of this sentiment in the Western tradition (koan like in its seeming self-contradiction) is the Austrian philosopher Ludwig Wittgenstein's (1922) famous final statement from his "Tractatus Logico Philosophicus." Echoing Lao Tzu, he affirms the inchoate character of the mystical experience and the limitations of conceptual thought. After rigorously developing his argument regarding the limitations of language and its relationship to reality, he ends by stating, "My propositions serve as elucidations in the following way: anyone who understands me eventually recognizes them as nonsensical,when he has used them—as steps—to climb up beyond them. (He must, so to speak, throw away the ladder after he has climbed up it.) What we cannot speak about we must pass over in silence" (pp. 576–577).

The paradoxical nature of Wittgenstein's project, at once an articulation of the principles of reason and its repudiation, echoes the dual character of human consciousness: a thinking, abstracting self, and an embodied, emotional unconscious self acting as its silent, but decisive, partner. I will examine this idea in more detail when we discuss the nature of consciousness.

Psychotherapy and Spiritual Practice

What does all this have to do with the practice of psychotherapy? A better question might be: is it possible to deny the spiritual dimension of psychotherapy? The central issue of who we are and how we relate to the rest of the cosmos is the focus of both. The stoicism which underlies much of cognitive behavioral therapy is an attempt to end suffering in terms not dissimilar to the texts of Buddhism or Taoism (Murguia & Díaz, 2015). In a similar fashion, the therapy office represents the secularization of the cathartic aspects of the catholic confessional. The humanistic existential tradition as well represents an acknowledgment of some intrinsic value to the human experience which, irrespective of one's belief in otherworldly phenomena, seems to point to some essential worth beyond mere biological machine; the spiritual being paired down for export to secular society but still retaining some remnant of its previous luster.

All of these sentiments were rather new to me prior to my meditation practice. Given my lifelong skepticism and discomfort with spiritual matters, dealing with the issue of patient's beliefs has always been a thorny subject.

For Felicia, a science teacher who identified as an atheist, the idea of incorporating spiritual practice into her daily life seemed ridiculous.

"I've tried meditation, and I just can't stop my thoughts. It just seems like a complete waste of time; there are so many other things I could be doing. I just don't see the point."

In these scenarios there are usually a flurry of overlapping beliefs reinforcing the reluctance. First, that meditation involves somehow stopping one's thought which, experientially, particularly when dealing with upsetting thoughts, only reinforces the likelihood of them re-occurring (Tolin, Abramowitz, Przeworski, & Foa, 2002). Next that one's life is too consumed with activity to make room for a practice that apparently, from an external point of view, involves doing nothing (never mind the time you might have wasted throughout your life pointlessly worrying about things that never come to pass, or that are out of your control).

Buddhism has in particular enjoyed a recent celebration of its methods in the psychotherapeutic community through the current fascination with mindfulness (outlined in one of the early Buddhist texts *the Sattipatthana Sutta*) and meditation practice (a broader term outlining a variety of practices of which mindfulness is one). Because of its emphasis on an experiential psychological process, making it perhaps the earliest example of psychotherapy, one need not have any particular belief system to practice it, a selling point for people like Felicia who find religious ideas repellent or irrational. Sam Harris (2014), author and neuroscientist (and one of the so-called "Four Horsemen of Atheism"), in his book "Waking Up: A Guide to Spirituality without Religion" addresses these concerns of non-believers. He acknowledges the discomfort that many individuals have with assumptions regarding mystical experience and spirituality, while at the same time discussing his own spiritual experiences with psychedelics and through his training in the Tibetan Buddhist practice of Dzogchen. The problem of rejecting spiritual experiences as self-delusion on the part of practitioners is "that millions of people have had experiences for which spiritual and mystical seem the only terms available" (p. 11). As the title of his book suggests, one need not reject the experience of spirituality on the basis of non-belief. It becomes problematic only when one draws conclusions based on these experiences regarding the broader nature of reality.

Through the work of Jon Kabit Zinn and others, the beneficial effects of mindfulness-based practices have been validated empirically (Grossman, Niemann, Schmidt, & Walach, 2004) and are now available through numerous cellphone apps (most notably "Headspace" and "Calm") and local programs throughout the world. Kabat-Zinn (2003), the founder of the Mindfulness-Based Stress Reduction (MBSR) program, defines mindfulness as "the awareness that emerges through paying attention on purpose, in the present moment, and nonjudgmentally to the unfolding of experience moment by moment"(p. 145). Elsewhere, he elaborates on the nature of the egoic process:

> We all take ourselves too seriously because we believe that there's someone to take seriously. That "me." We become the star of our own movie. The story of "me", starring, of course, me! And everyone else becomes a bit player in our movie. And then we forget that it's a fabrication. It's a construction. And that it's not a movie and that there's no "you" that you can actually find if you were to peel back.
>
> *(Mindful.org, 2019)*

This explanation of the egoic process brings us back to Felicia's question at the outset of this chapter. If there is no "you," if this idea of yourself is not only experienced as fraudulent but is actually a fiction, we are returned to the question of just what is left in its place?

Advaita Vedanta (literally "non-secondness"), or the non-dual school of Hindu philosophy, represents the earliest iteration of this idea of the self (atman) as identical with the universe (brahman), a way of simultaneously affirming the reality of some essential consciousness while denying the reality of a personal self. Based on the Upanishads, Bādarāyaṇa's Brahma Sūtras (Menon, n.d.), it shares much of the basic tenets of various schools of Buddhism, particularly the Dzogchen school. Zen, while differing in language, puts forth a similar idea, that "awareness of oneself as a discrete individuality, is an illusion" noting "the dualism of myself and not myself" leads to a differentiation of oneself from the external world (Kapleau, 2013). The emphasis here is in the non-conceptual basis of ultimate reality in which the knower and the known are indistinguishable – not a matter of intellectual awareness in a conventional sense, but a kind of reframing of one's perception. On one hand, nothing changes; on the other, the basic foundation of experience is upended.

Finger Pointing at the Moon

Returning to our earlier discussion regarding the failure of language to articulate the notion of enlightenment, if the experience is in some sense incommunicable from the Eastern perspective, what exactly are we talking about when we discuss spiritual awakening, and what do such experiences look like in a Western context?

Since Jung's time, the great popularization of Buddhist and other meditative traditions in the West has led to a number of instances of enlightenment outside of the cultural context of the East. This has brought us some sort of scientific awareness of the biological impact of meditative practices and of the neurological correlates of these experiences.

An account, strikingly similar to the classic enlightenment experience, is Jill Botte-Taylor's description of the brain hemorrhage she suffered in December of 1996, popularized in her TED talk entitled "Stroke of Insight" (2008). A brain researcher at Harvard University, Bolte-Taylor begins the talk with a discussion of her personal family experiences with mental illness, in particular her brother's struggles with schizophrenia, which spurred in her a lifelong interest in mental health issues. She works with NAMI providing education to the public regarding mental illness. On the day in question, Bolte-Taylor experienced the subjective side of brain dysfunction, noting a complete loss of control over her body over the course of four hours. There is a final utterance from her deteriorating left hemisphere:

"And I'm asking myself, 'What is wrong with me? What is going on?' And in that moment, my left hemisphere brain chatter went totally silent. Just like someone took a

remote control and pushed the mute button. Total silence. And at first I was shocked to find myself inside of a silent mind. But then I was immediately captivated by the magnificence of the energy around me. And because I could no longer identify the boundaries of my body, I felt enormous and expansive. I felt at one with all the energy that was, and it was beautiful there." After a long protracted effort attempting to dial the phone, she contacts a coworker who sends emergency services. After surrendering to the possibility of her impending death, she loses consciousness. Later she awakens in the hospital, amazed at her survival.

"Because I could not identify the position of my body in space, I felt enormous and expansive, like a genie just liberated from her bottle. And my spirit soared free, like a great whale gliding through the sea of silent euphoria. Nirvana. I found Nirvana. And I remember thinking, there's no way I would ever be able to squeeze the enormousness of myself back inside this tiny little body." (Taylor, J. B., 2008).

Bolte Taylor's account of the dissolution of her internal chatter in the midst of her aneurysm bears a marked resemblance, minus the physiological complications, to Eckhart Tolle's account of his spiritual awakening in the "Power of Now" (2004). Prior to this event, Tolle reports a long history of anxiety and suicidal depression throughout his life. At age 29, he describes a literal dark night of the soul, awakening in the middle of the night feeling "a deep longing for annihilation, for nonexistence was now becoming much stronger than the instinctive desire to continue to live" (p. 3).

A repetitive thought, almost like a mantra, focused on his self-loathing and the fact of not being able to live with himself, provokes a moment of clarity: "Then suddenly I became aware of what a peculiar thought it was. 'Am I one or two? If I cannot live with myself, there must be two of me: the "I" and the "self" that "I" cannot live with.' Maybe, I thought, only one of them is real" (p. 4).During the panic attack that follows, he experiences auditory hallucinations telling him to "resist nothing" as he is sucked into a void which is mysteriously described as both outside and inside himself. He awakens the next day to discover that the inner voice which has plagued him his whole adult life has become silent, thrusting him into a state of presence or awareness of the present moment.

It has long been noted that the experiences occasioned by the use of psychedelic drugs have approximated the ego dissolution experiences that I have just described, as well as the accounts of mystics since antiquity. Timothy Leary (1964) along with his colleague Richard Alpert, following their personal and professional experiences with psychedelics (later known as Ram Dass), famously reinterpreted "the Tibetan Book of the Dead" as a sort of guide to managing the experience, making explicit the connection between the soul's journey and the phenomenology of Lysergic Acid Diethylamide (LSD) use. More contemporary researchers Nour and Carhart-Harris (2017) noted that "distortions of self-experience are a central feature of a number of altered states of consciousness, such as the psychedelic state and the mystical experience" (p. 177). While early applications of these drugs for clinical purposes showed much promise for the relief of suffering (Bill Wilson, one of the founders of Alcoholics Anonymous, was reportedly an early advocate of the therapeutic use of LSD) (Vargas-Perez & Doblin, 2013), the banning of these substances has prevented, until recently, the investigation of its healing potential for mental health issues.

Tim, a patient who recently participated in several Ayahuasca ceremonies at one of the many retreats that have arisen to treat trauma and addictions of all types, agreed to speak with me regarding his own mystical experiences brought forth by this ancient psychedelic. His descriptions correspond quite closely with those of Bolte-Taylor and Tolle.

The "Story" of Tim

"Look, I've been on a bunch of SSRI's and SNRI's, taken benzos for sleep and anxiety issues, what's a little trip to the Amazon?" he jokes. Beneath the laugh is the frustration with the side effects and limitations regarding the clinical effectiveness of such drugs and the promise of a more effective treatment.

Ayahuasca, a potent hallucinogenic tea (essentially an orally active form of the hallucinogen N,N-Dimethyltryptamine (DMT)) made from the bark of Banisteriopsis caapi together with various other plants, has reportedly been used in a ceremonial context from as early as 2000 B.C. according to archeological evidence (McKenna, Callaway, & Grob, 1998). Today, its usage has expanded beyond its employment by shamans in the Amazon basin to various religious sects which use the substance for sacramental purposes as well as therapeutic rehab centers who employ the substance for the treatment of psychological issues and addiction.

The use of various types of psychedelics for therapeutic purposes has experienced a recent resurgence. A Johns Hopkins-funded study involving terminal cancer patients reported that "a single dose of psilocybin produced substantial and enduring decreases in depressed mood and anxiety along with increases in quality of life and decreases in death anxiety in patients with a life-threatening cancer diagnosis" (Griffiths et al., 2016, p. 1195). Ayahuasca has shown similar promise for the treatment of psychiatric disorders and addiction. A study with individuals with treatment-resistant depression "found evidence of rapid anti-depressant effect after a single dosing session with ayahuasca when compared with placebo" (Palhano-Fontes, Barreto et al., 2019).

Tim's lifelong struggles with depression and anhedonia helped him to overcome his reticence about the drug. In light of his later experiences with medication, he recalls his early introduction to the subject:

"You know, I was the archetypal hyperactive kid. I think I spent every day of kindergarten sitting out in the hallway outside the classroom for not being able to sit still, breaking the rules, you know. It gave me perspective about why kids behave the way they do. They kept pushing for me to go on medication but when they took me to a child

psychiatrist, he said I was a normal kid. I wonder how different my life would be if it had gone differently. I don't think that anyone knew the chaos I was experiencing at home. I don't think they have a pill yet for fixing a broken family."

He paused for what seemed like an uncomfortably long time.

"My Dad lived far away, and I didn't have much contact with him. My mom had to work all the time, so I was basically raised by my Aunt. At some point I remember my mom going to the hospital because she got depressed after losing her job at a car dealership. She says that they diagnosed her with bipolar disorder, but I don't know much about what her treatment was like, other than the fact she seemed to be zonked out on whatever drugs they were giving her. Whole years went by, I think, where she didn't seem to get out of bed. When she wasn't sleeping, she was out most of the time. I was always embarrassed by her erratic behavior and the inappropriate things she would say to my friends. She always seemed to be fighting with the rest of the family because of her issues with spending. I remember resenting how she would spend all her money on her friends and on gifts for their kids; she was so needy and thought she could buy people's affection. I didn't seem as important to her. When I was very young, I remember being terrified when the police came to our door looking for her. When I got older, it became really difficult to be around her or even to stay in touch with her. She was so paranoid that she would always be changing her phone number and moving to different apartments. I always felt like I had to be the adult around her, that I couldn't count on her to make the right decisions. One day I got a call that she had gotten arrested and injured herself because she thought somebody was following her. I went to the hospital to see her, and she was handcuffed to the gurney. I felt so frustrated and angry by her behavior and attitude that I just stormed out. When I tried to call the hospital to find out about her treatment they wouldn't release any information to me. Months went by before I received a call from a social worker and discovered that she was in a psychiatric hospital. I went to visit her, and I found out that she thought I never wanted to speak to her again."

I asked him about what had inspired him to go to an Ayahuasca ceremony.

"I heard about these retreats for years, mostly celebrities with drug problems who were trekking down to the Amazon. I have always wanted to believe in something bigger, there being some greater purpose to life."

"So yeah, I booked a place, not in the Amazon, but with a shaman who had trained there. A company that works out of the country where it's legal. The first time I made the reservation I had a bunch of problems with the payment. Turns out one of the ex employees had scammed a bunch of people and ran off with the money. I was upset, but I went to the place anyway. My girlfriend at the time was going to do it, but we broke up so I figured I would have been paying for her anyway. I just felt like I needed some guidance. I mean, I tried all the other things to try and get better, like yoga, meditation, exercise… Don't get me wrong, they help, but I just needed something more."

"The people I spoke with were really quite pleasant, you know stereotypically spiritual, kind of hippie-ish. They sent this whole, like, manifesto about the medicine and how to prepare, asking about medications and mental health history, even what your favorite music is."

"I met with a female guide, in her mid forties. She had her first experiences at the same center and had ended up training with her first guide. She said she had guided like a thousand people since then. Unbelievably grounded and welcoming, which was great because I was scared shitless."

"The first cup almost tasted like a mixture of like old coffee grounds and dirt, the second was kind of acidic. When I closed my eyes, it was like I could see the music in my mind's eye, just like this undulating ocean of color moving with the rhythm. I had this weird thought like "oh shit, this is what all those people were talking about", like there was some great secret that no one ever talked about that was being revealed to me. The patterns of color were like some living organism. And as I looked at it, it was like this shifting lush green, like the canopy of the rainforest, which then shifted into the desiccated brownish dead matter. It kept moving like that in waves, life and death, life and death. I felt this feeling of understanding, that the two tendencies were part of one thing, that you couldn't have one without the other and that everyone and everything was part of that pattern. I felt that if I zeroed in on it, I would see all the different moments of my life, all the things I had done and that were done to me, Mom and Dad and all that. People hurting each other and loving each other, coming together and breaking apart. Like the drop of an ocean, each drop thinking that it was moving of its own accord, but really just moving forward whether it wanted to or not. All parts of this large tapestry that the individual part could never see from their vantage point. I realized in that moment that I was part of that whole thing and when I had that thought, I started to feel like I was pixelating, like coming apart. 'So this is what it's like to go crazy' I remember I said out loud. It felt like I was in heaven and hell simultaneously, not like in a bad way. I know that probably doesn't make sense to anybody but that was what it was. It felt like it was somehow necessary to feel what I was feeling, like something that had been in me that had been weighing me down was being torn away. Then I felt this intense fear, like 'when is this going to end?' It felt like a thousand years had passed but it had really only been a few hours at the most. At that moment, it was like that process ended and it seemed like I was dying and that there was nothing to do about it but let it happen. It was this intense sensation, that I had stopped breathing, that my heart had stopped, but somehow I was still there. In that moment, I opened my eyes and felt like there was no longer any distinction between what was out there and what was in here, my mind was just totally quiet. It was the first time in my life that I felt the voice in my head stop jabbering."

"The second time I felt this sense of disappointment, almost like I expected it not to work for some reason. I kind of realized that was how I always feel, like I was able to observe what I was doing as it was happening. The guide offered me a second cup and this time I started almost to convulse. I have the situation all the time, almost like this restless discomfort, like I'm jumping out of my skin. Only this time it just kept going over and over again. My body was shaking, but I was completely present and calmly observing it. It reminded me of this documentary I had seen on these orphanages in Romania. All of these abandoned kids rocking themselves uncontrollably. I realized I was just like them. It was like my body was acting out all of this childhood stuff."

As Tim notes regarding his intense reactions during the ceremony, a relationship between traumatic attachment and ADHD, as well as various so-called personality disorders, has long been theorized. Conway, Oster, and Szymanski (2011) asserted that "children experiencing a series of adverse life events early in life, also referred to as Complex Trauma, share a constellation of symptomatology found in children diagnosed with ADHD" (p. 63).

If we may draw parallels with Bolte Taylor's experience, then we may make the following observations: for the unconscious implicit self, time exists as an endless now. For traumatized individuals, early dissociated formative circumstances are acted out again and again, disconnected from conscious awareness. The compulsive hyperactive acting out of the verbally mute right brain exists in order to gain the attention of the detached conscious self which it is dissociated from. In Tim's case, perhaps in the same way a therapist may evoke unconscious experience within a session, Tim is able to observe and acknowledge what has happened to him due to the greater hemispheric connectivity afforded by the drug.

"I became aware of myself as the abandoned kid, wanting so badly to speak but being unable to. I was crying and telling the guide and she asked me what I wanted in this moment and it came all at once like a flood. 'To be seen.' As I said it, I had this awareness of all the people for whom I had been invisible, but instead of anger, I had this understanding that they were doing to me what had been done to them. That we were all the same abandoned neglected child. The feeling persisted. I starting thinking about all the people suffering, not even just people either. Afterwards, I even started becoming aware of the preciousness of everything and everyone, human, animal, plants even. Just this kind of overflow of compassion for everyone and everything. I realized we're all in this together. Literally all part of the same energy."

Tim's description calls to mind a story author Joseph Campbell (1988) related in "The Power of Myth." He described a high ridge in his native Hawaii, where individuals would often go to commit suicide. A police officer witnessing a man jumping to his death follows him over the edge without regard for his own safety, barely looking back to see if his partner was there to grab him. All thoughts about the probable loss of his life fall away from him in this decisive instant. Campbell interprets this in light of Schopenhauer's metaphysics (inspired by readings of Buddhist and Vedic philosophy). The officer has a spontaneous realization that the man about to kill himself is somehow a part of him, "and that the separateness is only an effect of the temporal forms of sensibility of time and space. And our true reality is in our identity and unity with all life" (pp. 272–273). In the more prosaic explanations of contemporary neuroscience, we might recast this idea in terms of mirror neurons. Watching another individual perform an action causes a corresponding reaction in the brain of the observer. This means essentially that seeing someone jump to their death is to vicariously experience yourself doing the same thing. The foundation of empathy is perhaps this recognition that the boundaries between self and other (brought forth in some psychedelic experiences and mediation practices) are tenuous. The consequences of the loss of this feeling of connection and empathic engagement with the world and its inhabitants, in a cultural and political context, may be dire indeed.

Recent revelations regarding the nature of mind highlight the importance of our affective, implicit self on our ability to navigate the world (see the case of Elliot in Antonio Damasio's book "Descartes error,"(2006) a man who after the removal of benign meningioma in the area of his frontal lobe was unable to function in the world due to his loss of emotional response, despite the intact nature of his intellectual functioning). This brings us back into Bolte Taylor's experience of the world as her damaged left hemisphere went off line in the midst of her stroke. The two distinct modes of being in the world (represented by the left and right hemisphere) have their place, but are unequally represented in our cultural landscape. Psychiatrist Ian Mcgilchrist (2019) builds upon these ideas in his book "The Master and His Emissary" exploring the cultural implications of hemisphere lateralization and predominance of left brain thinking in the postmodern era with its privileging of the quantifiable, evidence based, and cognitive over other ways of knowing. A kind of alienation from some central aspects of our experience has led us to an endless wrestling over data abstracted from our core sense of connection and meaning.

I have often encountered these tendencies when I have introduced the concept of meditation in therapeutic settings. In particular, individuals who pride themselves on their intellect struggle with the idea of not thinking (the common misapprehension of the experience). It strikes them as some type of self-imposed idiocy, even if the negative bias of their relentless self-talk is a source of extreme pain or, as is often the case, constant procrastination as they circle forever between equally justifiable alternatives. Indeed, the need to intellectually analyze one's experience in order to, as it were, solve the problem of ourselves (a succinct parody of the Freudian approach) divorced from the dimension of emotion becomes merely an obsessive ritual. To allow ourselves to feel what we feel and to recognize the ruminative quality of much of our self-talk is the last thing that many of us want to do. Enlightenment might be this state of integrated function of the hemispheres, where the emotional embodied self is understood and recognized by its twin; a state of nonduality where total unity is greater than the sum of its parts. This does not come from the left hemisphere talking over its silent partner, but a kind of attentive engagement much like what we call mindfulness.

Criticisms of Mindfulness Practices and New-Age Spirituality

Amidst the discussion of transcendence rests the likelihood of failure. There are individuals for whom certain types of practices may seem difficult or impossible. Beyond this fact, the majority of those involved in mindfulness meditation are not employing it to become enlightened and have no specifically spiritual intention behind it. Is it possible that the co-opting of strategies of mindfulness for the purpose of maintaining the destructive status quo (perhaps in the same way that psychotherapy does) may console us or lead us to accept things that ultimately we should be fighting against? What is the end result of divorcing the practice from its ultimate aim, as was the case with the popularization of some types of yoga as a form of exercise? In attempting to popularize the methodology of self-knowledge, we have perhaps sold out its fundamental character, that of defending the uniquely human from the onslaught of a relentless meritocracy that inevitably ends in the eventual devaluation of ourselves and everything else on the planet. That being said, from my own perspective, observing one's inner experience without judgment has a tendency to foster a more compassionate, engaged stance toward others. Ultimately it is this position of empathic engagement which allows us to act for the benefit of the world. Referring back to the quote which I began this chapter with if it is seen as merely an exercise in self-betterment, it is in some very real sense, not true meditation.

On Narrative

In transcribing and utilized excerpts from conversations with my patients throughout this chapter, I must acknowledge the political dimension in my own tendency to construct "stories" out of these discussions, both in my editing practices and in embedding narratives within my larger discussions. As Gilmore (2010) suggests, regarding stories within the self-help genre like Eckhart Tolle's, "The reproduction of redemption creates a preference for certain kinds of narratives that seem to substantiate through repetition the impossible access to mobility promised by the American dream. Indeed, narratives that succeed in this market point away from a critique of the systemic nature of inequalities, and promote an increasingly non-specific and generic self" (p. 658). From a more academic angle, Woods (2011) notes in regard to narrative practices in the humanities, there are numerous ethical quandaries involved in the presentation of illness narratives, questions revolving around the veracity of the speakers, assumptions regarding the values of narrative coherence in the well-lived life, as well as the centrality of narrative to a conception of self and identity. To counteract these tendencies, Woods invokes Kirmayer's suggestion that "We can only find 'a way to enter into the making and breaking of narrative' in clinical settings if we attend first 'to what is unfinished, incomplete, and tentative – the myriad forms of 'non-narrative' communication," including all the dimensions of embodied interaction (as cited in Woods, 2011, p. 76). In our discussion of story, as in Wittgenstein's discussion of the limits of language for the mystic, there is always a tendency to divorce us from the incommunicable aspects of experience, from the embodied, non-conceptual nature of life.

Biological Criticisms

From the neuroscientific perspective, Turjman (2018) has presented a critique of the phenomenology of enlightenment experiences, noting that the internal observational stance (an observing "true self" identified with pure consciousness and a "false self" identified with the ego) discussed by writers such as Eckhart Tolle is in fact an epiphenomenon arising from a misapprehension of a purely physical process, "what is referred to as Ego is not a psychological construct, but is rather driven by two integrated systems (the "echo-mirror neuron system" and Default Mode Network (DMN)) that support a wide range of functions, and in which the inner self-voice plays a central role" (p. 746)The issue is that the inner voice which Tolle and others suggest is the false self is in fact a necessary component to our experience of being a conscious presence. To separate the two is a functional impossibility or to experience one's inner voice as auditory hallucination. Meditation practices focused on the stilling of this inner voice are seen as being dangerous for some individuals resulting, "in the impairment of vital functions that allow one to interact intelligently with the surrounding environment" (p. 746).

Turjman's neurobiological critique of "the delusion of self-realization" concludes with a final indictment of the present moment experience extolled by Tolle noting that to be in the state "requires the cessation of the inner self-voice and, thus, the multisensory simulation process that perpetuates the past, which is something that cannot be achieved through any volition. But even if this does become possible, the cessation of the simulation processes would consequently disrupt the continuity of Self-Consciousness. So how would it be possible, then, to experience being in the present?" (p. 749). This, in a sense, brings us full circle, in effect that there can be no self in the absence of this inner self voice, almost an inadvertent confirmation of the somewhat contradictory affirmations of the mystic.

One supposes that identifying and exposing the underlying mechanisms of brain function which go into our experience of the self would settle the matter definitively. Given the motivation for much of the practices which are the focus of the critique is the alleviation of suffering, it would seem to be a tragic error that people utilize such practices to attempt to improve their mental health only to worsen it. And yet it seems that, despite this pulling back of the curtain, many people appear to benefit from these practices. I asked Felicia about the effect meditation practice has had on her life and mental health.

"It took me awhile to really get it but when it took hold I finally started to understand. The practice has made me more calm. What happened in the past is in the past. It is not who I am now, I matter. Sometimes, before, I couldn't leave the house. Bill would ask me to stop at the grocery store because we ordered the groceries delivered but they forgot to bring the bread and he like to bring sandwiches for work. Getting through the parking lot would be next to impossible. Half the time I wouldn't even make it in. My friends joked with me that it took me so long to get into the bookstore from the parking lot that the chain went out of business. To go into a store I would need so much

Xanax that I wouldn't remember what I came there for. Now it's totally different. I haven't needed any PRNs. (short for pro re nata; medications that are taken on an as needed basis). Before, just the thought of not having the pills in my pocket book would send me into a panic. I just tell myself to just be in the moment. It doesn't matter if people run into you."

"I went to the Dharma center and I saw that there was a place where people would kneel and pray before the statue of the Buddha and I thought that wasn't how I understood him, like I thought of Catholicism and how you're not supposed to pray to idols. That's not what Buddhism means to me. It's not something you pray to...it's a way you live your life. Before, when I was an atheist and we had to come up with some sort of higher power, I figured well...If I have to pick something, I'll pick aliens. That way I wouldn't have to deal with all the baggage connected to God. When I think about god I would think about how you deal with all the problems of the world and that he would have to be responsible for it, for all the misery and suffering."

"Now there is this spiritual awareness that I never had in my life. It's much better than my aliens were haha. There's a degree of self compassion. It taught me to let go of the need to be perfect. I get to nurture myself in a way that I never had before. You know how I grew up, it was that experience that never got from my parents. It gave me permission to make mistakes, to live with the thoughts. My eyes are welling up."

"There is no right or wrong. Just being. Even though much of what I've read says that meditation is still like doing something. I know I always tell you how many days I've been doing... Not like I'm trying to prove anything by it but just with this sense of awe. It's this time, this thing that I look forward to. It's not just appreciating the calm before the storm, it's the calm that prevents the storm."

Felicia's perspective is far from unique. At least from a clinical perspective, the evidence for the utility of meditation practice and so-called entheogens like psilocybin in the management of suffering (a fact which is acknowledged though minimized by the author) is considerable. The impairment of "vital functions" that are alluded to is usually temporary in nature and conducted in relatively safe settings (no one that I know of advocates doing mindfulness meditation while surrounded by lions or while crossing the freeway), acting more as an antidote to the "content" of much of our thoughts. No doubt there are individuals for whom contemplative practices are ill advised, just as the use of psychedelics is contraindicated in individuals with thought disorders. But the vast majority seem to be helped rather than hindered by these practices.

Turjman's rejection of the validity of spiritual experience recalls Freud's disdain for the oceanic feeling (interestingly enough it is a novelist, Romain Rolland, who defends the mystical intuition to the uncomprehending Freud) and the practices associated with it. The motivation for the rejection of mystical experience, while often couched in rationalist terms, seems to extend from a lack of experiential knowledge. The consequences of excessive religiosity are numerous (possibly the result of the emphasis on dogma in the absence of experience of the spiritual dimensions of life) and myth taken on a literal level becomes ridiculous.

As a consequence, the self in the machine, a mere artifact of the mechanical, finds its content and importance are subject to doubt and suspicion.

Spiritual Machines?

Since Freud delivered his revelations regarding the structure of the mind, we have had to come to terms with the notion of human behavior as determined by unconscious forces of which we have only the dimmest awareness, remaining in a sense strangers to ourselves. This project has continued to the present day, albeit in form which would be unrecognizable to its Viennese progenitor. The fact of the unconscious implicit self, in the aftermath of behaviorism, is a relatively uncontroversial matter as everyone from corporate interests to foreign governments seeks to subtly influence the direction of our dollars and votes beneath the threshold of our awareness. In light of this deterministic landscape, how are we to formulate this concept of spiritual awakening? What does it mean to achieve a higher state of consciousness when consciousness itself is in dispute or merely an incidental byproduct of more fundamental mechanisms? While the subject is a vast one that is beyond the scope of my present discussion, certain aspects are relevant to our subject.

As a clinician, I have rarely encountered these questions regarding the philosophy of mind as a matter of serious consideration amongst my colleagues. Social workers in the area of mental health often function as an adjunct of psychiatry, beholden to the tenets of the medical model. The assumption has been that the mind is something that, through some undefined process, arises from the mechanisms of the brain, and is reducible to the chemistry and biological processes contained there. One such determinist perspective, a natural consequence of confusing the neural correlates of an internal mental state with the subjective experience, is the view that our conscious experience is epiphenomenal, that is, a completely accidental byproduct of brain function and completely irrelevant to the functioning of the organism. This begs the question why consciousness should exist in the first place? Yet the subject of how matter should come to be conscious of itself, a basic fact available to all of us, is forever postponed in our analysis. The philosopher David Chalmers (1995) refers to this situation as the "Hard Problem" of consciousness which he defines as "the question of how physical processes in the brain give rise to subjective experience. This puzzle involves the inner aspect of thought and perception: the way things feel for the subject" (p. 81). Central to this question is the concept of qualia, that is the subjective aspect of perception. Thomas Nagel famously framed this aspect of the mind/body problem in his famous essay "What is it like to be a Bat" (1974). Nagel questions how private aspects of experience could be understood in physical terms, "Does it make sense, in other words, to ask what my experiences are really like, as opposed to how they appear to me? We cannot genuinely understand the hypothesis that their nature is captured in a physical description unless we understand the more fundamental idea that they have an objective nature (or that objective processes can have a subjective nature)" (p. 9). One may describe the chemical composition of vanilla ice cream, but the experience of coldness or sweetness or creaminess is essentially a private affair. I may share my ice cream with you, but the experience is mine alone.

We have yet to formulate a satisfactory resolution to this "Hard Problem." Chalmers and various other theorists (Stuart Hameroff, Roger Penrose, and Donald Hoffman to name a few) have proposed the premise that consciousness is a fundamental aspect of reality, like the laws of physics, a situation which synchronizes with Eastern mystical conceptions of the universe. This orientation, referred to as panpsychism, fails to account for how this fundamental constituent consciousness of matter could be assembled into something recognizably like a self.

Neuroscientist Antonio Damasio (2012) addressed this problem, framing his discussion regarding the nature of consciousness with two fundamental questions: how does the brain construct a mind? How does the brain make the mind conscious? He believes there are two aspects to conscious experience, a self-process which is added to a basic mind process. The self is not viewed as a fixed entity but rather a process which is present whenever one is conscious. This self develops in steps: a proto self with primordial feelings, an action-driven core self, and finally the autobiographical self which incorporates social and spiritual levels. Contrasting William James' notion of a biologically grounded self versus David Hume's conception of the self as a sequence of perceptions in constant flux, he posits maps of perceptual information which are experienced as images in the mind (images which can relate to different types of sensory experience, i.e. visual, auditory, tactile, etc.). These images may be present in the mind, even in the absence of a self/protagonist. Consciousness is seen as not something distinct from the physical but as something which is rooted in the body. A proto self arises from those perceptual maps mentioned earlier, represented in the brainstem and cerebral cortex. This proto self and the body form a feedback loop which links primordial bodily sensations like pain and pleasure (the foundation for our emotional experience) to representations within the brain. This in turn forms the foundation for a core self and later an autobiographical self which adds conceptions of past and future.

This autobiographical self perhaps collapses in the face of the spiritual awakening, awaiting the opportunity for a new conception or story of the self to emerge. As much of my work as a psychotherapist involves helping people with significant traumatic experiences, the discussion brings to my mind psychiatrist Judith Herman and her book "Trauma and Recovery." Herman notes the importance of self-narrative in the process of healing. Once safety and security needs are established, the central theme of treatment focuses upon the development of a coherent narrative of the traumatic event. The original fragmented memory and the often dissociated or repressed material associated with symptoms are translated from their wordless, disconnected state to the realm of verbal coherence. The slow and often painful reconstruction precedes various types of exposure or desensitization techniques (flooding or some type of formalized testimony) which are accompanied by relaxation techniques and other methods for facilitating emotion regulation. The process of reconstruction and the mourning of losses resulting from the traumatic experiences lead to a period of reconciliation and reconnection with others, the development of a new self which may require the facing of feared situations and a casting off of the former victimized self. All of these aspects of the treatment process have in my experience been enhanced by meditation practice on both the group and individual level. While in meditation the point is not to necessarily construct stories, we are able to step back from our often painful self-narrative and observe them without judgment.

Conclusion

The creation of meaning is perhaps the central impulse behind the spiritual "search," an attempt to answer the question of who we are by locating our relationship to the greater whole. From a scientific perspective, we may conclude by creating an exhaustive description of the mechanisms for the "how" of spiritual experience, but it remains for us to determine the "why" of it. The significance of such experiences in terms of developing a new relationship to both our individual and our collective stories exists in a realm outside the deterministic structures of our biology. Perhaps it exists in the space beyond narrative. As Tim noted at the conclusion of our interview,

"When I got back from the retreat I was watching TV and it struck me how we spend so much time creating stories, we watch them, we play them out in our imagination, wondering what our friends and families think, running all these ridiculous situations through our head and none of it is real. The biggest change I've had from this experience has been that. You stop seeing yourself as that old story. It deepened my experience of meditation. It's definitely not for everybody, but I think there are different paths for different people. I used to wonder who I would be if I stopped playing all these tapes in my head from my past. Now I know…"

Close Reading Questions

1. Jarrette-Kenny locates a conundrum during his work with Felicia; he says, "If there is no 'you', if this idea of yourself is not only experienced as fraudulent but is actually a fiction, we are returned to the question of just what is left in its place?" How would you respond to a client who is experiencing this kind of spiritual questioning?
2. Why does Jarrette-Kenny connect Wittgenstein and Lao Tzu? What does this connection tell you about the foundations of Eastern and Western mental health practices?
3. What does Jarrette-Kenny's title mean to you? What does he mean when he explores the notion that "the ego can toss itself away by a tug at its own bootstraps"?

Prompts for Thinking and Writing

1. Why do Blasoni and Jarrette-Kenny make it a point to reference Jung's personal and professional spiritual practices? Seek out Jung's works as primary sources in your answer.
2. Listen to the podcast on the spirituality of children, featured on the E-Resources Page. How do you think the ego changes from childhood to adulthood based on the podcast in connection to what you have learned in Kenny's chapter?
3. Seek out a relationship between Garbe's description of meditation and a Kundalini Awakening and Jarrette-Kenny's description of meditation during an Ayahuasca treatment. How do these descriptions of meditation change your ideas about the now common practice of mindfulness?

References

Chalmers, D. J. (1995). The puzzle of conscious experience. *Scientific American, 273*(6), 80–86.

Conway, F., Oster, M., & Szymanski, K. (2011). ADHD and complex trauma: A descriptive study of hospitalized children in an urban psychiatric hospital. *Journal of Infant, Child, and Adolescent Psychotherapy, 10*(1), 60–72.

Damasio, A. R. (2006). *Descartes' error.* New York, NY: Random House.

Damasio, A. (2012). *Self comes to mind: Constructing the conscious brain.* New York, NY: Vintage Books, A divisions of Random House Inc. .

Epstein, M. (2013). *Thoughts without a thinker: Psychotherapy from a Buddhist perspective.* Basic Books a Member of Perseus Books Group.

Freud, S. (1989). *Civilization and its discontents.* 1961. New York, NY and London: WW Norton.

Gilmore, L. (2010). American neoconfessional: Memoir, self-help, and redemption on Oprah's couch. *Biography, 33*(4), 657–679.

Griffiths, R. R., Johnson, M. W., Carducci, M. A., Umbricht, A., Richards, W. A., Richards, B. D., … & Klinedinst, M. A. (2016). Psilocybin produces substantial and sustained decreases in depression and anxiety in patients with life-threatening cancer: A randomized double-blind trial. *Journal of Psychopharmacology, 30*(12), 1181–1197.

Grossman, P., Niemann, L., Schmidt, S., & Walach, H. (2004). Mindfulness-based stress reduction and health benefits: A meta-analysis. In Database of Abstracts of Reviews of Effects (DARE): Quality-assessed reviews [Internet]. York (UK): Centre for Reviews and Dissemination (UK); 1995–. Retrieved from https://www.ncbi.nlm.nih.gov/books/NBK70854/

Harris, S. (2014). *Waking up: A guide to spirituality without religion.* New York, NY: Simon and Schuster.

Herman, J. (1992). *Trauma and recovery.* New York, NY: Basic Books.

Jung, C., & Suzuki, D. T. (1964). *An introduction to Zen Buddhism.* New York, NY: Grove Weidenfeld, pp. 9–29.

Kabat-Zinn, J. (2003). Mindfulness-based interventions in context: Past, present, and future. *Clinical Psychology: Science and Practice, 10*(2), 144–156.

Kapleau, R. P. (2013). *The three pillars of Zen.* New York, NY: Anchor Books, a division Of Random House Inc.

Kirmayer, L. J. (2000). Broken narratives: Clinical encounters and the poetics of illness experience. In C. Mattingly & L. C. Garro (Eds.), *Narrative and the cultural construction of illness and healing.* Berkeley and Los Angeles: University of California Press.

Leary, T. F., Metzner, R., & Alpert, R. (1964). *The psychedelic experience: A manual based on the Tibetan book of the dead.* New Hyde Park, N.Y. University Books.

McGilchrist, I. (2019). *The master and his emissary: The divided brain and the making of the western world.* New Haven, CT and London: Yale University Press.

McKenna, D. J., Callaway, J. C., & Grob, C. S. (1998). The scientific investigation of Ayahuasca: A review of past and current research. *The Heffter Review of Psychedelic Research, 1*(65–77), 195–223.

Menon, S. (n.d.). Advaita Vedanta. *The Internet Encyclopedia of Philosophy,* ISSN 2161-0002. Retrieved September 25, 2019 from https://www.iep.utm.edu/adv-veda/

Mindful Staff. (2017, January 11). Jon Kabat-Zinn: Defining mindfulness what is mindfulness? The founder of mindfulness-based stress reduction explains. *Mindful.org.* Retrieved from https://www.mindful.org/jon-kabat-zinn- defining-mindfulness/

Mitchell, S. A., & Black, M. J. (2016). *Freud and beyond: A history of modern psychoanalytic thought.* London, England: Hachette UK.

Moyers & Company. (2015, March 30). Joseph Campbell and the Power of Myth, Ep. 4, Sacrifice and Bliss. Retrieved April 8, 2016 from http://billmoyers.com/content/ep-4-joseph-campbell-and-the-power-of-myth-sacrifice-and-bliss-audio/

Murguia, E., & Díaz, K. (2015). The philosophical foundations of cognitive behavioral therapy: Stoicism, Buddhism, Taoism, and Existentialism. *Journal of Evidence-Based Psychotherapies, 15*(1), 37.

Nagel, T. (1974). What is it like to be a bat?. *The Philosophical Review, 83*(4), 435–450.

Nour, M. M., & Carhart-Harris, R. L. (2017). Psychedelics and the science of self-experience. *The British Journal of Psychiatry, 210*(3), 177–179.

Palhano-Fontes, F., Barreto, D., Onias, H., Andrade, K. C., Novaes, M. M., Pessoa, J. A., … & Tófoli, L. F. (2019). Rapid antidepressant effects of the psychedelic ayahuasca in treatment-resistant depression: A randomized placebo-controlled trial. *Psychological Medicine, 49*(4), 655–663.

Sahn, S. (1976). *Dropping ashes on the Buddha.* New York, NY: Grove Press.

Sheline, Y. I., Barch, D. M., Price, J. L., Rundle, M. M., Vaishnavi, S. N., Snyder, A. Z., … & Raichle, M. E. (2009). The default mode network and self-referential processes in depression. *Proceedings of the National Academy of Sciences, 106*(6), 1942–1947.

Taylor, J. B. (2008). Stroke of insight. *TED: Ideas worth spreading.* Retrieved from https://www.ted.com/talks/jill_bolte_taylor_s_powerful_stroke_of_insight/transcript?language=en

Tolin, D. F., Abramowitz, J. S., Przeworski, A., & Foa, E. B. (2002). Thought suppression in obsessive-compulsive disorder. *Behaviour Research and Therapy, 40*(11), 1255–1274.

Tolle, E. (2004). *The power of now: A guide to spiritual enlightenment.* New World Library.

Tolle, E. (2008). Practicing the power of now: Essential teachings, meditations, and exercises from the power of now. Retrieved from ReadHowYouWant.com

Turjman, O. (2018). Enlightenment: Exploring the neural basis of pure consciousness. *Journal of Consciousness Exploration & Research, 9*(8), 739–753.

Vargas-Perez, H., & Doblin, R. (2013). Editorial (Hot topic: The potential of psychedelics as a preventative and auxiliary therapy for drug abuse). *Current Drug Abuse Reviews, 6*(1), 1–2.

Watts, A. W. (1989). *The book: On the taboo against knowing who you are.* Vintage Books Edition. (Kindle DX Version) Retrieved from Amazon.com

Wittgenstein, L. (1922). *Tractatus logico-philosophicus.* London, England: Kegan Paul.

Woods, A. (2011). The limits of narrative: Provocations for the medical humanities. *Medical Humanities, 37*(2), 73–78. doi:10.1136/medhum-2011-010045

6

A POWER GREATER

Exploring Spirituality in Addiction Recovery

Debra Ruisard

Pre-Reading Questions

1. Try "close hearing" the podcast on addiction that attends this volume on the E-Resources page. With the voices you've heard in mind, embark on Ruisard's scholarship.
2. Why do you think that recovery from addiction has historically been tied to religion and spirituality?
3. What are your assumptions about parents who temporarily or permanently lose their children due to addiction? What are your assumptions about people who attend Alcoholics Anonymous?

"Religion is for people who are afraid of going to hell, spirituality is for people who have been there" (Dossett, 2013). Reflecting a deeply held belief that there is a strong spiritual and/or religious component to addiction recovery, this statement is often quoted by members of the widely known self-help recovery groups Alcoholics Anonymous (AA) and Narcotics Anonymous (NA). Spiritual transformation is a common theme threaded throughout the hellish stories heard at AA or NA meetings of the destruction that drug or alcohol use brought to someone's life and their arduous path to recovery. References to God, a higher power, prayer, and meditation are embedded in the language of the 12 steps. And, as the quote infers, there is a distinction made between being spiritual and being religious, with many people promoting the former over the latter despite the religious overtones of the language used. The only criterion for joining the 12-step community is a desire to abstain from all drug and alcohol use, attracting a diverse group of individuals with varying opinions of what it means to be spiritual. Therefore, despite the risk of being too reductionistic, offering a basic definition of spirituality for this chapter is necessary to provide clarity. If you remove all the religious and secular themes that are commonly attached to this sometimes provocative concept, it can be understood simply as the innate instinct that someone has to seek greater meaning and purpose in one's existence and life experiences.

As a clinical social worker in the addiction treatment field, I've witnessed how spiritual growth was sometimes an unexpected and valued outcome of the personal introspection and behavior changes that occurred in individuals seeking to overcome their addiction. Many people who attempt to stop drinking alcohol or using drugs find themselves attending an AA or NA meeting and are exposed to the idea that spirituality is part of the recovery process. For those who have had a positive exposure to religious beliefs and spiritual practices, the emphasis on spirituality could be helpful. For those who do not believe in the existence of a higher power, God or otherwise, or have had negative experiences with religion or spirituality, this focus can create a barrier to participation in the 12-step community. Yet the connection between spirituality and recovery is not reserved only for those who attend AA or NA meetings, as many individuals who do not ascribe to the 12-step philosophy embrace spirituality and use it as a resource to sustain recovery. At times, the spirituality of the 12 steps becomes inadequate for the spiritual growth a person may experience, and they will turn to religious beliefs and practices to support them in their process of recovery. And there are those who do not consider spirituality to be important to their recovery at all. Given the variety of ways that spirituality and/or religion could impact recovery, social workers working in the field of substance use would benefit from understanding the construct of spirituality as it relates to addiction recovery and develop specific competencies in exploring this complex topic with clients.

This chapter will examine the history of the spirituality of the 12-step program, consider the research around spirituality and recovery, offer a broader framework for the exploration of spiritual topics, and, through the examination of individual narratives, provide a way to explore spiritual themes with substance using clients. It is essential that social workers not simply accept the commonly held understanding of both lay people and professionals that recovery requires a particular type of spiritual or religious component. Nor is it adequate to formulate our conversations around the narrow understanding of spirituality that is propagated by the 12-step approach, as this may lead to resistance and potentially unexplored strengths and resources that can be useful for an individual seeking to establish long-term recovery.

Spirituality and the 12-Step Program

Spirituality has been considered an important aspect of recovery from alcoholism and drug addiction since the origin of AA. According to Bill Wilson, the founder of AA, "belief in the power of God, plus willingness, honesty and humility to establish and maintain the new order of things, were the essential requirements" for recovery from alcoholism (Alcoholics Anonymous, 2001, pp. 13–14). His words, recorded in what is called the *Big Book* of AA, set the stage for the foundational assumption that a spiritual component is necessary for recovery from an addiction. According to AA's history, Bill Wilson, having had a "white light" experience during his fourth detoxification from alcohol, reached out to psychiatrist Carl Jung for his opinion. Jung communicated to Wilson the importance of this spiritual experience, and hence, spirituality became a central principle of the 12 steps of AA, particularly of the 1930s American Protestantism kind (Schaub, 2013). Individuals following the 12-step path to recovery "came to believe that a Power greater than ourselves could restore us to sanity" in Step Two, and consequently "made a decision to turn our will and our lives over to the care of God as we understood Him" in Step Three (Alcoholics Anonymous, 2001, p. 59). God is mentioned in four of the other eight steps, and prayer and meditation are part of Step 11, recommended as strategies to make contact with God. Recognizing that referencing God might be off-putting to non-religious or anti-religious individuals, the fourth chapter of the *Big Book*, "We Agnostics," sets out to convince those who claim to be atheist or agnostic that they must give up their resistance to spirituality in order to recover from the destructive use of alcohol. In fact, the *Big Book* provides only two alternatives: "to be doomed to an alcoholic death or live on a spiritual basis" (Alcoholics Anonymous, 2001, p. 44). Such a dire prediction does not bode well for the non-believer. Dissent from one early atheist member was the catalyst for the inclusion of the phrase "as we understand Him" in the third and eleventh step. In 1975, AA for Atheists and Agnostics was formed, and in the 1980s, the Secular Organizations for Sobriety and Rational Recovery were founded as secular counterparts to AA (Kurtz & White, 2015). Between 2011 and 2014, six books were published that offered "concrete suggestions on how those who resisted the 'God-talk' in Alcoholics Anonymous might nevertheless live that program and its spirituality within that fellowship" (Kurtz & White, 2015, p. 64). Since the origins of the AA fellowship, attempts have been made by members of the group to be more inclusive of alternate or a lack of religious and spiritual beliefs. Consequently, many non-religious people find the 12-step program to be a valuable resource for their recovery without having to accept the religious aspects.

Research on Addiction and Spirituality

The spirituality and recovery connection espoused by 12-step programs has been a focus of researchers seeking to understand how people recover from addiction. Dermatis and Galanter (2016) conducted a review of empirical studies on the role of spirituality and religion in 12-step recovery programs. In their review, they found that a number of spiritual and religious characteristics increase once someone achieves sobriety and can predict clinical outcomes relevant to relapse risks; "Feeling God's presence on a daily basis, believing in the universality of a HP [higher power] and program involvement in the form of sponsoring fellow AA members" were the characteristics most predictive of sustained recovery (p. 519). Dr. William Miller, a long-time researcher of addiction treatment, believed that there is enough evidence to support on-going research on the impact of spirituality on addiction. In fact, he stated "religious involvement (one aspect of spirituality) is one of the strongest empirical risk/protective factors predicting addiction, comparable in size to family history" (Miller, 2013, p. 1258). The evidence that religiosity can protect someone from developing an addiction gives credence to the idea that it could also be a factor that supports recovery. Gabor Maté, renowned addiction physician, writer, and speaker about trauma and addiction, considered addiction to be one consequence of spiritual deprivation and believes that "at the core of all addictions lies a spiritual void" (Maté, 2010, p. 83). He saw value in combining spiritual work and psychological work during the recovery process so that seeking to fill the spiritual void does not become another addictive process. Carlo DiClemente, a contributor to the modernization of addiction treatment, predicted that "we will find from both neuroscience investigations and recovery practices that there are important connections between spiritual practices and recovery especially for individuals with the most devastating consequences related to addiction" (DiClemente, 2013, p. 1260). Neuroscience has already increased our understanding of how addiction impacts the brain leading to the development of the disease model of addiction. Future neuroscience research on the connection between recovery and spirituality will hopefully provide empirical evidence to support this connection and lending credence to the necessity of attending to the spirituality of addiction recovery.

There are, of course, critics of any serious consideration that spirituality and religion have an impact on the addiction recovery process. Walker, Godlaski, and Staton-Tindall (2013) have been concerned that "in the 21st century we predominantly rely on what is called a *spiritual approach* to address what is thought to be a *neurophysiological disorder* or *disease condition*" (p. 1234). They challenged the field of substance use to measure and analyze what exactly is meant by spirituality because the current concept that is promoted by addiction professionals does not appear to be informed by theology. They also propose that any measurement of spirituality should include a qualitative assessment to determine what role spirituality actually plays in the lives of recovered individuals. Maia Szalavitz – a reporter, author, and self-disclosed person in recovery – is a vocal critic of the 12-step approach to recovery. She endorses the use of evidence-based interventions to treat this disease rather than using the traditional 12-step spirituality. In her view, "if addiction is a medical disorder, spirituality should not be central to treating it. Whether or not you want to believe in a Judeo-Christian 'God as we understand him'...should have nothing to do with medical care" (Szalavitz, 2014). These viewpoints promote a pragmatic approach to a very ethereal subject matter and support evidenced-based practices which can be observed and measured.

A Framework for Understanding Spirituality

The distinction between religion and spirituality common to the recovery community is reflected in academia, where there has been a noticeable shift in focus from religion to the broader concept of spirituality. Belzen (2004), a psychology of religion professor, delineated the difference between religion and spirituality: "religion is a phenomenon on a macro, cultural level, whereas spirituality is a phenomenon on a micro, personal level...religions always require some kind of spirituality, whereas spirituality on the other hand can be totally non-religious" (p. 302). Religion is now often placed under the umbrella of spirituality as one of many ways that individuals attend to their spiritual selves. The Pew Research Center reported that 80% of Americans believe in God and 75% say that they try to talk to God or a higher power (Pew Research Center, 2018), although the number of people who claim to be atheist, agnostic or nothing is climbing from 17% in 2009 to 26% in 2019 (Pew Research Center, 2019). Still, it is highly likely that the majority of substance using clients who seek the services of a social worker will have religious and/or spiritual beliefs and practices that can be assessed and used as a potential resource in treatment. However, the percentage of mental health professionals who profess to be spiritual or religious is lower than the people who seek their services (Delany, Miller, & Bisono, 2007), a point that is also true for licensed clinical social workers (Oxhandler, Polson, & Achenaum, 2017). This void might contribute to a reluctance or resistance on the part of the social worker to initiate conversations with clients about how spirituality impacts their recovery. Hodge (2002) found that in the past few decades there has been a proliferation of studies that point to the value of developing a level of competency in addressing spirituality in clinical social work practice. He encouraged social workers to "develop the skills necessary to utilize spirituality in practice settings to ameliorate problems in a manner consistent with the profession's ethical mandates" (p. 86). What is needed is a broader framework within which social workers can explore spirituality that encompasses, and yet goes beyond the confines of the spirituality of the 12 steps and religious beliefs.

Miller, Forcehimes, and Zweben (2011) suggested using Paul Pruyser's framework of spirituality that can be expressed in either religious or non-religious language, a helpful choice if there exists resistance to religiosity/spirituality on the part of either the social worker or the client. Pruyser (1976), a clinical psychologist, developed this framework for pastors working with parishioners struggling with issues of faith and it is easily applicable for a social worker working with a client struggling with addiction. He conceptualizes spirituality around seven core human experiences that provide insight into an individual's overall sense of meaning. The first core experience is awareness of what is holy or sacred in one's life. What does a client revere above all else – a place, a possession, an experience, a relationship, a deity? What in their life creates a sense of awe? The second experience is providence – do clients see the world as a friendly or a dangerous place? How does their outlook inform how they function in the world? Faith, or one's belief system, is the third core experience. Do clients believe in something, transcendent or not, that makes them feel safe and secure when life becomes challenging? Gratefulness is the fourth core experience. Are they able to see the good things in their life and accept themselves as deserving of them? The fifth experience is repentance. Are they remorseful for what they have done and able to take responsibility for making changes in their life to improve their well-being? Connection, or communion, is the sixth experience to explore. Is the individual seeking relationship with others, or are they isolating? Do they find meaning in participating in a larger group? Vocation is the final core experience. What provides the client with a sense of purpose in life – a job, a career, a vocation, a role? All seven core experiences have the potential to prompt the client to move beyond the biological, psychological, and emotional dimensions of recovery and discover that part of the self that we often label as "spiritual" could actually be enlisted to support the recovery process. It is not necessary to examine all seven; however, these themes can direct a conversation with a client who is building a meaningful life of recovery.

Personal Narratives of Spirituality and Recovery

Spirituality is impossible to quantify; therefore, a qualitative approach to examining its role in recovery is warranted. In this exploration of spirituality and recovery, eight unstructured interviews were conducted with individuals who were open about their status as a person in recovery and who responded to an invitation to be interviewed about how their recovery is or is not connected to spirituality. The use of an unstructured interview was purposeful so to not direct the interviewees in a biased direction. This method of interviewing is recommended when the goal is to gather in-depth information about a topic the interviewer has little knowledge (Gill, Stewart, Treasure, & Chadwick, 2008). The demographics of the eight interviewees were as follows: 50% were females, 50% were males; 75% were Caucasian, 25% were African American; the age range was 32–55 years old; the years of active addiction ranged from 5 to 32 years, with the average length being 17.5 years; the age range for entering recovery was 22–50 years with the average age being 35.5 years; and the range in years of recovery was 4–13 years, with the average length of 7.8 years.

The interviews were not clinical in nature; however, the information provided by the interviewees is similar to what is gathered in a clinical interview and similar themes can be identified. Pruyser's (1976) framework did not guide the interviews; however, it was used to analyze each narrative after they were conducted to demonstrate how this framework could be used to broaden and direct a clinical conversation around spirituality and recovery.

Spiritual beliefs are deeply personal and often held with great religious conviction. When we enter into conversations with our clients about spiritual matters, this opens up the possibility that our own beliefs, or lack thereof, may influence our approach and put us at risk of being perceived as biased or judgmental; attitudes that are antithetical to foundational social work values. As a person raised in the Protestant tradition, I am aware that I am most comfortable engaging in conversations with my clients about Christian beliefs. My religious views were impacted by my social work education and this translated into an openness to all forms of spirituality in my clients with strong boundaries around the disclosure of my own religious views. The majority of the individuals interviewed for this project speak of spirituality influenced by Christian values; however, this does not reflect the reality that spirituality in recovery is influenced by all faith traditions, as well as agnostic and atheist perspectives.

Spirituality of the 12 Steps

For many people, finding or reconnecting with their spiritual self happens through their involvement in the 12-step approach to recovery. The 12-step concept of God is often very different than the religious one many people grew up with, and as they begin to open up to the idea that recovery has a spiritual component, they begin to view God from a different perspective.

Sheryl. Sheryl found her spiritual self through her involvement in NA, and this has sustained her in long-term recovery. She has a solid conviction that spirituality is necessary for her recovery and speaks assuredly of how her journey into recovery was paralleled by her spiritual growth. Sheryl's drug use started around age 13 and became especially problematic in high school when she started dating "bad boys" who gave her easy access to drugs. The years after high school were when the worst of her drug use occurred: "My parents did not know what to do with me. They were unsure of why their smart little girl wasn't living up to her potential. They took me to all the best doctors and treatment and things like that; I wasn't what you call a first-time winner." She finally got to the point where she had enough and was willing to make a change. Sheryl was fortunate enough to meet a compatible group of people her age who were all finding recovery at the same time: "We became this ragtag crew and did everything together. I never knew that life could be that simple and fun; I was laughing and feeling again. Having those relationships made it so much easier to stay in recovery."

Sheryl grew up Catholic but stopped attending church at the age of 12 when her grandmother died. Entering the 12-step fellowship re-introduced her to God and spirituality: "I don't really believe in a Jesus and all these characters, but I can get with the message that there is good and there is bad; and you should choose the good, you should choose the light in the world versus the darkness." Through her experiences in the fellowship of NA her idea of God changed: "I can't really explain my sense of God now, but I say "God" because it is easier than trying to explain exactly who God is. There is something that loves me just the way I am, as crazy as I am, there is a power watching over me and I just have to continually align myself as best I can with that, rather than with the disease of addiction." Now, when she wants to escape the chaos and craziness in her life, she finds a quiet, peaceful place in her apartment, lights some candles, and meditates: "That is a spiritual thing in my life to just be like – okay, now it's time for me. Let's shut the world down and just turn everything off and kind of clear the space of tension and focus on the good stuff!" When asked what she would say to someone new in recovery about spirituality, she replies, "The most important thing is that my spirituality is connected so much to gratitude. I don't know if I glide through the world on this cloud of gratitude, but I think it is an essential piece to recovery and spirituality." A sacred space, a strong sense of providence, faith, and gratitude are four core experiences evident in Sheryl's narrative. The fact that Sheryl uses the term "God" yet acknowledges that this label does not capture her experience of a higher power is notable and should prompt social workers to explore what clients mean when they refer to "God" in conversations about spirituality.

George. George spent most of his life in active addiction. He looks a little rough with his tattoos and swagger, but when he starts to talk it is apparent that he is a gentle, compassionate man. In his family there are generational patterns of drinking, and this behavior was normalized for him. His addiction to drugs took hold in high school and progressed into his adulthood: "I always felt there was something wrong on the inside, there was a darkness. There was something lacking in my spirit." He eventually started to hate the life he was living, using drugs every day. But he found he could not stop, so he stopped trying. "I just said 'It is what it is; this is my life and this is the way I am going to probably have to live the rest of my life." Even with this growing acceptance of what his life was like, George continued to pop into treatment facilities and meetings, somehow knowing that was where he belonged. One day he learned in the 12-step literature that "while abstinence is the beginning, the only hope for recovery is a profound emotional and spiritual change." And the lightbulb went off! He became open to the possibility that there was a spiritual aspect to his recovery that he needed to explore.

The most compelling core human experience in George's narrative is repentance. He was taught as a child that God was punishing and, having done a lot of bad things, George thought he was condemned with all this sin in his life: "I thought I was the worst human being on the planet. I was considered a career criminal, hopeless; judges and police officers talked to me like I was the scum of the earth." This made him hesitant to embrace the spirituality of recovery, fearing condemnation from God, but as he became open to the spiritual aspect of the 12 steps, he "started to see a greater reliance on this God, for a relationship with a God I started to enjoy and feel better about having. I started to feel a lot of peace of mind behind living differently and having a prayer life and a spiritual life." George began attending a non-denominational church with people who had similar experiences and he began to help others find recovery, eventually becoming a Recovery Specialist. Now his whole life has a new sense of purpose. "How did this transformation happen? How did this guy become a completely different person that's trustworthy and honest?" George attributes all of it to his relationship with God. The most compelling aspect of his story is that it offers an illustration of how spiritual transformation can sometimes be the most powerful motivator for someone's recovery. In addition to repentance, vocation is a strong component of George's spirituality. He has found his purpose supporting people in active addiction to find recovery and he is also considering a vocation in ministry.

Spirituality through Religious Tradition

Even though the 12-step program of recovery is infused with spirituality, for some people, personal spiritual growth leads them to seek a deeper experience with religious faith. Sometimes a spiritual awakening or a spiritual crisis will lead to a more intense search beyond what the 12 steps offer.

Karen. Karen exudes an intense sincerity that is reflected in her dedication to ministry and addiction counseling. Her descent into addiction began when she was in her early 20s and used alcohol to cope with the death of her father. She was also prescribed pain medication for her back. After spending six months in jail for forging prescriptions, her addiction continued to progress as she began buying pain pills off the street, and then finally, in the last four months of her addiction, using heroin. It was during these last months that her life spiraled out of control. She had been able to hide her addiction from her family, but the truth came out when someone called child welfare, and she asked her family to take her children so she could enter a treatment program. That was transformational! "I think that was probably the time I felt the most free." she said as she remembered her year spent in rehab. "It was like they were putting words to how I was feeling. I just knew I felt so out of control inside. It was very awakening for me. And it just made sense, it just clicked." She successfully completed treatment, regained custody of her children, and has not used drugs or alcohol since that time.

As a young child, Karen attended church with her grandmother, and as a teenager, she went with her father. When she entered the military, she moved away from her childhood faith and stopped attending church. But she clearly remembers her spiritual awakening when she was in jail and had what she calls an "encounter" with God. "I was in this deep sleep and I was dreaming about cows and honey and the scripture came to me about 'the land of milk and honey'. And when I woke up tears were streaming down my face and it was like this overwhelming, warm, comforting feeling that just came over me. I will never forget it!" This sacred experience or encounter, as she calls it, kept her connected to God even as her addiction got worse. Karen was introduced to 12-step meetings when she completed treatment. Ultimately it was her realization of the role her higher power played in her recovery that transformed her. "I was like, oh my God, this is the focus! If I just stay connected to him, if I just continue to trust, believe, and work on this relationship, I will be okay." It was also the initial connections she made with people in early recovery – the bible study leader, her sponsor, people in the church she went to – that set the foundation for her strong commitment to her church that characterizes her life now, so much so that she is involved in an intercessory prayer ministry and has embarked on a path of becoming a deacon in her church.

Faith and connection are clearly the two core experiences in Karen's life that define her spirituality. When asked to define spirituality she said "Spirituality for me is my relationship with God, with the Holy Spirit, and with Jesus. It's just about a relationship for me. How am I relating to my higher power and where are we at in this relationship? It's all about relationship and it's all about Him!" Her involvement in the faith community also reflects how much she values connection. Karen's spirituality is clearly a religious endeavor and what is surprising was that she felt she needed to tone down her religious language in order to fit into the 12-step community. She ultimately moved away from NA and toward the church for support in her recovery.

Derek. Derek's narrative is defined primarily by spirituality rather than recovery. Derek does not consider himself to be "in recovery" in the way that most people understand recovery as he still consumes alcohol on occasion. Nor did he participate in the 12-step program as part of his recovery process. But he did struggle with certain vices in his late 20s, including excessive alcohol use, and overcame them through following a spiritual path. Derek is highly animated and engaging when speaking of his spirituality. "I was lucky that I was not raised under any dogma. My parents were Catholic, but it wasn't pushed on me." He speaks about his journey through the lens of a spiritual awakening, which he says came first. He drank alcohol heavily throughout high school and college, and alcohol became a buffer for the pain and anxiety he experienced after the ending of a significant intimate relationship in his early 20s. He considers this relationship loss to be the trigger for his spiritual awakening that began with physical illness and his search for what was making him so sick. It was at this time that he decided to stop using substances. "I stopped because my body didn't want it anymore. I wasn't feeling well, I was very symptomatic and I would try to get help. They would do all these tests, but they could never tell what was wrong with me and ultimately they would prescribe me mental health medications." His intuition told him that wasn't the answer; there was something else going on.

One night as he began to fall asleep in his bed it happened – a feeling of falling into his bed, of imploding into himself and then expanding into nothingness – an experience that felt like minutes but lasted for six hours. A few nights later while meditating, he felt heat at the base of his spine and his whole body started vibrating as the heat traveled all the way up his spine. At the time he did not know what was happening to him but his search for an explanation led him to eventually understand this experience to be a "kundalini awakening" from the Hindu tradition. After this occurrence, Derek began exploring Hindu and Buddhist ideas around spiritual awakenings, slowly developing his faith in transcendent energy. "I believe there is something playing out, that we don't know what that is, that we have to trust," he says. As he began to share about his spiritual crisis and awakening, he encountered people described similar experiences, "who didn't know why they were experiencing what they were experiencing and going to places where people were telling them they were crazy and they were obviously not."

As a psychotherapist, Derek now works with people who are navigating spiritual crises and awakenings such as his own, offering insight and support to these individuals. Derek's narrative can be characterized by these three core human experiences: his sacred experience of a kundalini awakening, his commitment to faith in something larger than himself, and a life purpose, or vocation, to help others who are in a spiritual crisis. Derek's story distinctly diverges from the others, not only due to his non-conformist view of recovery, but also due to his non-Christian spiritual awakening which was just as transformative as Karen's but less common. It is evidenced that the Judeo-Christian faith is not the only belief system in the recovery world.

Blending 12- Step Spirituality and Religion

Blending 12-step spirituality and religion in a balanced way takes intentional effort. For some, the pendulum swings from one to the other as life becomes more established in recovery.

Brian. Brian is a serious, thoughtful man who occasionally reveals his dry humor as he talks about his "long thirty years of drinking and drugging" and his path into recovery just six years ago. He started drinking when he was a young teenager and his alcohol use quickly turned into drug use. He joined the service when he was 18 and considers that the worst thing for him to do as he found the wrong crowd there. After leaving the military, he moved from job to job, and rehab to rehab. He eventually found himself divorced, estranged from his two children, and homeless on the street with a serious drug and alcohol problem. "I became good at it, real good at it. I could survive, I was in my element. And I survived better on the street than I did in 'normal life'."

Brian's recovery began with an experience that encompasses three of Pruyser's core experiences – a sacred moment, providence, and faith in God. On July 9, 2011 he got distressing news that unemployment was not going to give him any money. He sat outside the local library and broke down wailing, like a baby. "And this lady walks out of the library and all she says to me is 'If you give it to Him, He will take your pain away'. She invites me inside and gives me a glass of water, but that is all she says to me." He believes God sent him an angel. He found his way into the VA hospital and has been clean and sober since then. "God was looking out for me 'cause He knew I had a better purpose in life. He carried me straight through!"

Brian grew up in the American Methodist Episcopal Church and went to church because he was told to; at age 17 he just stopped going. Once he got into recovery, he began attending church because NA said he needed to have a spiritual side, so he was going just to check that box off. But when he started attending an evangelical church with his wife, he had a spiritual awakening. "One Sunday morning, the pastor was talking directly to a couple in the church and it got really, really dark in the room, true story! And the light was on them. It was really, really weird and there was nobody else you could see around them!" Brian felt like the pastor was talking directly to him, prophesying that he would find financial prosperity. "I felt something glowing, and then the next week I got three calls for jobs. Something did happen that day, I can't deny it!" Others may consider this just a coincidence, but for Brian it was another significant sacred moment that validated his faith in God. Having a profound religious experience such as Brian's can be found in many stories of recovery, although in the 12-step tradition such sudden transformations are considered exceptions rather than the rule. For most people the search for meaning and purpose is a gradual one.

Julie. Julie's story of addiction and recovery is impacted by traumatic loss. Julie started drinking and smoking pot when she was 18 but stopped when she became pregnant with her son. After he was born, however, she drank to excess when overwhelmed and stressed. She stopped drinking when she became pregnant a second time but turned to pills after her daughter was born. The pills helped her to function as a single mother, giving her energy to go to work, take care of her children, and do everything she needed to do. When she couldn't get any more pills, she turned to heroin and used it on a daily basis for three years. "I wanted to stop but I couldn't because I had to take care of a baby. I didn't think I could go to rehab because I had nobody to watch my kids." Eventually things caught up to her and one day child welfare came, took her daughter and placed her into foster care. "That is what it took to get me clean. That was the only, only thing that worked!" She attended an intensive outpatient program, started going to NA meetings, and has been in recovery ever since.

Julie grew up Catholic, but in the beginning, spirituality did not play a role in her recovery. "I grew up with a punishing God…and when I got into recovery, I was angry. I didn't know if there was a God or not, but if there was, I was angry at Him for punishing me for all the bad things I did." An image of God as punishing is often portrayed in the traditional church and it can be an obstacle for the development of faith in adulthood. However, as Julie talked more about her spirituality it was obvious that it is her faith in God that now sustains her in recovery. "I would take other people's image of a higher power – loving, caring, greater than me, not punishing – it sounded good so I would just hold on to that." And then the unthinkable happened – her son passed away from a drug overdose. Instead of blaming God, this tragedy pushed her closer to God and to religion. "I couldn't go to meetings because they were causing me more harm than good. People would talk about not wanting to live and I would be running out of the meetings crying my eyes out. I needed something to believe in after that. I needed to know that there is a God and there is a heaven. And this isn't all for nothing." She eventually found a local non-denominational church that provided the comfort she was seeking. She became active in the church, and now she is sustained spiritually by attending church services, reading spiritual books and trying to "be still, be quiet and just, you know, listen and pray." Her belief that her son is in heaven continues to bring her a sense of peace and acceptance about his death. "I believe in my spirit that even though I miss my son, that he is here. I know he is here even though I can't physically see him and I wish I could. And he is proud and he wants me to stay clean." She tears up as she remembers her son. "It's gotta be because of God because I didn't think I could do this and not have one of my kids here. I just do my part and not fall off course, and God takes care of the rest."

For Julie, her faith in God is the primary core human experience that defines her spirituality. She is seeking to embrace providence as she tries to make sense of her son's death and exploring this particular human experience would definitely be beneficial to her as she continues to cope with this traumatic loss while maintaining her recovery. Her understanding of providence is linked to her sense of purpose, vocation, which she strongly believes is to speak about her experience whenever she is afforded the opportunity to do so. Julie's story demonstrates how spirituality can strengthen recovery in the face of traumatic loss. Without a greater sense of meaning and purpose, Julie believes she would have relapsed.

The Non-Spiritual Approach to Recovery

Despite the common belief that spirituality plays an important role in addiction recovery, there are stories that refute this assumption.

Carol. Carol's sense of humor is very engaging, and it pairs well with her matter-of-fact approach to her recovery. She does not consider spirituality to have played a part in her recovery story at all – in fact she hesitated to volunteer to be interviewed as she didn't think that she would have much to say. Her path into addiction didn't start until she was in her 40s. Her social drinking was slowly increasing as her children got older and she was introduced to prescription opiates after dental surgery. Once she was no longer able to fill her prescriptions, she began to purchase them illegally. By the time she was 47 she had a full-blown opiate addiction, and she was drinking vodka around the clock. At her family's insistence she went into a detox, twice, but that did not stop her use. Finally, at her 50th birthday party things changed.

> I was so messed up that day, I don't remember anything about the day, but I was told it was really bad! The next morning my mom, my sister, and my daughter showed up at my door to take me to rehab. And I just said, 'I'm ready!' Carol spent thirty-two days in rehab and has been sober ever since.

Carol struggled with the spirituality of AA. She grew up Methodist, but what attracted her to the church was going to events with her sisters and her mother, enjoying everyone being together. The process of developing a religious belief system did not interest her and this perspective influenced her response to the spirituality of the 12 steps. "When we talk about a higher power, I believe in God but I wasn't really having any particular higher power other than just wanting to be healthy and happy and have my relationships back in check." She particularly struggled with the AA saying of "Let go and let God" that was told to her in meetings and she eventually found herself drifting away from the 12-step group she was a part of. "I just wasn't feeling that way. I thought recovery was more about motivation around myself and my family, and how things should be and how I wanted them to be."

Carol's family is her driving force for recovery. "Maybe that's spirituality, in terms of not wanting to hurt my family. I hated that I hurt my family, that I scared them, 'cause it goes against anything I would really ever do when I am not in addiction. I feel like that's a little spiritual." By the end of the interview, Carol began to consider the possibility that she was more spiritual than she originally thought. "This conversation is making it more apparent to me, I think that some of the things that lead people into their addiction are not based in spirituality. I think that you have to totally change your beliefs, to believe in something that motivates you and keeps you going in a better, more positive way." Connection is what motivates Carol. And gratitude. She has a daily practice of writing down things that bother her and then contrasting that with a list of what she is grateful for. "I always have much more than I am grateful for and it kind of helps calm me, or put things into perspective." Carol's story, despite her conviction that she is not spiritual, is the narrative that aligns most with the definition of spirituality provided at the beginning of this chapter – an innate instinct to find meaning and purpose in her existence.

Paul. Paul's energetic presence and personable style of communicating complements his role as a psychotherapist. He used alcohol in his late teenage years to self-medicate his anxiety and symptoms of obsessive-compulsive disorder and to cope with the death of his father when Paul was only 16. A college roommate introduced him to cocaine in his sophomore year. Through college and various jobs, he continued to use cocaine, desperately wanting to stop but not being able to. At the suggestion of his therapist, he attended an NA meeting. At that meeting he met some people in recovery who invited him to hang out with them the next day, answering his questions and telling him their stories. "They really did seem loving and welcoming. I went to another meeting that night and then I went home. And that was it. I haven't had a drink or a drug in over thirteen years!"

Paul embraced the spirituality of the 12-step program in the beginning because people told him to. "I was told when I first got sober to pray twice a day to stay sober and thank God at the end of the day that I am, so I just did it. And I prayed for two years, on my knees, and then decided I was just doing it out of worry and fear." This exacerbated his OCD symptoms and he wanted to drink every day for the first 18 months of his recovery. Realizing finally that the spiritual route was harming rather than helping him, he stopped these activities. Paul does not consider himself a spiritual or religious person and he shivers a bit when he hears those terms because of the association with dogma, about a right and a wrong way to do things. Connection is unmistakably the strongest core human experience that defines Paul's recovery. "I guess I always felt there was something in this world I was connected to, or that was looking out for me but I don't think it was a person, place or thing. It feels like this energy, or connectedness with other people." When asked, he tells people that his higher power is "the concept of the group – the group is where I go, and there are a lot of different people in the group and we have done this together." While seeing the group as a higher power is not uncommon, it is not considered to be a spiritual concept as defined by the 12-step philosophy. Paul is a good example of someone who, despite an aversion to religiosity, found a way to embrace the NA community and navigate around its spiritual expectations.

Discussion

Applying Pruyser's (1976) framework of spirituality to each individual narrative demonstrates how this broader perspective can inform the exploration of spirituality in addiction recovery. Each person identified in their narrative at least two core human experiences on Pruyser's list, and all of them alluded to themes that a social worker could pursue during a clinical session that might reveal additional core human experiences that could be considered spiritual in nature and an additional resource to support the recovery process.

For Sheryl, a core experience that would be valuable to explore would be how her connections with other people also give her life meaning. Her entrance into recovery was positively impacted by her relationships with a small group of people who were in early recovery, and she is currently very active in the 12-step community. Connection is also a theme that is woven into George's story – the connection he has with his sponsor, his network of support, and the various pastors who have mentored him in his faith. He remembers when "something clicked and I was like, yeah, I think I need other people" and now he spends most of his time and energy offering that connection to people who are still in active addiction, and early recovery. Based on this information it would be a natural bridge to examine with Sheryl and George how connection supports their recovery from a spiritual perspective.

Vocation is one of Pruyser's core human experiences that is not typically included as a component of spirituality but for some of the interviewees, it would be a valid topic to explore. For Karen, who is passionately pursuing both a role in ministry and a career in the addiction field, vocation is strongly connected to both her recovery and her spirituality. Karen speaks about her religious views and spiritual experiences with ease, and she would most likely welcome the opportunity to explore how vocation supports her spiritually in recovery. Julie agreed to be interviewed despite the difficult emotions she knew it would stir up in her because she believes that her purpose is to tell her story to everyone who asks. She shared that she says yes to every request she gets because it might help someone who is struggling with addiction and recovery. For Julie, this reflects the theme of vocation, how she makes sense of all that she has experienced in her life. Carol's choice to have a second career as a social worker reflects how vocation is also core human experience for her, which, if given the opportunity to explore this theme, she might also agree it falls into the spiritual category.

Providence is a core human experience that one could explore with Derek – based on his conviction that something is guiding him in a positive direction. He describes his spiritual awakening as very dark and very painful. He attempted to bypass it all with yoga and meditation but discovered that he had to deal directly with his pain. Spiritual awakening "magnifies whatever trauma you might have had so you have to deal with it, now. There is no off switch, alcohol doesn't do it, nothing works anymore – you have to deal with your stuff." And in doing so, he found hope and healing.

Brian's narrative could open up a conversation into the core experience of repentance. He speaks of himself as having two people inside – the tough Brian and the vulnerable Brian. The tough Brian abandoned his family, lived on the street, and did things that went against his values. The vulnerable Brian is trying to do the right thing, but he admits "there still is a portion of that person [tough Brian] in there." If a social worker spent time exploring remorse, guilt, acceptance, and responsibility – aspects of the core human experience of repentance – with Brian, this would strengthen his capacity to explore his vulnerable self without fear of retribution from God.

Paul, who identifies the most with being non-spiritual, finds meaning in his connection to his family – his wife, his 15-month-old daughter, his dog – and in being of service to others. He also says "Not doing damage gives me meaning, because I feel like I did a lot of damage in the world, I was very selfish and wrapped up in things. I try to practice more humility and be more selfless." Perhaps if Paul were introduced to Pruyser's framework he might be more inclined to consider that his connections to people, his vocation, and his acts of repentance have a spiritual component to them that extends beyond the narrow focus that he was introduced to through the 12 steps.

The narratives shared by these individuals have many common elements and yet reflect each person's unique experience with spirituality in recovery. Most interviewees had some exposure to religious involvement in early childhood, but this does not appear to be correlated with how important spirituality is in one's recovery. The majority of those interviewed initially found their way into recovery through the 12 steps, but this also does not appear to predict the importance of spirituality to their recovery. Another common theme was that for the most part, they all believed that every person who comes into recovery has to find their own connection to spirituality, if there is one to be found. Each of them was asked what they would say to someone early in recovery about spirituality. According to Karen, "There has to be something else that's there, I don't care what you call it. Because it doesn't have to be my God, it just has to be something greater than yourself. That's something I always say – there has to be something." Julie's advice is "Just listen and keep an open mind." Brian's suggestion is "Take your time with it. Find what works for you. If you jump into it, you can find yourself down the wrong trail." George doesn't force feed his spirituality on anyone else. "I try to let people be where they are at. I believe that everybody's process is a little bit different." Derek, comfortable with not knowing, surmises that "there is something playing out, we don't know what that is, and we just have to trust." And Paul's pragmatic belief is that "you can be in AA whether you are spiritual or not," although when newcomers ask him about it, he tells them he is not the best person to talk to them about it because he does not consider spirituality to be part of his experience.

Conclusion

Spirituality and recovery have been connected since the beginnings of the AA movement and addiction researchers, recognizing this connection, have conducted studies to build a scientific basis for this connection. People in recovery share stories that reflect varied themes of spirituality – both of the religious and non-religious kind. In the face of these realities, it is hard to deny that spirituality has something to do with recovery. But it remains a difficult topic to explore for many valid reasons. The social worker and the client come into the therapeutic relationship with different, sometimes opposing, religious experiences, beliefs, and practices. And they may not be in agreement about what it means to be spiritual. The distinction between spirituality and religion is a helpful one to make although it is recommended that the social work field embraces an expanded definition of spirituality beyond the 12-step concept of believing in a higher power. When exploring spirituality with people in recovery, simply asking "Are you spiritual or religious?" or "What is your higher power?" is insufficient. It is more fruitful to ask open-ended questions that open up the possibility for a deeper conversation. What creates in you a sense of awe? What guides you in your life? What do you believe about yourself or your life? What role does gratitude play in your recovery? What past actions do you regret? With whom do you seek connection? What is your purpose in life? These questions, reflecting Pruyser's (1976) framework, acknowledge that people long for meaning and purpose, and instinctively seek connection with others or something beyond themselves to find it. Creating space for the conversation might lead someone to be self-reflective and discover a valuable insight about their personal recovery as Carol expressed: "This interview makes me think that maybe I am more spiritual than I thought."

Informed Consent: Informed Consent was obtained from all the individuals whose narratives are included in this chapter. Names have been changed to protect confidentiality.

Close Reading Questions

1. Ruisard writes that

   > Individuals following the twelve-step path to recovery "came to believe that a Power greater than ourselves could restore us to sanity" in Step Two, and consequently "made a decision to turn our will and our lives over to the care of God as we understood Him" in Step Three.
   >
   > (Alcoholics Anonymous, 2001, p. 59)

   Why might critics of the 12-step program oppose the nature of these steps?
2. In what ways might repentance be considered a spiritual practice? How does Julie's experience of a "punishing God" affect her spirituality?
3. Why do the demographics of Ruisard's qualitative study matter in relation to spirituality?

Prompts for Thinking and Writing

1. Ruisard writes that "the percentage of mental health professionals who profess to be spiritual or religious is lower than the people who seek their services." Is there a definition of spirituality that aligns with your beliefs?
2. How might one's approach to spirituality change over 50 years? What would you add to Pruyser's 1976 framework in 2020 or beyond?
3. Paul's story reveals that spiritual meditation can lead to OCD symptoms. How does this connect with the descriptions of meditation in Garbe, Kenny, and Okuda?

References

Alcoholics Anonymous. (2001). *Alcoholics anonymous* (4th ed.). New York, NY: World Service, Inc.

Belzen, J. (2004). Spirituality, culture and mental health: Prospects and risks for contemporary psychology of religion. *Journal of Religion and Health, 43*(4), 291–316.

Delany, H. D., Miller, W. R., & Bisono, A. M. (2007). Religiosity and spirituality among psychologists: A survey of clinician members of the American Psychological Association. *Professional Psychology: Research and Practice, 38*, 538–546.

Dermatis, H., & Galanter, M. (2016). The role of twelve-step-related spirituality in addiction recovery. *Journal of Religious Health, 55*, 510–521.

DiClemente, C. (2013). Paths through addiction and recovery: The impact of spirituality and religion. *Substance Use and Misuse, 48*, 1260–1261.

Dossett, W. (2013). Addiction, spirituality and 12 step programmes. *International Social Work, 56*(3), 369–383.

Gill, P., Stewart, K., Treasure, E., & Chadwick, B. (2008). Methods of data collection in qualitative research: Interviews and focus groups. *British Dental Journal, 204*(6), 291–295.

Hodge, D. (2002). Equipping social workers to address spirituality in practice settings: A model curriculum. *Advances in Social Work, 3*(2), 85–103.

Kurtz, E., & White, W. (2015). Recovery spirituality. *Religions, 6*, 58–81.

Maté, G. (2010). *In the realm of the hungry ghosts: Close encounters with addiction.* Berkeley, CA: North Atlantic Books.

Miller, W. (2013). Addiction and spirituality. *Substance Use and Misuse, 48*, 1258–1259.

Miller, W., Forcehimes, A., & Zweben, A. (2011). *Treating addiction: A guide for professionals.* New York, NY: Guilford Press.

Oxhandler, H., Polson, E., & Achenaum, W. A. (2017). The religiosity and spiritual beliefs and practices of clinical social workers: A national survey. *Social Work, 63*(1), 47–55.

Pew Research Center. (2018, April 25). When Americans say they believe in God, what do they mean? Washington, DC. Retrieved from https://www.pewforum.org/2018/04/25/when-americans-say-they-believe-in-god-what-do-they-mean/

Pew Research Center. (2019, October 17). In U.S., decline of Christianity continues at rapid pace: An update on America's changing religious landscape. Washington, DC. Retrieved from https://www.pewforum.org/2019/10/17/in-u-s-decline-of-christianity-continues-at-rapid-pace/

Pruyser, P. (1976). *The minister as diagnostician: Personal problems in pastoral perspective.* Philadelphia, PA: Westminster Press.

Schaub, R. (2013). Spirituality and the health professional. *Substance Use and Misuse, 48*, 1174–1179.

Szalavitz, M. (2014, September 24). What I've finally concluded about 12-step programs after 25 years of writing about drugs and addiction. *Pacific Standard Magazine.* Retrieved from https://psmag.com/social-justice/ive-finally-concluded-12-step-programs-25-years-writing-drugs-addiction-91099.

Walker, R., Godlaski, T., & Staton-Tindall, M. (2013). Spirituality, drugs, and alcohol: A philosophical analysis. *Substance Use and Misuse, 48*, 1233–1245.

7

THE SPIRITUALITY OF INCARCERATION

Bianca-Ramos Channer

Pre-Reading Questions

1. Given Ramos-Channer's title, what first comes to mind when you think about spirituality in the context of a jail?
2. How is a therapeutic alliance similar to or different from alliance with another trusted guide, like a Rabbi, Pastor, Priest, or Imam?
3. How might a "religious background" impede one's "spiritual" growth?

"There is so much evil in the world, you know. Like real evil. It's hard to believe that there is a god, or a higher power, or something…" His voice trailed off, and his attention went back to somewhere outside the small window in my office. He'd just shared with me a horrendous trauma, which had occurred two days before he committed the crime that led to his incarceration. Moments later, his attention returned to me, and he continued, "There has got to be something, right? I mean, call it what you want—god, buddha, spirits, energy—all that. Some of it? I don't know. I have to believe in something. I can't survive this place without it."

In what appears to look like a college campus, if not for the layers of barbed wire, metal gates, and uniformed staff and police vehicles circling the inner and outer perimeters at all times, young men aged 15–23 are housed in the detention facility. The detention facility has multiple housing units, where anywhere from 10 to 30 young men live in a dorm-like setting. Here, they are referred to as residents by most staff. Each housing unit has a common area with chairs bolted to the floor, a game table also bolted to the floor, a small bookshelf, and a huge flat-screen TV that sits in protective casing secured high on the wall out of reach of both staff and residents. Upstairs, separated behind locked gates, are offices for the social workers and supervisor of the unit. Correction officers are the only ones on unit with the key to the gate that divides the residents living and recreational quarters from the staff offices.

As a clinical social worker in the prison system, I managed a caseload of primarily dual diagnosis young men, and Ty was assigned to my caseload due to holding an Axis I Mental Health and Substance Abuse diagnosis. The rates of dual diagnosis within juvenile justice populations have increased significantly within the last decade. Schubert, Mulvey, and Glashen (2011) found that "juvenile offender populations have disproportionately high rates of mental health problems compared with the general population of adolescents. A majority of the diagnosable youth in the juvenile justice system also have a co-occurring disorder" (p. 925). Even with high rates of co-occurring disorders, there are very few residents who independently agree to participate in mental health and substance abuse counseling. Ty was one of the few residents who came into the detention center requesting treatment.

Because spiritual means more than religious and is individually defined, creating spaces for both religious and spiritual activities in jails is necessary. Religious activities have been infused in prisons since their inception, but there has been little to no focus on spirituality or on a range of religious experiences and services. The limited religious activities offered in prison are unappealing to many young adults who are in the process of figuring out who they are and how or if their religious/spiritual identity is an important component to their identity. Upon entering jails, many turn to religion/ spirituality as a way to cope. Through my work with a young man who was, in his own words, "absolutely an atheist" when he entered the juvenile detention center, I examine how the therapeutic alliance can provide the opportunity and encouragement incarcerated young adults need to explore their religious/spiritual identity.

Incarceration can be a meditative and transformative space with the potential to deepen spiritual and/or religious connections, which are important parts of how many residents cope with their time. I have seen a significant process of spiritual change that occurs in youth during their incarceration. Some come in with a faith/religious/spiritual background and rediscover it, this part of themselves being reignited while in jail. Others are introduced or discover faith/ religion for the first time behind bars. Perhaps as a way to cope, or out of boredom, many young people turn to religion or spirituality during their incarceration. Regardless of religious affiliation pre-incarceration, and even during incarceration, many of the youth on my caseload mentioned spiritual experiences that got them through their time. In the detention center, spirituality encompasses far more than a particular religious connection. For many, the process of spiritual development starts when adjusting to incarceration, perhaps because incarceration is the first time when residents are safe enough to explore their spiritual beliefs.

The Case of Ty

In one of my first sessions with Ty, as I was gathering general information about him and reviewing programs available, he laughed when I mentioned religious services. "I am absolutely an atheist. I don't believe in God or anything like that. So, I will never be signing up for those religious services or programs or anything like that. You don't need to even mention that stuff to me!" At 16 years old, Ty looked much older than he actually was. He had a hardened look on his face, and even though he had bright green eyes, there was some darkness behind them. Ty's face, neck, and arms were covered in tattoos. He leaned back in the chair, with his arms crossed, avoiding eye contact for the first several months of individual sessions. Over time, I slowly learned about his past, what lead to his incarceration, and his family history. Ty was born into a family that had a strong religious background; his grandfather was a church leader. His birth mom had been raised in the church but was kicked out of the church when she became pregnant as a young unwed teen. "From that moment on, my mom basically gave up on religion, and so that's how I was raised. I went once to my grandfather's church, and it was all just...I don't know. It was too much."

Ty had a typical adjustment to jail in that he struggled initially. Throughout his first year, Ty was not involved in any programs or activities outside of what was mandated in the treatment housing unit: weekly individual and group sessions and a monthly family session. Despite coming in wanting treatment, during his first year, Ty was finding it difficult to participate in treatment. "You guys always want me to talk about things in the past. Bring up old stuff. Share stuff. That's just not what I am about." Ty had never participated in any treatment program prior to his incarceration despite being diagnosed with several axis 1 and 2 disorders. Ty was raised by his birth mother up until he was eight years old and had little contact throughout his life with his birth father. Despite being of mixed ethnicity, Ty solely defined himself with his mother's ethnicity because "I will never have, and have never had, any parts or anything to do with that man." At the age of eight, Ty was removed from his mother's custody due to negligence concerns reported by a neighbor. Ty shared that his mother worked long hours and that she was off to work before he went to school and came home around bedtime. When he was removed from his mother's custody, he was placed briefly with his maternal grandparents, and then was placed in foster care. "I couldn't stay with my grandparents. They were all about church. They preached to me all the time. It was like they were never involved in my life until they had to be, and then they were like on a mission to save me. I didn't need saving. I still don't. So, I acted up even more, ran away all the time, did a lot of dumb stuff to them and their house, and that got me out of there."

As I learned more about his past, I began to understand a little bit more about why he was "absolutely an atheist" as he shared several bad experiences he had with "evil church goers." When speaking of members of his grandfather's church, he often referred to them as evil church goers. It took two years before I learned why he used this term. Ty had been continually approached by an elder church member in a "way too friendly, super creepy way. This old dude always tried to get me alone, or get me to go somewhere with him, and other people just stood by and watched like it was totally normal for an old man to be like that."

Ty's first couple of months in the treatment unit were challenging because he wanted to sign out of treatment weekly and often was in trouble with peers for his arrogance of being "different from these crazy kids in here." Ty was very outwardly against all religions, thought spirituality was a joke, hadn't bought into treatment, and seemed to have it out for residents who fell into these categories. In the first couple of months, Ty defaced a resident's religious materials, hid a resident's prayer mat, and when a resident was writing in his journal, Ty took it from him and started reading out loud what was written. Ty rarely spoke in group, and would often antagonize and do things specially to irritate other residents during group sessions. He would make fun of other residents, especially residents who were at the highest treatment level, and he "enjoyed" picking on residents who attended religious ceremonies and/or had religious symbols/materials.

While having Ty in group counseling sessions was exhausting, he flourished in individual sessions. In fact, many times, the only reason that he was not removed from the treatment unit for behavioral reasons was that he was making significant progress in individual and family counseling. In individual sessions, Ty was opening up about his past, working through some long held anger at his family members and life circumstances. A lot of this work was centered on working on his relationship with his mother and his maternal grandparents. He blamed them both for some traumatic experiences in foster care. Ty experienced both verbal and physical abuse while in foster care. He blamed himself for not being "loveable enough" for either of them to accept him, or keep him home. Ty was unlike many of the residents that I worked with in that he demonstrated deep self-reflection and was trying to make sense of things and figure out himself. Not that this was always reflected in his actions, but I quickly learned that his focused attacks on religious/spiritual residents or residents at the highest treatment level were a cover up for his own insecurities in these life areas.

Ty remained skeptical until part way through his second year. Ty's birth mother had suddenly and unexpectedly become gravely ill. It was mid-afternoon, and I received a call from Ty's maternal grandfather stating that there was a family emergency. After completing the verification process, I gathered some basic information about the emergency. I learned that his mother had fallen ill at work and was taken to the emergency room. Ty's grandfather told me not to tell Ty that his mother was currently in a coma, and the doctors were not optimistic about her recovery at this point. I went downstairs, quietly informed the correctional officer that I needed to have Ty call home immediately, and went to get Ty from the day room where they were just lining up for showers. As we began walking upstairs to the social work offices, Ty asked, "OK. What happened? To who? How bad is it?" It was pretty well known that when social workers came downstairs and asked to bring kids upstairs immediately that something serious had happened at home.

I was often put in a tough spot by families in crisis, and I never knew how much to tell a resident before putting them on the phone. I told Ty that he needed to call his grandfather because there was a family emergency. With a confused look, he said, "My grandfather? Please. Before I get on the phone tell me what happened?" Internal turmoil. When Ty's grandfather asked that I not tell him all the details, I hadn't verbally agreed or disagreed. I sat trying to look calm attempting to make a quick decision that would be best for all. "Well, I don't know any of the specifics. All that I know is that something happened to your mom." He looked absolutely shocked, and my stomach dropped. I listened as his grandfather told him that something had happened to his mother at work, and that she was in the ER and before he could finish his sentence, Ty started questioning. "What happened? When did this happen? Which hospital? How is she? How can I talk with her?" My heart ached, as I listened to his grandfather stumble through responses to some of his questions.

The next day, we learned that Ty's mother had a hemorrhagic stroke and had undergone an emergency surgery to alleviate the pressure on her brain. She was put in a medically induced coma, and Ty had been told that if she does fully recover from this, she will likely never be the same and would be paralyzed, or partially paralyzed. Ty was devastated. He was angry that he wasn't home and couldn't be at her bedside. For several weeks, it was a waiting game, as Ty waited for any new information on his mother. He checked in with me multiple times a day to see if I had gotten any calls, and due to the circumstances, he was allowed to call his grandfather daily. During every single call, Ty's grandfather would say that there is an army of people praying, that prayers healed, that God is in control, and that Ty needed to get closer to God and he would provide him comfort and healing. Ty's grandfather always ended his calls in this manner, and usually Ty would dismiss him reminding him that he didn't believe in that. However, during this time, Ty simply said "yeah, okay."

During this time, Ty shared his fears of her dying and her "not really knowing that I love her...and that I forgive her...and that I truly appreciate her and all that she did to try and help me and provide for me and that I was so wrong about so much!" As part of a way to help him process these thoughts and emotions, I had him write a letter to his mother. We discussed keeping this letter in his treatment file or having his grandfather read it to her and initially he was completely opposed to the latter. Ty poured himself into writing, and when his letter was complete, he chose to have his grandfather read it to her, stating: "this helped heal me. She needs to hear this because maybe it will help heal her too." As each day passed, and there was no improvement in his mother's condition, Ty became more and more spiritual. He defined spiritual as "being more connected and concerned about others and about figuring out himself and how to improve." He shared with me that he had started praying and meditating daily. Ty was very clear that he wasn't praying to God, that he was praying to "all Gods and the Universe," as he believed that this was a way to include all "the greatest higher powers out there! I am still not sure that I believe in a God, but I need to believe that there is something spiritual out there."

Ty's mother made a complete and unprecedented full recovery. Ty's grandparents are convinced that the only reason she recovered completely was the power of prayer. "My grandfather is always talking about the power of prayer, and for a long time, I thought it was BS. But now? Now? I don't know, it kind of makes sense." Ty and his mother had parallel healing processes. Ty's relationship with his grandparents, his mother, and his peers both on the unit and on grounds improved. While he will perhaps always remain slightly skeptical, he experienced profound change in his beliefs, his outlook, and his behavior. I was able to witness how increased religious/spiritual beliefs decreased behavioral incidents for Ty, as the research reviewed above suggests. But perhaps more personally profound, I was able to witness the emotional transformation that came with the development of hope, connection, and excitement for the future.

Religious services in prisons have a long and complex history that has greatly impacted current faith-based prison programs: "Religious programs for inmates are not only among the oldest but also among the most common forms of rehabilitative programs found in correctional facilities today. This high prevalence of use is confirmed by the US Department of Justice, which reports representative data on America's prison population" (Hallett & Johnson, 2014, p. 668). In 1991 the Bureau of Justice Statistics conducted face-to-face interviews with nearly 14,000 inmates from over 250 facilities in 14 states. They found that of the "personal enhancement programs" offered, religious services were utilized the most, with 32% of inmates reporting involvement in bible studies or church services. Self-improvement programs were attended by 20% of those interviewed and only 17% of inmates interviewed reported participating in counseling (Hallett & Johnson, 2014). In the juvenile detention center, all residents were required to participate in counseling and had the choice, with strong encouragement from others, to participate in personal enhancement programming. Religious services were offered weekly and part of my responsibility was to ask residents on my caseload if they wanted to attend the services offered. In the detention center, there was a Christian bible study and service and a Muslim prayer service. Even though Ty had told me that I "didn't need to mention that stuff!" I asked him weekly.

Evolution of Faith-Based Programs in Prisons

Since their inception, prisons have strongly been influenced by religion. There have been drastic and continual changes in the delivery of religious services and programs that differ from state to state, and even year to year. Ever since the first penitentiary was built, religion has played a principal role in the efforts of correctional professionals to reform offenders. In fact, the word "penitentiary" is itself derived from "penitence" meaning "regret for wrongdoing or sinning." Thus, penitentiaries were originally seen by some as place where offenders could go and atone for their sins. Throughout penal history, religions continued to play an important role, and have possibly been employed more frequently than any other type of correctional intervention (Clear & Sumter, 2002, p. 126).

For a long time, and perhaps currently, the term "prison ministry" equates to prison evangelism. Prison evangelism has a long and complex history that is outside the scope of this chapter; however, it is worth noting that religious programs offered in jails vary and change continually based on social and political factors. Within the last several decades there have been significant changes from evangelical efforts to church-sponsored ministries to individual-led ministries in prisons. For centuries there has been an overarching belief that criminal behavior is due in part to a lack of religion, and that the more religious the people are, the less likely they are to deviate from societal norms (Chadwick & Top, 1993; Petterson, 1991). Some of the first US prisons, Auburn in New York and Eastern State Penitentiary in Philadelphia, were based on redemption ideals and "prisoners were confined to cells to study and receive religious instruction so that they might reflect on their offenses" (Thomas & Zaitzow, 2006, p. 247). Despite these deeply ingrained beliefs, prisoners' rights to religious expression developed gradually and were not protected under the constitution until the mid-20th century (Thomas & Zaitzow, 2006).

During the mid-20th century, religious programs became acceptable programs in nearly all US prisons, and prisons began employing chaplains and also utilizing lay people as volunteers for religious service needs. These rights were extended mainly to two Christian doctrines, Protestant and Catholic. During the 1960s due in part to the growth of black Muslim religion in prisons, litigations in the US District courts and then a few years later in federal courts, these rights (special diets, access to clergy, religious materials/publications, group worship/prayer) were expanded to non-Christians: "The rights of some religious groups were curtailed by prison administrators' fears that prisoners were using religion as a ply for political action, as a shield for gang activity, or as a means to obtain illicit resources" (Thomas & Zaitzow, 2006, p. 248). The literature on religion in prisons highlights many examples of prisoners using religion to recruit and promote gang activity, but many also highlight budgetary, staffing, and ideological concerns: "Because the primary goal of custodial institutions is security, and because providing resources for religious activities can strain budgets, the concerns are more than entrenched conservatism or rigid ideology" (Thomas & Zaitzow, 2006, p. 252). Rigid ideology is part of what is addressed in treatment with incarcerated youth.

There is an overarching presumption that all residents have a set of fixed ideas and behavioral problems that landed them in jail, such as anger management and drug use, and that these beliefs can be addressed through a series of workbooks correcting thinking patterns and moral decision making. The goal is to correct rigid beliefs and faulty thinking patterns. This assumes that all residents are the same, come from the same background, communicate and process things the same way, understand the world in similar ways, and have the same goals. In this treatment model, there is little to no focus on environmental, social, or spiritual factors. It is hard to address or "correct" thinking patterns without including spiritual and religious factors. Instead of seeing religion as aiding in helping correct thinking, it is often viewed as a hindrance or a concealment of other activities.

Administrators' fears of prisoners using religion as a shield for other activities have been a reality in many programs, including the detention center I worked in. After a large riot on grounds, it was learned that much of the organizing and planning was completed during religious services, and this led to immediate and drastic changes in religious program delivery in the detention center. In addition to the very real fears of prison riots, radicalization of prisoners is another concern of having religious gatherings and programs offered to inmates. Prisoner radicalization is not a new concept, and has been linked to a combination of religion, gang activity, and terrorism. With the recent heightened social and political concern of terrorism, there has been increased focus and concern regarding prisoner radicalization.

When exploring the literature on prisoner radicalization, religious conversion is an important part of the discourse. Religious conversion in prison is not a new phenomenon and has existed since the very first prisons were based on redemption ideals (Dix-Richardson & Close, 2002). These deeply ingrained beliefs that incarceration should transform a person's life and belief system is why religious programs are the oldest and most common interventions. While there is some debate on the effectiveness of religious interventions in jails, what is agreed on is that religion plays an important role in correctional security and in rehabilitation.

One of the most important components of correctional security is adjustment to prison. Clear and Sumter (2002) found that increased levels of self-reported religiosity were associated with higher levels of prison adjustment and lower numbers of disciplinary confinement. Some argue that increased religiousness or spirituality is only correlated with lower rates of disciplinary issues. Eytan (2011) reviewed results from 12 empirical studies on religion and spirituality in jails and correctional facilities finding that the "strongest reported effect of religion and spirituality on prison life is a reduction of incidents and disciplinary sanctions" (p. 294). In addition to reduced disciplinary issues, there is some research suggesting that religion plays a role in what type of crimes is committed. Burkett (1980) found that religion more effectively deters non-victim-orientated crime.

When people are confronted with severe and chronic stress, religious coping is prominent. Religious and spiritual beliefs provide a context for observing one's environment, themselves and others; and a way to contextualize past experiences and plan for the future. "More recent work in the sociology of religion and mental health has documented that religious involvement is associated with higher levels of psychological well-being and lower levels of mental health problems like anxiety and depression (Koenig, 1995; Levin 1997; Levin and Chatters 1998). By turning to religion and/or spirituality, individuals have access to a critical resource to draw upon to alleviate problems that come with unfavorable life conditions in a non-criminal manner" (Schroeder & Frana, 2009, p. 722). Relying on religion or spiritual beliefs to cope with adjustment to prison life and to get through the difficulties of incarceration was common not only in the youth that I worked with, but also in their family members.

With the concerns of safety forefront, the early research on religion in jails has focused on larger social and environmental impacts (lowered disciplinary sanctions, reoffense rates, and crimes committed). There is not as much research that looks at the emotional impact of religious activities and the transformative connection this can and does have on larger social and environmental factors. In a study done on 11 men ranging in age from 20 to 50 currently residing in a Midwest halfway house, Schroeder and Frana (2009) found that religion and spirituality provided the men with "positive feelings such as peace, tolerance and love and help alleviate feeling of anger, anxiety and depression… provide[d] these men a much needed distraction from the adverse life circumstances (unemployment, divorce, legal troubles, addiction) that often plague their lives…especially the process of religious and/or spiritual transformations (i.e. being born again or having a spiritual awaking), provide a distinct factor marking the transition to a more conventional life" (pp. 735–736). Religion and spirituality can have a profound emotional impact on adjustment to prison, behavior during incarceration, and also post incarceration adjustment.

While a lot of the research on religions in prisons has focused on adults, the impact of religiosity on youth offenders is relatively unexplored. Research on religion and youth delinquency has most commonly focused on understanding dimensions of religiosity or looking at the effectiveness of religious intervention strategies. The research on religion and criminal behavior shows that religion can be a protective factor that remediates the effects of delinquency (Baier & Wright, 2001). Sloane and Potvin (1986) found that higher rates of church attendance were associated with reduced frequency and severity of delinquent behavior. More recently, Gockel and Burton (2013) found that religion mediated the relationship between trauma suggesting that religion can inform treatment approaches. I include spirituality here to argue the necessity of including religion and spirituality in holistic treatment approaches for juvenile offenders.

Historically, criminology research has been focused on understanding the etiology of crime and delinquency. There has been a societal shift from wanting to understand why people commit crimes to figuring out how to help people stop committing crimes. Recently, criminologists have started moving beyond etiological explanations to researching the process of desistance from crime. There is currently not a lot of research explaining when, why, and how people stop committing crimes (Schroeder & Frana, 2009) or the role that religion and spirituality can play in these processes. Interesting, given the fact that the penal system was based on redemption ideals. With the anchor of faith programs based on and in religion, spirituality has not been fully incorporated into the focus, delivery, or activities of religious programs in prisons. For people who don't define themselves as religious or are not invested in a particular religion, like Ty, the programs offered in jail aren't appealing and may actually create more disinterest in religion.

Religious or Spiritual?

Religious or spiritual beliefs are fundamental aspects of our humanness. Religion and spirituality are generally considered separate concepts with some overlap. On one hand, Walsea (2005) defined religion as a voluntary and a personal relation of a person to God, arguing that religious development is transformative and transgressive. Religion is seen as having a social component or experience. On the other hand, spirituality is seen as a more personal experience that is focused on addressing questions about life (Fetzer, 2003). Spirituality can also be understood as an association with a supernatural or higher power whereas religion is seen as a formal connection to religious practices (King & Benson, 2006). These concepts are interconnected, but what I learned from my work with youth in the detention center is that these hold very different individual meanings and are different developmental processes. For this reason, I use religion and spirituality in general, and use my client's voice and definitions to specify his understandings.

For young adults, religion and spirituality can be especially significant during a developmental time of self-exploration. Young adults are trying on new identities, new ways of thinking, and new beliefs. Religiousness and spirituality develop together with a worldview, and during this time genuineness permeates all activities that young adults take on. "Religious authenticity helps adolescents to find their role and place in the world, it becomes the source of specific meanings and sense" (Rydz, 2014, p. 73). Young adults who are incarcerated during this time often struggle with unique issues related to making meaning and sense of their lives. This process usually starts with adjustment to prison life. When a young person becomes incarcerated it is common for the individual to go through an emotional, psychological and physical adjustment. Some theorists argue that individuals go through emotional and physical traumas as they adjust to prison culture and that creates a unique type of vulnerability. Clemmer (1958) was the first to coin the term "prisonization" to explain the adjustment process. While there is plentiful research that explores prison culture, generally speaking adjustment to prison culture can be broken down into two models: deprivation and importation. Sykes (1958) developed the deprivation model to show how prisoners are deprived of five basic needs: autonomy, personal security, material possessions, social acceptance, and heterosexual relationships. So, in order to cope with these deprivations, prisoners create a culture of their own. Proponents of the importation model in contrast argue that prisoners bring in their beliefs and values and that this influences behavior on the inside. So, obeying "prison code" is not a reaction to prison but rather a reflection of a person's characteristics and pre-prison experiences (Slosar, 1978). While these models have been highly criticized as being over simplistic, they can provide us with a basic understanding of prison adjustment (Clear & Sumter, 2002).

As a social worker at a juvenile detention center, many of the youth I worked with shared that hardest adjustment is getting used to the constant watching and control. Adjustment to the environment is a complex individual, emotional, and social process. Prisoners have little control over anything, and this is perhaps the most challenging adjustment: "Prisoners adjust to control by finding ways to adapt to unnatural surroundings" (Thomas & Zaitzow, 2006, p. 245). The adjustment to feeling completely out of control for some initiates a religious or spiritual awakening and developmental process. One of the ways that young people cope, and that is encouraged throughout treatment, is through trying to make meaning and sense of the past. For many, this is the beginning of a religious or spiritual connection.

Incarceration affords juveniles a unique opportunity to develop a religious and spiritual identity. Research on the development of religiousness in young adults outlines several components that include personal reflection, trying to understand the environment and then reconstructing one's self and internalized faith (Rydz, 2014). Incarceration forces many into personal reflection, and requires one to figure out the jail environment. In the detention center, the development of religiousness or religious/spiritual exploration is heavily influenced and complicated by environmental, political, and social factors. Young adults who are trying to adjust to prison culture, all while trying to figure out themselves and the world around them, are heavily influenced by the thoughts and opinions of others. In the detention center, there are cliques and gangs, and many young people feel that they cannot survive their time without being part of a prison subculture or group. While Ty stated that he could never be "fully a part of any group" he wanted more than anything to belong. His adjustment to the detention center was most heavily influenced by trying to figure out where and what he wanted to belong to.

As abstract thinking develops in the late teenage years, this can go hand in hand with the development of religiousness or spirituality as people begin to see and understand things in their world differently. Fowler (1981) proposed six stages of development for faith across the lifespan and his theory gives us the language to think about this process for incarcerated youth. In the early stages (stages 0–2), faith is characterized by the safety of the environment, and strong beliefs in justice and mutuality. Fowler (1981) developed these stages based on Kohlberg's (1958) moral developmental stages and Piaget's (1957) cognitive development stages. In these initial stages, our basic ideas about our faith develop as we begin to decipher fantasy from reality and then move to literal understandings. For children like Ty who grow up generally feeling unsafe in their environments and not introduced to any specific faith beliefs, they do not experience these stages early in life. In stage 3, Fowler (1981) proposed that a synthetic-conventional faith arises in adolescence and that many people remain in this phase throughout their lives. This phase is characterized by synthesizing many differing ideas into an all-encompassing belief system. Peck (1987) attempting to simplify Fowler's (1981) stages, developed what he believed are the four most common phases of faith. His second phase, called formal-institutional, aligns with Fowler's (1981) third phase but Peck (1987) proposes that people in this phase rely on institutions such as churches for their beliefs and they become attached to their religion. Fowler's (1981) fourth stage, Individuation and Reflection, is when people begin to critically examine their beliefs, and become disillusioned with their faith. Peck (1987) calls this phase Skeptic-Individual and characterizes this as a non-religious phase as people begin to question the world around them. Here is where many of the incarcerated youth I have worked with start.

Incarceration forces many into a reflective period where they become disillusioned with previous beliefs (not just faith based), and start examining and questioning the world around them. This is also encouraged through treatment, as the goal is to correct faulty thinking patterns. Incarceration is also where many young adults are introduced to or exposed to many new things. This can and does include religion and spirituality. Throughout their time behind bars, they start synthesizing many ideas to form an all-encompassing belief system (the early phases of religious development). Using the stages of faith development explored above as a guide, incarcerated youth have a unique trajectory because coping with and adjusting to incarceration initiates the development of religious/spiritual beliefs for many.

While Ty's spiritual awakening was ignited by a family emergency, he had already started exploring this part of himself way before his mother's illness. However, Ty's process was initiated in his adjustment to the treatment unit and his initially challenging interactions with his peers. He wasn't vocal or didn't give off any behavioral signs of religious or spiritual development, but I could see it in how he was wrestling with big life questions in individual sessions. Once Ty adjusted to the treatment unit, he began to feel a sense of safety there and then he began to let down his walls and started to explore his beliefs much like Fowler's (1981) early stages suggest. He remained skeptical, but had begun to open himself up to exploration. I saw this process unfold in the majority of youth that I worked with throughout their incarceration. Ty began to use his spirituality to cope with things on the unit, things happening on ground, and it became his prominent coping strategy when his mother became ill. One of the main goals of treatment is to help residents change their coping strategies and I witnessed how religion and spirituality were the most transformative influences for Ty, and many other young adults.

Religious coping becomes a particularly prominent strategy for those undergoing stressful situations. Petts (2009) found that religious importance changes significantly between pre-arrest and post-arrest: "Certainly, the incarceration event alone can spur enhanced reliance on religion (Clear et al, 2000), as there is a substantial loss of freedom and increased isolation. Youth may experience psychological transference, seeking to gain a sense of control, seeking understanding and hope, interest in connection and reassurance through religious means" (Yoder & Bovard-Johns, 2017, p. 129). Jail is a continually stressful situation. Combine that with stressful situations from home and then add in stress about the future, and we can begin to understand some of what young adults incarcerated go through and why religion and spirituality are so transformative during this time.

Positive social bonds are transformative, and there is abundant research on the power of the therapeutic relationship. Yoder and Bovard-Johns (2017) studied religiosity and the therapeutic alliance, and argue that the therapeutic alliance is partially responsible for the influence of religiosity in therapeutic services: "Supportive of social bonding theory, it is not surprising that the therapeutic relationship is associated with increases in religious importance. As the evidence base surrounding therapeutic alliance for youth non-sexual (Florsheim et al, 200) and sexual offenders increases, it is noted that a strong alliance is linked with several positive outcomes...Perhaps the interpersonal relationship sustained in the therapeutic setting encourages the interest in developing or solidifying an existential one" (Yoder & Bovard-Johns, 2017, pp. 129–130). Ty was surrounded by a support system that encouraged and inspired his spiritual exploration and journey toward more meaningful relationships. Coming from a religious background, having gone through my own religious and spiritual exploration, I often encouraged the young adults that I worked with to explore their own faith beliefs. I didn't know it at the time, but my encouragement was part of what aided Ty to become more spiritually connected. At the end of a session where we were discussing future plans he stated, "I think what has been best about this all is that I had to think. I had to figure stuff out. I had to learn to believe in myself by others believing in me, before I could believe in something bigger out there." Part of the power of the therapeutic alliance is belief bonding. When we believe in our clients, we help them believe in themselves. Real transformations come when they believe in themselves and believe in their futures. Incarceration is a life-changing experience that for many requires a religious/spiritual connection to make it through. There are vast and varied ways that people religiously and spiritually connect and it is often not through set activities or services, but rather through a belief in another person's abilities and greatness.

As social workers foster a therapeutic alliance with incarcerated youth, we need to honor the whole person and include the spiritual self: "Integrating respective religious or spiritual beliefs into the rehabilitative process may facilitate inclusive interpretations of the problem (Basham & O'Connor, 2005). It may be critical to include aspects of religion and spirituality in holistic rehabilitative practices for youth offenders" (Yoder & Bovard-Johns, 2017, p. 130). Through fostering respectful discussions and encouraging clients to explore or connect to their spiritual self, drastic treatment results can occur starting with a stronger therapeutic alliance. In our juvenile detention centers and jails, we need to do more in this area. While expansions of religious programs could be helpful, what perhaps would be more supportive to incarcerated youth would be a respectful exposure to different religious and spiritual practices and beliefs. To do this, we first need a broader and deeper understanding of spirituality and religiousness and the vital role these beliefs play in coping and transformations.

Holistic treatment approaches need to include the spiritual self as "utilizing religious or faith-based approaches could also support the larger systems" (Yoder & Bovard-Johns, 2017, p. 131). We need to start completing spiritual assessments at intake and throughout treatment, in the same way that we do mental health, education, and substance abuse assessments. One such assessment is the Spiritual Well Being Scale (SWBS) developed by Ellison (1983). The SWBS has been used with varied populations and proved satisfactory levels of validity and reliability. The scale incorporates measures of spiritual well-being, existential well-being as well as different aspects of religiosity. While this scale can help social workers start to understand a client's spiritual or religious beliefs more broadly, the FICA Spiritual History Tool (Puchalski, 2001) is a short tool designed to prompt discussions about patient's spirituality and effect on health care. FICA is an acronym for Faith, Importance, Community, and Address in care. These brief questions need to be included in the intake assessments for incarcerated youth as it provides insight into whether or not a youth defines themselves as religious/spiritual, the importance of this in their life, their desire to be part of a religious/spiritual community, and how to include religious/ spiritual care in treatment plans.

Had either of these tools been used at intake with Ty, it could have shown me the importance that he placed on spirituality, his desire to be part of a community, and thus I would have been able to incorporate spiritual well-being into his treatment from the beginning, instead of at the middle and end of his treatment. "Individualizing religiosity to youth, families, and ecological context is critical to integrating therapeutic alliance into treatment" (Yoder & Bovard-Johns, 2017, p. 131). Doing spiritual assessments at intake is not enough, as youth are continually exploring and changing their beliefs, especially in jail. Spiritual well-being needs to be assessed throughout and included in all treatment plan and release planning for incarcerated youth if we really want to treat the whole person and support change. As Ty so eloquently stated, "Had I not been locked up, and in this treatment unit, I never would have taken the time to reflect on my life and my beliefs. I didn't think that stuff mattered in the beginning, probably because I was so mad at the world. But now? Now it's really all that matters."

Close Reading Questions

1. What is prison evangelism? Radicalization? Prison conversion?
2. What is "an evil churchgoer" beyond the one example Ty gives in this case?
3. How might a spiritual partnership in mental health practice actually promote older adults' independence? Find examples from the text to support your answer.

Prompts for Thinking and Writing

1. Ramos-Channer cites a 1991 Bureau of Justice report that says 32% of the prison population engages in spiritual and religious programming during incarceration. Research what those numbers look like now. What surprises you about what you've learned from your research?
2. Why is adolescence such an interesting moment for one to begin a spiritual practice in isolation from his or her family?
3. How might concepts like "good" and "evil" become refrained in the context of incarceration?

References

Baier, C., & Wright, B. (2001). If you love me, keep my commandments: A meta-analysis of the effect of religion crime. *Journal of Research in Crime and Delinquency, 38*(1), 3–21.

Basham, A., & O'Connor, M. (2005). Use of Spiritual and Religious Beliefs in Pursuit of Clients' Goals. In C. S. Cashwell & J. S. Young (Eds.), *Integrating spirituality and religion into counseling: A guide to competent practice* (p. 143–168). American Counseling Association.

Burkett, S. (1980). Religiosity, beliefs, normative standards and adolescent drinking. *Journal of Studies on Alcohol, 41*, 662–671.

Chadwick, B., & Top, B. (1993). Religiosity and delinquency among LDS adolescents. *Journal for the Scientific Study of Religion, 32*(1), 51–67.

Clear, T., & Sumter, M. (2002). Prisoners, prison, and religion: Religion in adjustment to prison. *Journal of Offender Rehabilitation, 35*(3), 127–159.

Clemmer, D. (1958). *The prison community.* New York, NY: Holt, Rinehart & Winston.

Dix-Richardson, F., & Close, B. (2002). Intersections of race, religion, and inmate culture. *Journal of Offender Rehabilitation, 35*(3), 87–106.

Ellison, C. W. (1983). Spiritual well-being: Conceptualization and measurement. *Journal of Psychology and Theology, 11*(4), 330–340.

Eytan, A. (2011). Religion and mental health during incarceration: A systemic literature review. *Psychiatric Quarterly, 82*, 287–295.

Fetzer Institute National Institute on Aging Working Group. (2003). *Multidimensional measurement of religiosity/spirituality for use in health research.* Kalamazoo, MI: Fetzer Institute.

Fowler, J. W. (1981). *Stages of Faith the Psychology of Human Development and the Quest for Meaning.* Harper & Row.

Gockel, A., & Burton, D. (2013). Can god help? Religion and spirituality among adolescent male sex offenders. *Journal of Child & Adolescent Trauma, 6*, 274–286.

Hallett, M., & Johnson, B. (2014). The resurgence of religion in America's prisons. *Religions, 5*, 663–683.

King, P., & Benson, P. (2006). Spiritual development and adolescent well-being and thriving. In E. C. Roehlkepartain, P. E. King, L. Wagener, & P. L. Benson (Eds.), *The handbook of spiritual development in childhood and adolescence* (pp. 384–398). Thousand Oaks, CA: Sage.

Kohlberg, L. (1958). The Development of Modes of Thinking and Choices in Years 10 to 16. *Ph. D. Dissertation*, University of Chicago.

Peck, S. (1987). *The Different Drum: Community Making and Peace.* New York, NY: Touchstone

Petterson, T. (1991). Religion and criminality: Structural relationships between church involvement and crime rates in contemporary Sweden. *Journal for the Scientific Study of Religion, 30*(3), 279–291.

Petts, R. (2009). Family and religious characteristics' influence on delinquency trajectories from adolescence to adulthood. *American Sociological Review, 74*(3), 465–483.

Piaget, J. (1957). *Construction of reality in the child.* London: Routledge & Kegan Paul.

Puchalski C. M. (2001). The role of spirituality in health care. *Proceedings (Baylor University. Medical Center), 14*(4), 352–357.

Rydz E., (2014). Development of religiousness in young adults. In K. Adamczyk & M. Wysota (Eds.), *Functioning of young adults in a changing world* (pp. 67–83). Kraków: Libron.

Schroeder, R., & Frana, J. (2009). Spirituality and religion, emotional coping, and criminal desistance: A qualitative study of men undergoing change. *Sociological Spectrum, 29*(6), 718–741.

Schubert, C.A., Mulvey, E.P., and Glasheen, C. (2011). The influence of mental health and substance use problems and criminogenic risk on outcomes in serious juvenile offenders. *Journal of the American Academy of Child and Adolescent Psychiatry 50*(9), 925–937.

Sloane, D., & Potvin, R. (1986). Religion and delinquency: Cutting through the maze. *Social Forces, 65*, 87–105.

Slosar, J. (1978). *Prisonization, friendship, and leadership.* Lexington, MA: Lexington Books.

Sykes, G. (1958). *The society of captives.* Princeton, NJ: Princeton University Press.

Thomas, J., & Zaitzow, B. H. (2006). Conning or conversion? The role of religion in prison coping. *The Prison Journal, 86*(2), 242–259.

Walsea, C. (2005). *The human development of religiousness* (Vol. 1). Lublin: Wydawnictwo KLO.

Yoder, J., & Bovard-Johns, R. (2017). Religiosity and therapeutic alliance among youth who commit sexual crimes. *Child Youth Care Forum, 46*, 119–135.

8

WHEN LIFE REVIEW IS NOT ENOUGH

The Spiritual Present(ce) of Older Adults

Robin Wiley

Pre-Reading Questions

1. What kind of spiritual force can the young impart upon older adults? How do you imagine a spirituality as it transfers from one generation to the next? What special spiritual wisdom might older adults impart?
2. Does a clinician have to be overtly religious or spiritual to foster a spiritual connection?
3. What might keep the population of older adults from the experience of spirituality?

I am not a religious or spiritually based clinician. My personal beliefs regarding spirituality do not impact my work with clients. Yet, I would be remiss if I did not help to incorporate the role of formal religion or spirituality in the lives of my clients. A client's perception about spirituality provides the clinician with a potential valuable tool for intervention. My experience is that older adults increasingly use spirituality as a coping mechanism and navigation system in facing their daily struggles, not just as these struggles relate to their own histories or looming deaths. As we age, many of the tasks associated with younger age may become increasingly difficult. Certain elements of life, once taken for granted, can become a source of stress. Most of the older adults coming into my practice are referred to address adjustment to lifespan stressors and the associated emotional symptoms. The problem for older adults is when they cannot access spirituality from their lonely place, a place of being stuck in the past or worried about the future.

I have been trained to use interventions including Cognitive Behavioral Therapy, Reality Orientation, Reminiscence Therapy, and Life Review Therapy. These approaches are endorsed by the client referral sources that work extensively with this population. However, many of the associated interventions do not seem to tackle the main issues faced by aging clients. These older adults do not fit stereotypes for this age group. My population is cognitively clear with a desire to be more active. The cognitively clear older adult, or CCOA, is not ready to leave the productive life she has created. When there is loss, such as unemployment due to illness, limited mobility, reduced independence, limited social contact, or displacement from home, the aged experience an attack on their intersectional identities. I have found myself silently agreeing with older clients as they vent about the frustrations related to getting old. Empathetic listening has often proven to be my most effective intervention, and the presence of my empathy has been the spark to my clients' use of spiritual connection in times of struggle. At times, I question my role with older clients and wonder if the chosen interventions are making a difference in changing their experience. However, if my presence keeps them present, then I have learned that I am helping my clients to experience the spiritual journey that is the last stage of life.

We may assume older adults experience an uptick in spirituality due to their close proximity to death. Here, I will examine our assumptions about how older adults experience spirituality. My goal is to demonstrate how and why the incorporation of spirituality into mental health practice with older adults offers them solace in their present state in a way that Life Review therapy alone cannot. Because I work primarily with older adults (ages 70 through 100) suffering from varying levels of anxiety and depression, I help them to recognize the spiritual tools that help them to address these experiences and stay present. I offer the composite case of a client I'll call Joan to illustrate the role spirituality plays in aging mindfully – aging in the present, so to speak.

★ ★ ★

In beginning work with clients on staying present as a spiritual practice for the aging, I explain how we tend to focus our attention in the two areas of life where we have little, or no, impact. These two areas are the past and the future. We tend to rehash what we would have, could have, or should have done in the past, which can foster feelings of sadness stemming from remorse or regret. Of course, many people in the older population are trying to be prepared for the future. Specifically, many are trying to *predict* the future. This desire for prophecy would not be so harmful except that my clients tend to predict the future to be bleak. In short, we worry about situations occurring in the future that have not or may not even happen. The area of life where we have the most impact, really the only impact, is the present.

Historically, the focus of intervention has been that older adults benefit greatly from reconciling their past, specifically focusing on any regrets. This Life Review, resulting in reconciliation of the past, would lead them to a place of integrity, as opposed to despair, in old age. However, it is my experience in working with clients that older adults are not eager to review their life history. It is not that they do not reminisce on occasion. The past just does not tend to be their focal point. In my work, I have found that older adults are more willing to practice mindfulness because it reinforces skills they are already practicing: for example, older adults are hyper aware of space, time, flower petals, breathing, music, clouds, the energy it takes to rise; the practice of mindfulness in daily life allows for awareness of experiences which can promote peace and acceptance. Mindfulness, however, is not in the lexicon of the older generation, and older folks might be put off by the therapist's jargon of mindfulness practice. Therefore, my work is to seamlessly blend my presence into a way of keeping clients present.

Literature

Erik Erikson, as part of his well-known theory of development, discussed the importance of older adults navigating the last life stage, integrity versus despair, which involves reviewing one's life, coming to terms with past life decisions, and addressing possible regrets. Successful navigation of this life stage toward integrity allows the older adult to thrive emotionally. Failure to successfully address the interpersonal conflicts within this life cycle can result in despair. Erikson's last developmental stage of life is the foundation for much of the early therapeutic work implemented with aging adults (Goodcase & Love, 2016).

Dr. Robert Butler, psychiatrist and gerontologist, viewed aging adults as being naturally inclined to reminisce over their past; he is credited with creating Life Review therapy, which is a process for clinicians to facilitate the older client's navigation of the past (Achenbaum, 2013; Haight & Haight, 2007). Life Review therapy became one of the prominent interventions used with older adults. This view of the elderly, as being focused on the past, has inadvertently limited our perception of this age group and their psychological needs. Feldman and Howie (2009) found that Life Review therapy may not be helpful with some older clients. In their study, many of the elderly participants did not want to review their past, especially the negative events. Rehashing the negative opens up old emotional wounds which could lead to further emotional distress. However, Wu and Koo (2015) countered that reminiscence-type interventions, if more reflexive, can build hope and help the aging to cope by recognizing skills and strengths once forgotten. Goodcase and Love (2016) suggested that narrative therapy is more useful because it allows clients to fill in the gaps of their story, interpret their own identity, and create new meaningful narratives. This shift from Life Review to narrative allows for meaning making of experiences, past and present, in addition to opportunities for social acknowledgment (Villar & Serrat, 2017).

Literature that supports more "here and now" focused therapeutic interventions continues to surface. Miller (2005) suggested that Interpersonal Psychotherapy (IPT) is effective for treating depressed older adults. IPT focuses on the person in their environment as the trigger or a solution, focusing on the importance of relationships and socialization in the life of older adults. McCoyd and Walter (2016) included the therapeutic relationship as also being significant to older adults. Other therapeutic approaches, such as Cognitive Behavioral and Solution Focused therapies, are recommended to be supplemented with tenets from various theories of gerontology to ensure the appropriate application to aging individuals. CBT, in particular, is seen as more effective with the "younger-older" people, but has not been shown to work as effectively with older generations (Laidlaw & Kishita, 2015). In a study by Huang, Delucchi, Dunn, and Nelson (2015), Supportive therapy, which includes listening attentively, reassuring, and being comforting, is deemed as very effective with older clients.

Despite more contemporary therapeutic approaches, there continue to be barriers clinicians must consider that could impact effective intervention with aging adults. For instance, anxiety often goes undetected amongst the elderly because fear is assumed to be associated with old age. Older adults often do not use typical mental health jargon, but will speak of emotional concerns in terms of various physical symptoms. Also, assessments, commonly used by clinicians, do not typically cater to older adults and their experience (Bower, Wetherell, Mon, & Lenze, 2015). Older adults continue to be underserved in terms of psychotherapy. They receive fewer mental health services despite being at great risk for emotional difficulties (Bower et al., 2015; North & Fiske, 2012).

Perhaps the elderly have received less attention in therapeutic intervention because, as North and Fiske (2012) pointed out, the older population is the only group that suffers prejudice despite the fact that the offenders (younger folk) will all eventually join that group. Ageism – whether through infantilization and exploitation – enjoys a stealthy social approval in media and nursing homes, which may explain why age discrimination is considered "drastically under-investigated" (North & Fiske, 2012, p. 982). Discrimination against the aging may be seen as justified because it is in the aging's best interest. Some younger folks may think that older folks have lived their lives and now need to allow room for the young to flourish. Older individuals cannot help but internalize these social constructs related to aging. Peck (2001) discussed how external and internal perceptions, along with the meaning placed on them, form our schema and, by extension, our clinical ways of treating the elderly. Elders may have an increased awareness of aging or become preoccupied with aging based on the expectations projected by society, even from clinicians who should know better (Robertson & Kenny, 2016). As a result, they may engage less in social activities or minimize their issues based on believing no one will view their concerns as important.

We may miss the potential opportunity to see older adults as still developing, adjusting, exploring, and learning. Thompson and Thompson (1999) proposed that the elderly have become a disenfranchised group based on the lack of attention to their specific mental health and behavioral needs. The early literature (Garfinkel, 1975) described how attitudes toward the elderly impacted clinicians' desire to work with them. The elderly were perceived as not talking and, therefore, presumed to be uninteresting and not requiring any social interaction. Since our assumptions about the aging have the potential to impact their well-being, our social support and mindful presence during engagement are very helpful in promoting their emotional health (Goodcase & Love, 2016; McCoyd & Walter, 2016; Shank & Cutchin, 2016). Jarrott and Savla (2016) recommended increasing our contact with aging individuals to reduce our assumptions about how they are or should be. Opportunities for contact will become plentiful as the group of people over age 65 is constantly growing and will become an even larger part of society in years to come (Goodcase & Love, 2016).

Thell and Jacobsson (2016) asserted that age is used as a lens to assess the validity of problems experienced by clients. Age puts people in a certain stage of life, which may result in less emphasis being placed on certain presenting issues. This life course, which most clinicians tend toward reviewing, refers to society's view of certain common experiences one should encounter in a certain time span of life. Adulthood is the predominant section of life with childhood, and old age is considered separate, which is a view of age that may negatively influence clinicians' formulation of problems presented by aging adults. We may normalize loss, for instance, because it is associated with old age. Therefore, we may not see a need for intervention. Thell and Jacobsson (2016) noted more information is needed on how age influences the therapist's interpretative nature within therapy. As demonstrated in my experiences with Joan, our need to come to a mutual agreement on the presenting issues and best course of action, which ultimately resulted in our mindfulness practice.

The Case of Joan

On the day of our first session, I telephoned Joan, age 70, to confirm and let her know I was on my way. When I arrived at her door, she yelled for me to come in. As I entered, she was sitting in a recliner watching television. She stated that she left the door unlocked in anticipation of my arrival. She laughed as she said this in a sarcastic tone. As I began to explain why I was visiting, her body language indicated that she had little interest in what I had to say. She looked away from me and stared at the television as if I was not in the room. I was losing her. I realized I was regurgitating the same spiel that her previous therapists had been trained to deliver.

I switched course to an actual conversation about the present moment. We talked about the show she was watching on television, her beloved dog, and, eventually, her past experiences with therapists. I found her to be candid with a dash of sarcasm. I could appreciate her witty sense of humor. She confirmed my thoughts that she experienced therapists to be too formal. She felt they were preoccupied with her depression and potential for suicide. She joked about being old lending itself to thinking about death "because that is what happens after old." Although I smiled at her statement, I could not help but wonder how she was experiencing aging and all it entails. I felt that her age gave her a certain wisdom that made me a sort of imposter.

Joan was one of my first clients who would be considered an older adult. At age 70, she lived in a senior apartment complex not too far from one of her two adult children. I reluctantly accepted the referral from her primary care physician based on my own apprehensiveness about working with elderly clients. He felt she would benefit from talk therapy in addition to medication to address her anxiety and depression. He did not present her as a willing participant in therapy. Frankly, he described her as chasing therapists away in the past. I tried hard not to have preconceived notions about Joan. I wondered if she was resistant to therapy or maybe did not believe in it. Considering Joan's age, it was not hard to believe she may not view therapy, or a therapist, as helpful. I anticipated she may believe that seeing a therapist meant that something was wrong with her. She was compliant with her prescribed psychotropic medication. I remained optimistic.

When I sit with older clients, I am reminded of what it might be like to become old. The idea that, as we age, we will experience losses of great proportions can seem unfathomable. In my work with aging adults, I see individuals with a wealth of knowledge and experiences. I often wonder how they view my role in relation to them. Officially, I am their therapist. However, rarely do they, or I, use that description when referring to me. I do not want older clients to view my role negatively based on possible generational and/or cultural perspectives regarding therapy. I prefer to make reference to my prescribed purpose to offer them support where needed.

From my first session with Joan, I realized how her life had changed tremendously within less than a ten-year time span. She was forced into early retirement due to chronic medical issues. Her children convinced her to sell her house of 20 plus years and move into the senior apartments in an unfamiliar town. She ruefully said she could have worked another ten years. She told the story of her transition to less independence as if it were a short bedtime story. All the pertinent details were neatly placed in order so as to give a full picture of this experience to anyone who needed to know. She was practically dissociated from the story in telling it, and I gleaned that this picture of the past was not what was meaningful for her in the present.

Our sessions, which were every other week at her insistence, were characterized by conversations about Joan's dissatisfaction with various aspects of her current life. We would often discuss how she spends her days. She typically laughed, gave a serious look, and on one occasion stated, "I hate it here." She was referring to the isolation she felt being in her one-bedroom apartment. She felt her best friend and companion was her dog, Gary. She acknowledged having a couple of friends in the building with whom she spoke infrequently. She felt she could not relate to most of her neighbors because of differing interests. She wanted to talk about books or current events. In her opinion, they only talked about their grandchildren or other gossip. She had no interest in their conversational topics. During this time in our work together, she drove herself to do errands, including doctor's appointments. Otherwise, she filled her day by cleaning her apartment, watching television, reading, and occasionally participating in a scheduled activity in her complex. She joked that doctors' appointments had become part of her social entertainment. She went on to share that it becomes difficult on some days to want to do anything due to her mood. Here was a woman yearning for connection as a conduit into a life that seemed to be happening around her, without her being a part of it. Without real connection, her life was practically an out-of-body experience.

Joan defined our client-therapist relationship on her terms; usually, in a spiritual exchange, the guide sets the terms, but Joan either wanted to be the guide or didn't know how to let me guide, because of her need for autonomy at a time when most things were out of her control. She was consistent with our biweekly sessions. This schedule was atypical for the beginning therapeutic relationship because it minimized the optimal interaction. Nevertheless, I began to assess her needs as we continued to meet. Although Joan lived in a senior apartment complex amongst her peers, she remained socially isolated. I think we assume that the senior community provides much needed socialization because all the "old folks" will automatically gravitate toward one another out of necessity. However, just like any other age group, individual interests impact who we choose to associate (Shank & Cutchin, 2016). Joan did not feel connected to her peers. She was living in an unfamiliar neighborhood. Usually, it is hard for older adults to leave neighborhoods where they had attended a community church, but Joan never had a religious community to begin with, which may have caused her to want to avoid people with overtly spiritual connections. In fact, she avoided the religious programming of her new residence. Despite driving herself to her doctors' appointments, she did not wish to venture to places unfamiliar to her. Joan had a daily routine that I initially saw as a strength because it filled space in her day. This routine did not fulfill Joan's needs because it was not time meaningfully spent. Joan's mood also impacted her ability to complete her routine. Joan was somewhat insightful about this area of her life. She could always describe her mood to me in great detail. She was not reflective about why she felt the way she did. Because Joan and I did not see each other often, I spent more time with her during our scheduled sessions. I could easily speak with her for two or three hours. I enjoyed talking to her. In between our sessions, I started to question the direction we were going in therapy. We spent all this time talking, but was there any impact for Joan? I believed our sessions were always productive. Joan seemed to feel open to discussing whatever was on her mind. However, she did not fit into my schema about the therapeutic needs of "the elderly." She was dealing with issues related to her current daily life, not issues from her past. In an effort to meet her where she was, I was reluctant to guide our sessions toward what theory might be directing me to discuss. After all, I was still building rapport with her. Implementing interventions from Life Review or Reminiscence therapy would not fit her needs. Discussing her past seemingly had no significant impact on her present. Although she discussed past memories occasionally, it was not the ever-present theme of our sessions.

The more I worked with Joan, the more I began to feel like I understood how to effectively assist her; because she never had a sense of what it meant to be present, she experienced the severe anxiety of feeling cut off from the world since childhood. One rare occasion, we discussed her family history. She reported being an only child of parents whom she described as being very protective. When I asked her to elaborate on how they protected her, she indicated they made her scared of everything. She felt they constantly warned her against trying anything, even truly trusting or connecting with others. She believes she has always had anxiety, which, in her opinion, derived from her childhood. She described herself as never taking risks, even in adulthood. When Joan shared this perception, it helped me recognize how this experience may have molded her spiritual void. I attempted to move toward a more task-centered and problem-solving approach with Joan. We discussed various coping strategies such as reading, visiting a friend, or calling family. We also reviewed community activities she could explore. Her reluctance to attempt my suggestions confounded me. She seemed open to hearing the suggestions and even showed enthusiasm. However, she did not follow through. She did not feel motivated to accomplish the goals we established. As I reflect back on those earlier sessions, I guess I believed the solution was simple. Joan just needed to get out of her apartment more and engage in activities she enjoyed. She had verbalized her interests and she still had the ability to drive. She was older, but her life was not over. I just needed her to see that. I realized her struggles with depression and anxiety impacted her willingness and motivation, but, moreover, her resistance to others' presence kept her locked in her isolated childhood habits.

As I attempted to transcend Joan's barriers, I wondered what messages she was receiving elsewhere. When I asked about her children, she described her son and daughter in terms of their interactions with her. She referred to her son as the "judge" and her daughter as the "faraway fun one." She described how her son criticized her about her lack of effort to do things or go out. He also asked her "to get past her emotions." She did not know what he meant by that, yet she must have taught him that somewhere along the line, if only tacitly. She acknowledged that she did not see either of her children very often. She attributed their absence to their busy work schedules. Her son, who lived the closest, seemed to have a lack of understanding of how Joan's emotional concerns could impact her productivity and motivation. His interaction with her was very limited as he handled all her affairs via phone or computer. He rarely visited her. Her daughter, who lived in Georgia, seemed to have a closer relationship with Joan. They spoke almost daily by phone. The physical distance kept them apart. Joan often thought of moving to Georgia, but did not think it was the right time. This may have represented too big a risk for Joan. I realized that the connection I was forging with Joan may be her first connection of spiritual presence; unlike her children, who were apart not so much due to their physical distance but more so emotional distance – behavior they learned from her, I provided a closeness that was the space for her to be emotionally present.

Working with Joan helped me to rethink my role as her therapist. Joan was on her own to deal with the day-to-day issues she faced. She had virtually no interactive support. The messages she received from her son asserted that she needed to get herself together and just do something. When she shared this with me, I reflected on the message I was sending as her therapist. I saw Joan's potential to be more productive, but the message may have come across as a reminder of her son's messages. Perhaps this is also indicative of society's view of the high functioning elderly. Some may believe aging adults just need to adjust and move on to be successful in aging. Joan was not able to do this on her own. She also could not adjust in the ways I was suggesting. Feeling a bit useless and unproductive, I asked Joan directly how I could help her. She simply said it was good to have someone to vent to about what she was feeling. She felt I listened to her without judgment. She knew I could not fix all her problems, but she appreciated that I was willing to try to help her. I was speechless and a bit overcome with emotion. All this time, I was focused on how to eradicate the issues and help to improve Joan's mood. When I hit roadblocks to achieving those goals, I felt defeated and ineffective as her therapist. She was more focused on my presence and our relationship. I was there consistently every other week to listen to her, laugh with her, and give her a much-needed dose of socialization.

Letting go of my perceptions of how my relationship should be with Joan allowed me to be more effective with her. I looked forward to my sessions with Joan. As she shared more, I felt like I was beginning to know her better. Each little story she told was filling in the sections of the puzzle. I was beginning to make connections between her view of herself and her emotional life. Joan constantly worried about a multitude of subjects. She was concerned about her prescriptions running out, what her children thought of her, and her dog. On one occasion, she was frantic because her dog had somehow misplaced his favorite chew toy. She felt he would not be able to survive without this toy. Meanwhile, Gary, the dog, was sitting calmly in front of us. She just could not figure out where the toy could be. The whereabouts of the toy consumed her. We spent almost an entire session looking around the apartment for the toy. Although our efforts were futile, I think that session was a pivotal moment in our therapeutic relationship. Often, in our spiritual searches, we come up empty handed, or without the answers we were searching for, but if we have someone that we are searching with, then the search is in and of itself meaningful and productive.

Joan finally saw me as an ally, a support that would be there for her unconditionally. Joan seemed to be comforted by someone helping her. When the session was over and I was about to leave, she stated, "I'll see you next week." Joan conceding to weekly sessions further validated that the mere existence of the helping relationship was the key intervention for her. Of course the relationship with our clients is important, but it is typically the foundation created prior to implementing the interventions. The sessions with Joan gave her something to anticipate without the associated worry. As shown by the incident with her dog, her anxiety could be consuming. It was how she approached most events, other than our sessions. But the session time became like time for gratitude about the present moment we could share.

Over the next month or so, Joan seemed to be improving. Although not much about her situation had changed, she continued to process her concerns in our weekly sessions. She was going out at least once per week to run errands, participating in a weekly bingo game in the building, and interacting with a couple of ladies in the building she considered to be friendly toward her. She still worried a lot. She knew that her mood could be a barrier to her social efforts at times. Nevertheless, she was trying to be active as best she could.

As Joan experienced further age-related struggles, I realized I had become an integral part of her support system. Joan rarely contacted me between sessions. I would reach out to her to simply confirm our appointment. One particular week, she called me to cancel because she did not feel well. I thought nothing of this cancellation. Then she canceled the next two weeks. This time, she told me she did not feel like seeing anyone. I remember thinking she may feel she no longer needed therapy because she was doing well. I waited another week and then I called her to follow-up. After I expressed my concerns about not seeing her for a while, and the possible need to discharge, she asked if I could visit her the next day. When I arrived at her apartment, I saw her sitting in her recliner with her arm in a sling and a neck brace on. She proceeded to tell me she had gotten into a car accident a couple of weeks before. She got a ticket for reckless driving. She was scheduled to appear in court in the next couple of weeks. She felt bad about canceling our sessions, but she also felt ashamed about the accident. She was afraid of potential outcomes. I tried to ease her mind, but she said that she knew this would be the end of her driving. Her son had already taken her keys and the car. She knew she would never drive again. In her mind, this was her last semblance of independence. The ability to drive herself was a pathway out of her apartment on her own terms. I could only imagine how she felt. I held her hand as we spoke. I told her I could accompany her to court if she would like. She agreed. The weeks leading up to her court date were spent using our sessions to reassure Joan she would get through this.

I realized Joan felt little control over who she was or had become at this stage of life. In addition to losing her license and ability to drive, she was also on the mend from the injuries sustained in the car accident. Her anxiety increased as she expressed concerns about her ability to heal. She believed she would be even more limited in her ability to care for herself, more negative prophecy. During one session, she was feeling particularly sad and hopeless. As in previous sessions, she continued to focus on what she was unable to do. I asked her if she was aware of all her options to bring her back to the present. She questioned what options I was talking about. I pulled out a pad and pen, and we began to brainstorm what could help her in this current stage of her life. At the time, I did not know if this would make her feel better or worse. I had strayed away from solution-focused suggestions. I just wanted her to know options were available so she could begin to make some choices. I believed this might begin to help her feel more empowered. Among other things, we discussed options for her living arrangements, ways for her to get around without a car, and who could be part of her support system. I explained she did not need to use all these options, but it would be beneficial for her to have knowledge of her choices. Joan was open to many of the ideas we generated. We increased our sessions to twice per week so I could be more supportive to her during what she determined was her time of great need.

As promised, I accompanied Joan to her court hearing. As we sat in a courtroom waiting for Joan's name to be called, I watched as she stared down at the driver's license in her hand. The fender bender had resulted in the recommendation of surrendering her license. She reluctantly agreed to give up driving at the insistence of her children. When asked, I let her know I too believed it might be in her best interest. As we waited, I could not help but ponder how monumental this event must be for Joan. When we are young, obtaining a driver's license is a rite of passage toward independence and adulthood. If someone younger gets into an accident, no one assumes her ability to drive is permanently lost. Yet, in old age, what does surrendering one's license mean? Does this remove Joan's adulthood or independence? I wondered how this would impact her emotionally as well as socially. This was another loss associated with aging. I was happy to be there for her in that moment. I was showing her our relationship was a constant in her life. I hope this gave her some comfort.

Discussion

Joan's narrative caused me to question what I thought should be addressed within our sessions. The story she shared is quite common. She worked in a fulfilling career and engaged in social outlets on her own terms. She was not ready to relinquish her home, let alone the independence she had taken for granted. There is no way she could have been prepared for this major life transition. Her difficulty adjusting is having an impact on her emotionally which is characteristic of Erikson's stage of despair. As humans, we are aware we will age and eventually be considered "elderly." However, we may not be fully cognizant of the dynamics associated with aging. The concept of "successfully aging" has given meaning and perhaps unrealistic expectations to how we should age. Aging is no longer viewed as growing old gracefully and rocking away on a porch watching the growing grass. Being healthy, active, and socially engaged are all key elements associated with being successful at the aging game (Shank & Cutchin, 2016). In addition, spirituality can play a key role. As her therapist, I could assist her in reframing her negative thought patterns by bringing her attention back to the present. However, Joan did not discuss aging in terms of how society viewed her. She did not question if she was aging successfully. Contrary to my assumptions, she also did not reflect on past regrets or unresolved conflicts that would aid her in navigating the last developmental stage of life.

Conclusion

Throughout my work with Joan, and my other aging clients, I have realized we have much more to learn about the aging experience, and one way we can learn is to be the guides of the elderly's mindfulness practice. Aging adults' individual needs are not static nor based on the ascribed characteristics of their age group. This awareness needs to inform clinical practice with this group. What I thought she needed was a solution to her problems that we could create together in an effort to alleviate her emotional symptoms. Fortunately, she had the patience to allow me to learn, through trial and error, what would be most effective in working with her. I never could have imagined mindfulness could be as simple as meeting with Joan in ways that made us both evaluate what the term "presence" really means. The relationship we created served a need that had therapeutic value. Practicing mindfulness with the client instead of talking at the client creates meaningful and fulfilling use of present time. Joan knew her problems were associated with age and could not be solved. Her mindfulness of her thoughts and associated emotions that she could explore with me was what she felt she needed. Pennington (2009) reflects on the significance of the relationship with her older clients as related to the longevity and consistency. The therapeutic interaction mindfulness practice with aging adults is less about change and more about the interaction with one's spiritual self in communion with therapist as spiritual companion.

Close Reading Questions

1. How is solution-focused therapy at odds with keeping present?
2. What is Life Review therapy and how does it fit in with other treatment modalities mentioned in the literature section of Wiley's chapter?

Prompts for Thinking and Writing

1. Why might it be difficult for younger mental health clinicians to connect with older adults on a spiritual level? How might spirituality serve to bridge generational gaps?
2. Aside from the efforts Wiley made in this case, what other access to spiritual practice might a spiritually competent clinician provide?
3. How does Wiley's chapter on spiritual presence and keeping present connect with Ordille's chapter on hospice work and the podcast, featured on the E-Resources page, about the spirituality of children?

References

Achenbaum, W. (2013). *Robert N. Butler, MD* (1st ed.). New York, NY: Columbia University Press.

Bower, E., Wetherell, J., Mon, T., & Lenze, E. (2015). Treating anxiety disorders in older adults. *Harvard Review of Psychiatry, 23*(5), 329–342. doi:10.1097/hrp.0000000000000064

Feldman, S., & Howie, L. (2009). Looking back, looking forward. *Journal of Applied Gerontology, 28*(5), 621–637. doi:10.1177/0733464808330081

Garfinkel, R. (1975). The reluctant therapist 1975. *The Gerontologist, 15*(2), 136–137. doi:10.1093/geront/15.2.136

Goodcase, E., & Love, H. (2016). From despair to integrity: Using narrative therapy for older individuals in Erikson's last stage of identity development. *Clinical Social Work Journal.* doi:10.1007/s10615-016-0601-6

Haight, B., & Haight, B. (2007). *The handbook of structured life review* (1st ed.). Baltimore, MD: Health Professions Press.

Huang, A., Delucchi, K., Dunn, L., & Nelson, J. (2015). A systematic review and meta-analysis of psychotherapy for late-life depression. *The American Journal of Geriatric Psychiatry, 23*(3), 261–273. doi:10.1016/j.jagp.2014.04.003

Jarrott, S., & Savla, J. (2016). Intergenerational contact and mediators impact ambivalence towards future selves. *International Journal of Behavioral Development, 40*(3), 282–288. doi:10.1177/0165025415581913

Laidlaw, K., & Kishita, N. (2015). Age-appropriate augmented cognitive behavior therapy to enhance treatment outcome for late-life depression and anxiety disorders. *Geropsych, 28*(2), 57–66. doi:10.1024/1662-9647/a000128

McCoyd, J., & Walter, C. (2016). *Grief and loss across the lifespan* (2nd ed., pp. 259–287). New York, NY: Springer Publishing Company, LLC.

Miller, M. (2005). Late life depression: Focused IPT eases loss and role change. *Current Psychiatry, 4*(11), 40–50.

North, M., & Fiske, S. (2012). An inconvenienced youth? Ageism and its potential intergenerational roots. *Psychological Bulletin, 138*(5), 982–997. doi:10.1037/a0027843

Peck, M. (2001). Looking back at life and its' influence on subjective well-being. *Journal of Gerontological Social Work, 35*(2), 3–20. doi:10.1300/j083v35n02_02

Pennington, S. (2009). Aging with my clients. *Women & Therapy, 32*(2–3), 202–208. doi:10.1080/02703140902852078

Robertson, D., & Kenny, R. (2016). "I'm too old for that" — The association between negative perceptions of aging and disengagement in later life. *Personality and Individual Differences, 100*, 114–119. doi:10.1016/j.paid.2016.03.096

Shank, K., & Cutchin, M. (2016). Processes of developing 'community livability' in older age. *Journal of Aging Studies, 39*, 66–72. doi:10.1016/j.jaging.2016.11.001

Thell, N., & Jacobsson, K. (2016). "And how old are you?": Age reference as an interpretative device in radio counseling. *Journal of Aging Studies, 39*, 31–43. doi:10.1016/j.jaging.2016.09.001

Thompson, S., & Thompson, N. (1999). Older people, crisis, and loss. *Illness, Crisis & Loss, 7*(2), 122–133. doi:10.1177/105413739900700202

Villar, F., & Serrat, R. (2017). Changing the culture of long-term care through narrative care: Individual, interpersonal, and institutional dimensions. *Journal of Aging Studies, 40*, 44–48. doi:10.1016/j.jaging.2016.12.007

Wu, L., & Koo, M. (2015). Randomized controlled trial of a six-week spiritual reminiscence intervention on hope, life satisfaction, and spiritual well-being in elderly with mild and moderate dementia. *International Journal of Geriatric Psychiatry, 31*(2), 120–127. doi:10.1002/gps.4300

9

THE ASANA OF BEING WITH LIVING AND DYING

Reflections from a Day of Hospice Work

Joan Ordille

Pre-Reading Questions

1. Have you ever practiced yoga? What did the poses feel like? If you've never tried yoga, try it now by finding a tutorial online.
2. Why might the need for spiritually focused self-care be great among workers in hospice settings?
3. What assumptions do you have about a dying patient's need for spiritual connection? How might a mental health practitioner in a hospice setting provide spiritual connection?

Prologue

Waking up to a new day is a life cycle activity most of us get to take for granted. For those dealing with a terminal, life-limiting illness, it is not. One day a patient, Nate, mentioned having difficulty sleeping despite the pharmaceutical interventions the hospice nurse had put into place to relieve his anxiety and help him sleep. "I haven't had a good night's sleep since the doctor told me there is no more treatment. I doze, but I don't sleep soundly," he told me.

"So, you're dozing but not getting restful sleep? What do you think is behind your difficulty with sleep?" I asked him.

He shook his head. "I don't know," he replied.

Nate, in his prime, weighed in at about 230 pounds, and it was clear from pictures in his home it was a little extra weight on his 5-foot 11-inch frame. He worked in construction most of his life and had been a heavy drinker back in the day, his second wife, Myra, told me the first time I had visited. Nate had three children from a first marriage. There had been no contact with two of his children for years. A lot of anger, a lot of recriminations. "Their choice and his," Myra had said. At the end of the first visit to Nate's home, as I was leaving, I heard him say, "Why do I need a social worker anyway?" to no one in particular.

The cancer diagnosis had come almost two years before our first meeting. I had been at Nate and Myra's home a few times since he had been told there was no more treatment and admitted to hospice. During those visits, most of the psychosocial support had been provided to Myra in relation to her feelings of loss and anticipatory grief, as well as the day-to-day demands of her life and role as Nate's primary care giver. Nate, himself, had little to say to me up until the day he spoke about his trouble sleeping. He was sitting in his favorite worn, brown leather recliner, skin hanging loosely on his exposed arms from the weight loss associated with the cancer. His black Labrador, Duchess, was snoring nearby, an affront to Nate's sleeplessness. His sleep difficulties had become bad enough for him to mention it to me. I could have encouraged him to talk about his anxiety, but I would have lost him because Nate was not one to explore his feelings. I could have tried to be the hero and offered to reach out to his children asking them to visit their father, but I knew that could end in disaster for all the good willed intention. I could have offered to contact the nurse about the possibility of more medication to help him sleep but thought that more medication was not going to help with the underlying issues affecting his sleep.

"Are you afraid if you go to sleep that you aren't going to wake up in the morning?" I asked.

"You nailed it," he replied.

My heart went out to his man who had many things that could have been inhabiting his psyche and inhibiting his sleep. Over the years of work with hospice patients, I have encountered many who were afraid to go to sleep and had opportunity for similar conversations. I considered how to respond to Nate. While his condition was terminal, he did not appear to be in the actively dying phase of his disease.

"I don't have a crystal ball," I told him, "but I can tell you that barring a heart attack, which could happen to any of us, I have every reason to think that you will wake up tomorrow morning." I noticed a slight shift in his demeanor, a small sigh of relief as he settled more deeply into his recliner and reached out to stroke Duchess. "Nate, do you have unfinished business that could be affecting your sleep?"

He closed his eyes for a moment before he answered me. I could picture the wheels turning in his brain as he considered my question. "Yes, but I don't want to go there right now," he said. I knew he didn't have a whole lot of time left to "go there," but respected his reply, wondering if we could build a therapeutic alliance that would allow him the safety to explore both his immediate and his existential concerns.

Nate was one of a growing number of individuals with terminal illness to receive hospice services. The term "hospice" can be traced back to medieval times. It was a place of shelter for tired or ill travelers. Physician Dame Cicely Saunders is credited with founding the modern hospice movement in London in the 1940s. Saunders had the unique combination of training as a physician, nurse, and social worker, along with a strong religious faith. This combination of expertise and personal belief gave rise to Saunders' concept of "total pain," which included physical, psychological, social, emotional, and spiritual considerations in care for the dying, rather than the prevailing idea of pain as a physical sensation alone (Clark, 1999). Saunders visited Yale University in the early 1970s, beginning a conversation on this side of the Atlantic that would take root as the model for care of the terminally ill.

In parallel development to the work of Saunders was that of Elisabeth Kübler-Ross, whose book *On Death and Dying* was published in 1969. This important work by Kübler-Ross was based on hundreds of interviews with dying patients and described five stages of grief that terminally ill patients experience. A few years later, Kübler-Ross testified at a national hearing on the subject of death with dignity, indicating that we live in a "death denying society" that isolates the old and infirm to die in institutional settings. She felt that better, more personal care could be given to the terminally ill at home with the support of a team equipped to provide physical, emotional, social, and spiritual support to the dying person (National Hospice and Palliative Care Organization [NHPCO], 2012). She believed that dying patients should have the ability to participate in their health care and that "there was not a single dying person who did not yearn for love, touch or communication" (Clark, 1999, p. 729). As a result of the work of Saunders and Kübler-Ross, hospice care developed as an interdisciplinary approach requiring doctors, nurses, chaplains, and Master's-prepared social workers.

The census of hospice patients has grown steadily since the opening of the first hospice in the United States in 1974 when annually about 5,500 patients were served, to a census of 25,000 patients in 1982 when the legislative act that funded the Hospice Medicare benefit passed into law (NHPCO, 2012). The Center for Disease Control and Prevention (CDC) estimates there were approximately 1.4 million hospice patients in 2015 (2015, para. 2). Continued growth in the use of hospice services for end-of-life care is an expectation as the baby boomer population ages. There is, and will continue to be, a growing need for social work practitioners in hospice care, as well as a need for research to support their work. The myriad psychosocial issues that arise in hospice work require flexibility and a strong knowledge base to adequately address patient needs. A focus on care of the practitioner and how it is essential to safe and ethical clinical work is important to the preparation of hospice workers, based on the reality of working daily with living and dying, the associated effects of cumulative loss, and the immediate and existential suffering encountered in work with the dying.

This semi-auto-ethnographic account of a typical day in hospice social work will introduce *practice fusion* as a response to the complex and often unpredictable needs of the dying patient and their caregivers. It will also illustrate how this practitioner's self-care practice of yoga and meditation fuses with theory to enhance therapeutic presence and the processing of countertransference. It will emphasize the phenomenology of dying for the patient, and the related experience for their care givers and the clinician, and it will illustrate why social work education for those who work in the hospice setting needs to focus on multi-theory practice. It will also address Nate's question, "Why do I need a social worker, anyway?"

Daily Practice

My typical day begins with *surya namaskar*, Sanskrit word for sun salutations; it is a conscious choice to welcome a new day that celebrates and emulates the rising of the sun. Sun salutations are a moving yoga meditation that aligns and energizes the body. *Surya namaskar* links together several yoga poses in constant flow with breath and is a salute to life and the cycle of sunrise and sunset. I am not alone in this practice. Yoga was introduced to the United States from India by Swami Vivekananda around the turn of the 20th century and had a slow, steady growth over the first 100 years, with recent growth being exponential. A 2008 Yoga in America study reported the number of adults practicing yoga grew from approximately 4 million in 2001 to almost 16 million in 2007 (Miller, 2012, p. 83), illustrating that yoga, as a practice, has had significant impact since being introduced to the West.

My daily ritual that begins with yoga, breath work, and meditation is a practice that utilizes a blend of different schools of yoga, Eastern meditation practice, and philosophy: a *practice fusion*. Fusion is a combination or merging of diverse, distinct, or separate elements into a new, unified whole—a union. Yoga, derived from the Sanskrit word "*yuj*," also translates to union, or to yoke, as in the harnessing of energy (Boccio, 2009; Carrera, 2006; Mithoefer, 2006). Fusion has become a popular term in music and cuisine, the joining of different genres or ingredients to produce something new that retains an essence of the original elements while becoming something unique unto itself. *Practice fusion*, in self-care and in social work practice, is a thoughtful and deliberate blending of philosophy and methodology and is designed to enhance clinical practice and personal well-being.

My daily practice could include gentle Hatha yoga or a vigorous vinyasa flow that would include variations of sun salutations, also from the Hatha lineage, developed from the Hindu or Vedic tradition. It may draw from the grounding practice of Yin yoga, coming from a Taoist perspective, which focuses on the balance of yin and yang, interdependent opposites. Yin yoga focuses on deeper tissues in the body through holding poses for longer periods, balancing stillness and action. Kundalini yoga with its focuses on charkas, the energy centers of the body, and removing blockages through movement, breath, and mantra—a vibrational sound technology, developed from a Sikh tradition—may be the practice of the day. Sometimes, I practice from a single lineage, and other times I combine schools within a single practice session. I assess what my body, emotions, and spirit need, and I respond accordingly. While some schools would suggest that the best results are achieved from practicing a certain style or lineage of yoga, Swami Vivekananda blended several traditions together as he taught yoga in the United States, and there is also a history of blurring traditions in India (Miller, 2012). Seemingly, yoga itself fused elements together as the tradition evolved.

With a working knowledge of the history, philosophy, mechanics, benefits, and limits of various schools of yoga, a fusion practice meets the varying needs that arise in daily life and in my profession as a hospice social worker. It enhances the ability to be present to the lived experience of clients, as well as to my own phenomenology, or lived experience within that work. Yoga master Erich Schiffmann explains, "Yoga is a way of moving into stillness in order to experience the truth of who you are. It [yoga] is also way of learning to be centered in action so that you always have the clearest perspective on what's happening and are therefore able to respond most appropriately" (1996, p. 4). I suggest that the practice of yoga enhances therapeutic presence and the ability to be flexible and client-centered.

In parallel process to daily yoga practice, I began to recognize my clinical approach to work with hospice patients and their families was evolving into *practice fusion*, a blending or union from multiple theoretical orientations and practice modalities, and a practice that like yoga is physically, emotionally, and spiritually informed. In *Social Work Treatment: Interlocking Theoretical Approaches*, Francis Turner stated, "It has only been in the past four or five decades that attention has been drawn to theoretical commonalities across methods and hence the possibility and indeed the necessity of multi-method and multi-theory practitioners" (2011, p. 6). With the recognition of the need for multi-theory practitioners, I will define and illustrate the idea of practice fusion and differentiate it from what has commonly been called "eclectic practice."

Eclectic is defined as taking things from many different sources or selecting what appears to be a best choice in various doctrines, methods, or styles, a sort of a "patchwork" or "kitchen sink" approach. As stated earlier, fusion is the merging of diverse elements into a unified whole or a union. Additionally, fusion is an energy-producing phenomenon in physics. The sun is constantly converting matter into energy in a fusion reaction. According to Charles Seife, "In fusion, light atoms stick together and the whole resulting atom is lighter than the sum of the parts that made it. The missing matter—the stuff that disappears when the light atoms combine—becomes energy" (2008, p. 12). The process of fusion is like the powerful release of energy that can take place in therapy. Fusing theory in social work practice, like a well-designed yoga practice, has a seamlessness; the transitions are part of the practice, and there is flow, differentiating it from eclecticism and its pick-and-choose nature. In practice, I attempt to maintain a common, underlying light element, a client- or person-centered, relational approach, and blend it with other theories to holistically meet the needs of hospice patients and their caregivers.

The day-to-day reality of hospice social work requires a practitioner to draw from multiple theoretical frameworks and blend them together, sometimes over the course of several individual patient or client contacts, sometimes within the same visit. It would not be uncommon to utilize family systems, client-centered, crisis, and existential theories within a single visit to a patient and their family. Fusion and not eclectic: because where one theory distinctly ends and another begins is less important than utilizing theory in practice to meet the needs of the dying and their caregivers. A clinician must be well grounded in theory to effectively utilize a fusion practice, again, with knowledge of the history, philosophy, mechanics, benefits, and limits of a particular social work theory. I acknowledge the nay-sayers. There are benefits to being true to a single theory in social work practice, as well as in yoga and meditation, but I would suggest that many of the theories we utilize in practice today have arisen out of a fusion of ideas and practices. Turner asserted, "to make effective and ethical use of these theories they must be understood as individual conceptual constructs and also as bodies of thought that are inter-influencing, inter-connecting and interlocking" (2011, p. 4). A visit to a psychoanalyst today would look different from the psychoanalysis Freud practiced and illustrated in his case studies, but it would include some of the same principles. Likewise, the yoga practiced thousands of years ago would look very different from that which is practiced today, but it retains some common, underlying elements.

My clinical *practice fusion* draws significantly from client-centered theory or the person-centered approach as developed by Carl Rogers, as well as from psychosocial, existential, narrative, and crisis theories; it includes elements of family systems, of mindfulness, and of other Eastern philosophical frameworks. Phenomenology, specifically, the experience of being with patients in their lived experience of dying, informs my work; additionally, my own embodied experience of working with dying, which I process both literally and figuratively through yoga, breath work, and meditation. Self-care and support within the interdisciplinary team are not separate from the clinical work but an integral part of practice in a hospice setting.

Client-centered theory or the person-centered approach, as developed by Carl Rogers, is the basis of my practice fusion, the *Tadasana* or mountain pose, the strong and balanced starting point. Rogers' approach itself was a fusion of sorts, as stated in Rowe: "What is unique about Rogers' influence on client-centered theory is that even though he was its parent and chief proponent, his force was derived more from the integration and organization of existing concepts than from the generation of new ideas. This may account for the lack of authoritative rigidity and dogma that is characteristic of client centered theory" (1996, p. 70). Therapeutic presence and the building of relationships became the cornerstone of his work and theory development: "Rogers first became interested in effective therapeutic methods as opposed to psychological ideologies" (1996, p. 70). The hallmark of Rogers' work with clients was in the use of the therapeutic relationship, which is based on genuineness, congruence, accurate empathy, reflection of client feelings, and a non-authoritarian or non-directive stance (Rogers, 1951, 1980, 2013; Rowe, 1996).

The use of the term "person-centered approach" is an acknowledgment by Rogers that his humanistic theory of growth can be used in both clinical and non-clinical settings (Levant & Schlien, 1984; Rogers, 1980; Rowe, 1996), as well as in any circumstance where growth is the goal. As stated in Levant and Schlien (1984), "The person-centered approach was conceived to accommodate the expansion of client-centered therapy beyond its original boundaries of counseling and mental health. The relabeling recognized the increasing emphasis given to working with a wide range of people, few of whom would define themselves as 'clients' seeking therapy" (p. 14). The client- or person-centered approach widened to include medicine and health care, making it an ideal starting point for work with clients in a hospice setting.

For this chapter, the use of the term "patient" will reflect an individual's status as a hospice patient with a terminal condition, but it does not necessarily indicate an underlying psychopathology. As caregivers for the dying person also receive support from a hospice social worker, the use of the term "client," again, should not automatically point to an assumption of pathology. Change itself can be stressful and compromise coping. Psychosocial support to those facing death, with all its practical and existential implications, with the accompanying feelings of actual and anticipatory loss and vulnerability, either real or perceived, is essential and begins to scratch the surface of the question "why do I need a social worker?" It is important to enter the helping relationship in hospice social work with a lens that does not assume psychopathology but which understands that it may be an aspect of the experience of the "patient" or a "client" within the caregiving system. The client- or person-centered approach, through philosophy and practice, is a highly effective theory from which to approach hospice social work. As the vignettes in this case study will demonstrate, however, it is useful and necessary to draw from other theoretical applications to best serve the patient and/or client. The Rogerian approach makes room for the clinician to "draw from the process components of other theories of counseling and human behavior" (Rowe, p. 81), providing a baseline element for use within the flow of *practice fusion.*

A discussion of the Rogers' client-centered approach and my intention to explore countertransference through the use of yoga asana is appropriate, as traditionally, countertransference, which comes from the psychodynamic tradition, was not recognized or named as such in client-centered theory. Rogers would have referred to this phenomenon, the feelings that arise for the counselor within the therapeutic context, as congruence and non-congruence (Owen, 1999). However, countertransference has become a term almost universally used when therapists or counselors discuss and process their work with clients in a supervisory setting or when reflecting for self-understanding. As stated in Schore and Schore (2010), "There is now a growing consensus that despite the existence of a number of distinct theoretical perspectives in the field of social work, the concepts of transference and countertransference represent a common ground" (p. 67). I struggled with the choice to use the term "countertransference" in conjunction with Rogers' theory but decided it was appropriate to name and address feelings that arise in work with clients in this way. Owen (1999) addressed this issue in his article "Exploring the Similarities and Differences Between Person-Centered and Psychodynamic Therapy." Owen claimed:

> Both [theories] require the disclosure of some of the therapist's own reactions. Whether these are psychodynamic interpretations or reflections, they are in both cases based on countertransference feelings. Both practices aim to set aside and work through non-therapeutic therapist feelings through supervision and personal reflection. They also share a similar understanding of psychological problems in as much that incongruence in the person-centered tradition is similar to intra psychic conflict in the psychodynamic tradition.
>
> *(p. 186)*

Regardless of the specific name of the experiences that arise in a therapeutic setting, I have found yoga asana effective in processing the conscious, unconscious, or embodied feelings that arise in daily practice, agreeing with Owen's claim that, "at a level of honesty and openness to one's own reactions in the therapeutic situation, both models share a set of fundamental similarities to do with empathy and insight" (1999, p. 168). In addition to countertransference, the concept of encounter, as discussed in phenomenology and existential psychotherapy (Ellenberger, 1958), has implications and applications to the therapist's processing of client experience and insight. Having addressed and hopefully added some congruence to the use of concept and language, I proceed with a description of other theories important to daily practice, which are illustrated through the use of case presentations.

Complimenting Rogers' person-centered approach, psychosocial theory has applications to hospice social work. Woods and Robinson (1996) affirm the importance of the therapeutic relationship as central to the psychosocial approach:

> Research and 'practice wisdom' confirm that the worker-client relationship is crucial to the success of psychosocial treatment and one of its most powerful tools. The worker's effort is to demonstrate nonpossessive warmth and concern, nonjudgemental acceptance, genuineness, accurate empathy, a profound respect for the importance of self-direction and realistic optimism about change.
>
> *(p. 556)*

The psychosocial approach fuses nicely with client-centered theory, utilizing many of the same components, but it places additional emphasis on the role of the social worker as case worker: "The science and art of psychosocial treatment usually involves the use of a blend of treatment procedures and worker client communications and, often, 'concrete' services" (p. 556). Psychosocial theory includes a focus on the environment as well as on the individual. The very nature of hospice social work dictates that some patients and families will need support beyond psychotherapy. Successful support in obtaining needed concrete services builds trust in the therapeutic relationship. Components of psychosocial theory in conjunction with tenants of client-centered and crisis theory become evident in the case of Beatrix. Less important than where one theory ends and another begins is how they work together to meet the needs of constantly changing circumstances and client presentations.

The dying process disrupts the state of equilibrium within a patient and their caregiving system, making tenants of crisis theory important to hospice work. Kathleen Ell (1996) states that traumatic life events, such as a life-threatening illness or the death of a loved, can produce severe distress and that crisis is "frequently accompanied by feelings of confusion, anxiety, depression, and anger and by impaired social functioning and physical symptoms" (p. 176). A crisis may be the precipitating event that quickly builds a therapeutic alliance, or the previous work of building such alliance and trust can be the decisive factor in helping a client or family to navigate a crisis. The practitioner's role in crisis interventions is active and includes providing practical information and tangible support (Ell, 1996). It requires a more directive approach than client-centered theory, but I would suggest that the two can combine to complement each other to restore competency and coping.

Case vignettes will demonstrate the use of social work theory in the hospice practice setting while illuminating the need for a broad base of theoretical knowledge and expertise that illustrate why the ability to be flexible in the use and application of theory is essential. Turner asserted, "to tap the potential of differential use of specific theories, each of us must be familiar with all of them" (2011, p. 4). In interaction with my own journey, I will illustrate issues and interactions that may arise in a day of hospice social work while highlighting the concept of *practice fusion*, the art of blending theory in practice. I will also illustrate how the use of yoga and Eastern contemplative practice complement Western biomedicine in the hospice setting and that practitioner self-care of body, mind, and spirit enhances and informs clinical practice.

Coming to the Yoga Mat

Over the years of working with hospice patients and their caregivers, the interdisciplinary team chaplain, a fellow yogini, and I found creative ways to process our work. One day, as I was describing to her what had been an especially challenging patient encounter, she looked at me thoughtfully and asked, "What asana did that feel like for you?" Asana is a yoga pose or stance, one aspect of the eight-fold path of yoga. We had often talked about the challenges in our own yoga and meditation practices, and she took it a logical step forward, as yoga practice and lived experience reflect one another. I pondered the question she posed to me about our patient, Beatrix, and smiled. "Definitely *revolved triangle pose*," I answered. That began the journey of processing patient encounters through the metaphor of yoga asana.

Dealing with end-of-life care poses challenges and contradictions to Western ideas about attachment, denial, suffering, and being with discomfort and ambiguity, all of which can be informed by Eastern thought and contemplative practice. Unlike Western thought, the Eastern philosophies of Hinduism and Buddhism view the scientific and the spiritual as inseparable and complementary. They also view the physical, emotional, mental, and spiritual aspects of being human as integrated components of a whole and recognize a connection between all living things. This parallels hospice philosophy in the holistic integration and attention to body, mind, and spirit.

Eastern philosophy and the practice of Buddhism have been studying death and dying for thousands of years. Ira Byock claimed, "While the dominant orientation of Western culture toward death is avoidance, for over 2,000 years Buddhists have studied the question of how one can best live in the presence of death" (quoted in Halifax, 2009, p. xi). The eight-fold path of yoga is a science and philosophy that is thousands of years old. Yoga asana is one aspect of the eight-fold path. Yoga helps relieve stress and quiet the mind. It teaches one to be comfortable with ambiguity and contributes to therapeutic presence. In his book *Transform Compassion Fatigue How to Use Movement and Breath to Change Your Life*, Karl LaRowe states, "Becoming body aware makes you more sensitive to your own internal movement of energy, sensations, affects, various tension levels and most important, breathing. When you maintain this awareness, you're more able to identify which physical and emotional sensations are responding to what your client is describing to you, allowing you to separate the client-caused reactions from those arising from your own personal history" (2005, p. 14). LaRowe goes on say that breath and movement are important aspects of self-care for therapists and others in the helping professions and can be an important component in avoiding compassion fatigue and burn out. Yoga has been a cornerstone of my own development as a clinician and my personal healing journey. As LaRowe states, "Any honest and persistent pursuit in self-healing will lead a survivor at some point back to the body" (2005, p. 5). Yoga practice opened up a new way of being while informing my life and my professional practice. The body work inherent to yoga asana, along with the practice of sitting meditation, has enhanced my clinical skills and intuition while providing a grounding experience for dealing with the cumulative effects of loss associated with hospice work.

Why Do I Need a Social Worker?

The role of a hospice social worker is multifaceted. The ability to build rapport, relationship, and trust is essential to the work. Support to patients and their caregivers can include individual counseling and psychotherapy, family counseling, case management, crisis intervention, psychosocial education, facilitation of support groups, and advocacy (National Association of Social Workers [NASW], 2004). Social workers assist the dying in life review, an activity that supports building narrative to help make meaning of the life journey. Social workers facilitate legacy building activities that include letter or song writing, creating a blog, preparing "memory boxes" for loved ones, or creating audio or video tapes to be shared with family at special life occasions. Social workers support patients in repairing or accepting and grieving broken relationships and unrealized dreams. They assist patients with practical end-of-life issues and decisions while supporting the reality of terminal illness and dying, with a focus on maintaining quality of life, independence, and dignity. Addressing existential concerns, once thought to be solely the domain of the chaplain, also crosses into the care a hospice social worker provides. Additionally, as part of an interdisciplinary team approach, a hospice social worker strives to balance the medical model of care within cultural, developmental, and socioeconomic considerations, as well as the goals of the patient and/or client system.

The following vignettes enter a day of working with living and dying. They are examples drawn from my experience. In order to maintain the privacy and confidentiality of clients and their caregivers, these cases reflect composites of patients and demographics, surroundings and presentations have been modified. However, they are typical examples of daily work viewed alongside the phenomenological experience of this social worker's self-care practice. Quinn-Lee, Olson-McBride, and Unterberger (2014) reported that a phenomenological approach, which examines hospice social workers' lived experiences, "would provide additional insight as to how individuals make sense of their experiences in this field" (p. 235). My phenomenological approach is very much part of my writing below.

John, Susan, and an Open Heart

The workday starts with the morning death report, a listing of the names of patients who died over the past day. Following the death report, I review a nurse's hospice admission for a new patient. John's admission report ends with the not uncommon statement, "Oh, and the family does not want us to use the word hospice or to talk about dying." That statement brings up conflicting feelings while weighing values of self-determination, informed consent, and honesty, but I have learned most dying patients, on some level, know that they are dying and that patients and families often need time and support to approach the reality of terminal illness. Cain (2002) described this phenomenon of telling and not telling, knowing and not knowing from a different practice setting, but his work has universal implications. He claims, "No doubt, the clinicians involved feel they are in principled fashion, refusing to participate in what Beall keenly describing in other contexts a 'corrupt clinical contract.' But, alas, they are also buying into a dichotomy of knowing/not knowing, telling/not telling, a dichotomy that is as dangerous as it is psychologically false" (2002, p. 126). I have found that starting where the patient and family are is not only important in building rapport and therapeutic alliance but can allow conversations to evolve from a place of compassion and healing, rather than simply one of telling.

John was an 85-year-old man dying of lung cancer. He was, for the most part, alert and oriented but did occasionally show some mild signs of confusion. John's wife, Della, died about a year ago in the hospital, and family reported he had never really gotten over her death. True to the dynamics of the family, they did not talk to each other about that loss.

John is my first visit of the day. His daughter, Susan, greets me at the door to his home. Family members are taking turns staying with John, as he is declining rapidly and no longer able to take care of his own daily needs. Susan appears nervous, talking in clipped sentences a little above a whisper. Her eyes light on me, and she tells me that I cannot talk about dying with her father. I have a choice here, because there are issues related to patient self-determination and the right to know information about his condition. I can tell Susan that, thereby increasing her anxiety, or I can meet her where she is, assess what her fears are, build rapport and trust, and clarify my role.

"The admissions nurse mentioned in her report that you don't want us to talk about dying. I know you lost your mother just about a year ago, and so the possibility of losing your dad must be difficult. Tell me how this is for you?"

Susan's eyes dart back and forth, and she continues in the near whisper, "My mother gave up hope and died shortly after the doctor told her that there was nothing else they could do for her. I don't want my father giving up hope, too."

"You are worried that your dad will give up hope?"

"Yes," she replies, "and I can't stand to see him sad."

"So, seeing your dad sad is really hard for you. How was he after your mother died?"

"I don't like to bring it up, because I think it will just remind him of how much he misses her. We don't talk about it, but he has not been the same since she died."

"Susan," I ask, "what does your dad know about his condition? My understanding is that he is alert and oriented, so I wonder if he knows that something is going on? He is the one who is living this experience and sometimes not being able to talk about it can be painful, too."

"I think the doctor said something about six weeks, but they are wrong sometimes," she says.

"Yes, sometimes they are. But if your dad was told that, and he is no longer able to take care of himself, do you think he knows something is going on?"

At this point, Susan begins to tear up. I reach out and place my hand on her shoulder and say, "I see this is really hard for you." A tear runs down her cheek, and she has not yet moved out of the spot she has been in since I entered the door, like she's a shield between her father and me.

"I miss my mother so much," she says. "I cry every night. It was like I just got my life back to normal after my mom died, and then Dad was diagnosed and we got back up on the treadmill of doctor appointments, chemotherapy, radiation, and me not knowing what tomorrow will bring, if I will make it to work, be able to spend some time at my granddaughter's softball game or not. Nothing feels normal."

"That's probably because nothing is normal for you," I reply. "This is a lot of loss you are dealing with, and what we in hospice refer to as the emotional roller coaster on a day-to-day basis. I want you to know I am here to support you and your dad, not to hit him over the head with his terminal illness. If your dad asks me a direct question, I have to answer him honestly. Your dad may have things on his mind that he wants to talk about. I will not push him. I will let him take the lead. Do you think that we could go in and you could introduce me to him?" She nods her head and begins to move toward her father's room.

Following Susan toward John's room, I reflect on my morning practice. Warrior II or *Viravadrasana Dwi* comes to my mind. In the pose, the arms are wide open, with one pointing forward and the other to the back, there is an energetic pull from back fingertip to front fingertip, and the gaze is gently forward. The pose can feel like being pulled in opposite directions, but the stability comes from the core, the middle of the body and the legs, which are also set wide apart. The open arms make it a heart opening pose. I am reminded of the principle of being easy and comfortable in asana, not pushing toward the fullest extension, easing in gently. I acknowledge to myself feeling pulled in different directions by Susan and John's needs in this moment, and thinking that if I don't approach this encounter balancing both, I may not get a second chance because of Susan's role as gatekeeper. But, I look forward to what I expect will be John's "knowing."

John is lying on his back in a hospital bed, oxygen pumping through a cannula into his nose. His eyes flutter open when we walk into his room. I introduce myself and ask him how he is doing. "Tired all the time," he replies. There is a pause, and I am not sure if he will keep going. I let the pause stretch out a bit. "Three weeks ago I was still able to get my own meals, get out of the house every now and then, sit and read the newspaper. Today, I don't have the energy to do much more than get myself out of bed to the toilet," he says shaking his head. I can feel Susan's eyes on me, I am thinking that she is still not so sure she should have let me in. I have gotten used to the idea that some patients call their hospice workers angels, and some see us as the grim reaper.

"That's a lot of change for you in a short time. How are you dealing with it?" I ask.

"As best as I can," he replies.

Once again, silence hangs in the air. Susan has not moved since we entered the room. I see John glance over at her, and I wonder if they are both in protection mode. I sense that he is not going to say much more with his daughter there, and I take a breath and turn to Susan and say, "Could I have a few minutes alone with your dad." She gives me a long look and reluctantly leaves the room.

"I am ready to die," John says. "I just want to be with my wife. I feel like a burden to my family. They take real good care of me, but I don't know if they realize how bad off I am." I validate his feelings and sit with him in his reality. "I miss my wife something awful," he says. "We all do. She died in the hospital; we weren't there. I still feel guilty about that."

"Tell me about her," I say. John went on to tell me about his wife's illness. "That must have been, and sounds like it still is, hard for you. I hear that often from family who aren't with their loved one at the time of death. I've heard it said that sometimes the dying person will wait until they are alone to let go. It sounds like you were there for her during her illness, so I hope that moment alone won't define the loss for you." I realize that I can't change his feelings, but I can support his experience and share from mine. I ask John if he needs support to talk to his daughter, as it is very clear that he knows full well he is dying. He shakes his head yes. Susan comes back into the room, glancing back and forth between her father and me. I am sure she is wondering if I told her father he is dying, and so I attempt to create an opening for John.

"Do you have any questions for me?" I ask.

His reply is simply, "I know I'm dying. How long do I have?"

John and Susan are sitting next to each other, each with tears in their eyes. This change in roles, parent needing care, adult child as caregiver, is that place of paradox that contains challenges and gifts. John looks at Susan and says,

"When you were young and you were upset, you would come and place your head right here," he motions toward the middle of his chest.

I decide to take a risk, hoping that Susan can hear her father's plea in his voice. Susan's demeanor is still tense, but has softened a bit, and I can see a slight shift in her posture. "John, would you like Susan to put her head there now?" I ask.

"More than anything," he replies. I look at Susan and ask her if she hears what her dad is asking. She shakes her head yes but doesn't move.

"Is it something you can do?" I ask her, motioning toward John's heart. She shakes her head yes and moves toward her father, putting her head on his chest. His arms wrap around her. They both have tears running down their faces. I hope they are too consumed in their own moment to see the tears in my eyes.

Client-centered, existential theory and family systems informed work with John and Susan. This encounter could have been very different had John not wanted to talk about loss and his terminal status. Sometimes, patients remain complicit in the code of silence around their illness, and at times, people die without talking about their experience of dying and loss. Pushing toward a conversation that a patient is not ready for can create tension in the therapeutic relationship. Yet, there is a fine line that exists between being client centered in approach and knowing when to be more directive in discussion about end-of-life issues so the patient is able to participate in decisions about their care wishes and move toward closure.

I can't hide behind theory to shield myself from the reality of pain, suffering, and uncertainty that patients encounter or to increase my own comfort level. Theory can only be a guide. While I am not as comfortable in a therapeutic role that requires more directiveness, sometimes it is necessary, and sometimes only a crisis can precipitate change and healing.

Beatrix and Revolved Triangle Pose

Checking my phone, I have an e-mail from the receptionist alerting me to call the family of my patient, Beatrix. Bea is 78 years old and dying from heart failure, and I wonder if it is from a broken heart. Bea has three sons: Joshua, Jeremy, and Josiah. Her relationship with her children is often riddled with conflict, and over time, I came to realize that they maintained roles they had since they were young—protecting their mother.

Thinking back to the first time I visited Bea's home on a hot, early summer day, I recalled entering the house into the formal living room, complete with plastic covers on the aging furniture. There was a layer of dust on the plastic and it seemed that no one had sat in that room for a long time. What the room lacked in apparent comfort, it made up for with character. In addition to the plastic-covered, vintage, 1960's sofa and chairs was an eclectic collection of bird cages and glass figurines. Jeremy had greeted me at the door and led me through the living room and dining room into a family room that had every inch of sitting space covered by a collection of dolls. There were rag dolls and porcelain dolls, dolls that represented holidays, antiques dolls, and dolls that were hidden behind other dolls. For me, the room had a heavy feel to it that I could not explain, and in the dim light filtering through a hazy window, the room and all it dolls had a haunting air.

Bea's room was at the back of the house. As I continue to reflect back to that first visit and how Jeremy ushered me into a back bedroom, where I had met Beatrix Filmore in her bed, surrounded by symbols of her day-to-day life, including a pocketbook, calendar, magazines, remote control, Post-It notes, snacks, medication bottles, oxygen concentrator, and more dolls. Compared to a picture I spied on my journey to her room, Bea had shrunk to about half of her previous physical self. She was an attractive woman, despite her illness, with short cropped hair, smooth skin, and intense gray eyes. I had introduced myself, made some small talk, commented on photos in her room, and eventually asked how I could support her in her current situation. She seemed to have little interest in me and answered my questions with short, quick answers. I felt like I was in a standing forward bend or *uttanasana*, a pose that requires core strength and flexibility, one that gets easier over time. *Uttanasana* requires that you breathe into the resistance your body feels to move further into the pose. I wondered whose resistance I was feeling, hers or my own. That initial visit had focused on connecting Bea with some concrete services that would decrease her dependence on her family.

At other visits, bits and pieces of the story of Bea and her family had emerged. Bea had endured years of abuse, first at the hands of family members who raised her after her mother's death when she was young and later to the man she thought had rescued her from her early abusers, only to find that he was an abusive alcoholic. Her husband had died years earlier, but the years of abuse he had perpetrated continue to affect the family.

Both Bea and her children had a very difficult time accepting her terminal diagnosis. Sadly, she is not going to be able to escape dying from her failing heart. Family dynamics pose some real challenges to maintaining her physical comfort, and crisis is not uncommon in Bea's home. Despite the information and instruction the nurse has given to the Bea and her family related to medication to maintain her comfort, Bea's sons are reluctant to provide her with medication for comfort when she becomes symptomatic, fearing the medication may harm her. This is often a complicated issue in hospice care that takes control away from the patient, and a more complicated issue with Bea's family who believe they are protecting her by denying her pain medication.

At one visit I asked about her doll collection. Bea explained that over the years her sons had given her dolls at every holiday, and each one held a significant meaning for her. She cherished them. I noticed a perceptible softening in Bea when she talked about the dolls, which somehow seemed to provide a connection she was reaching for with her adult children but couldn't quite make. It was like someone had plugged in a string of lights and lit up the room.

I hadn't planned a visit with Bea today, but Jeremy called to say his mother had recently been talking about taking her life. Jeremy was distressed, and I wondered what kind of physical and emotional pain Bea was experiencing. Suicidal ideation in the hospice setting is not uncommon, and can raise conflicted feelings for the patient, the family, and the hospice worker. There can be a complicated dance of wanting to live and wanting to die that takes place during end-of-life experience. Helping patients to give voice to these feelings is an important aspect of hospice work, but many patients are able to do so without the desperation Bea felt. When a patient does voice suicidal ideation, there seems to be some irony in the conversation that ensues, as the reality is that the patient is looking death in the face daily. In the absence of Right to Die legislation, which might provide an opening for a different focus, the threat of ending one's own life requires protective action on the part of the clinical team, as in any other clinical setting. Jeremy ushers me through the house to Bea's bedroom. She does not appear to be in physical distress. I proceed into her room and ask, "Is it okay if I sit with you."

"Sure," she replies.

I check in with her, ask how she is feeling—is she having pain, or is she short of breath? She denies both but reminds me that nights are difficult for her. She had been arguing with one of her children last night and had been unable to sleep, unable to get herself out of bed, unable to get comfortable. She is still angry about the argument and the feeling of abandonment during the night. Bea has told me that she is not afraid to die, but she is afraid of dying in pain and alone. I ask her if she was able to use any of the relaxation techniques we had worked on previously to help her when she feels anxious at night, and I know the answer before she says it: "No." I know it was small solace in the face of her progressing illness and family troubles of the day. I also know I need to be direct with Bea in order to address her suicidal threats. I continue to be vigilant of signs of pain or shortness of breath, as it's impossible to continue a difficult conversation when Bea is symptomatic. Aligning with her self-report, I see no overt signs of physical distress and continue an assessment.

"Bea, Jeremy is concerned about some things he heard you say recently. He said that you've been making comments about ending your life. It that right?" I ask.

Bea looks at me and replies, "Sometimes I feel so bad that it seems like the only way to find relief."

Feelings of empathy for Bea float to the surface, considering the space she's in—somewhere between living and dying. "I'm sorry you're in so much pain sometimes. Bea, do you have a plan to harm yourself or end your life?"

"No, I don't have a plan to do anything," she says.

"Are you feeling suicidal now?" I ask.

Bea pauses and considers my question. "Right now, no. But I do when I'm in pain, and it can get really bad, especially at night."

I exhale—a sigh of relief—there is no immediate concern for her safety, but I am concerned about how to best support her. I continue to address her feelings and issues related to her comfort needs.

Looking directly at Bea, I reach out and place my hand on top of hers. "It's the job of the hospice team to help you when you are in such pain that suicide feels like the only option for relief. What I hear you saying is that you don't have a plan, and you don't currently feel suicidal. Are you willing to make a contract with me that you won't harm yourself in the future?" I am aware that there is controversy about the role of contracting and suicidal ideation, but have found it to be helpful, especially in cases like Bea's where there is no assessment of imminent danger. The fact that hospice patients normally have a lot of medication at their disposal for their comfort is both a safety and a liability consideration. Families experience such complicated grief around suicide, even when dealing with terminal illness. I try to balance concerns about safety with validation and accurate empathy.

"No, I can't do that because I may not be able to keep my word. I need that option when I'm in so much pain, and I feel so alone. It gets really bad at night sometimes. My sons want me to keep fighting and I am too tired and in too much pain to keep fighting. I am ready to die, but my boys don't want to hear that."

I am thinking that Bea's children have been protecting her for as long as they can remember, and they are not able to hear her need for comfort above their own need to act as her protector.

"I hear you saying that you feel stuck between not wanting to disappoint your family and getting your own needs met. You must feel really hopeless and stuck if you feel that suicide is your only option to end your pain and suffering. I want to help you to find options other than suicide and work with you and your family around your safety and comfort, but I also hear you saying you are not willing to work with me about how to maintain your safety in the future." After I say it, I realize for Bea, there is not much future left.

The discussion continues and I wonder how to let Bea maintain control. She eventually starts to engage in planning for her own safety, and together we develop a plan that lets Bea know she has options other than suicide when she feels alone and in physical and emotional pain. Bea agrees to reach out for nursing support for help her with pain and to consider hospice inpatient care for managing her symptoms. It has been a long conversation, and I see Bea starting to breathe harder. I begin to bring the discussion to a close and ask Bea if she is tired. Her reply is not what I expect.

"Yes, I'm tired and you have upset me," Bea says.

"How did I upset you?" I ask her and notice that keeping my voice level is taking some effort. I feel as though I am holding a difficult asana with Bea. In practice, working into a challenging pose requires a focus on the breath, not the pose. I recall the advice of the Yoga Sutras, the reminder to be easy and comfortable in a pose, but I only feel myself tightening.

"I don't feel good and you kept on talking about this," she says, looking away. I look at this woman who is trying to hold onto control and dignity, trying to remain in her own familiar asana. I breathe. "I'm sorry if I upset you. This was hard for you and for me, too, because I take your safety and comfort seriously. You now have options other than suicide when you're feeling hopeless and alone, so while I'm sorry that I upset you, I'm not sorry we had this discussion."

I know I am tired too, and feel like I've been holding a complicated pose, revolved triangle, a variation of *Trikonasana*, for too long. This asana requires standing with the legs apart and lined up longitudinally, and it involves a complex twisting of the trunk across the body while opening the chest and trying to get the arms to make a perfect line vertically from fingertip to fingertip, one arm reaching for the sky, the other for the earth. For me, it is a tricky pose to get into, and difficult to hold, requiring strength, flexibility, and balance. Feeling the challenges of working with Bea and the unspoken, unresolved issues and occasional crisis that twist through her life and the life of her sons, I gather myself and my belongings and pass by the watchful eyes of the dolls as I head toward the door.

Crisis theory is often utilized in hospice work. Kathleen Ell described crisis as "a severe emotional upset, frequently accompanied by feelings of confusion, anxiety, depression, and anger and by impaired social functioning and physical symptoms" (1996, p. 176). In addition, she states that successful adaptation to crisis enhances the ability to cope with future events (1996). At various times, support to Bea and her family included a flow through client-centered, crisis, psychosocial and family systems theory.

I know that Bea has more difficulties to face as her condition worsens over time. Leaving Bea's home, I am relieved to get back into my car, to sit quietly for a few minutes and regain my center before moving on to my appointment with Jewel.

Balancing with Jewel

Jewel is too young to be dying of cancer. I had been meeting with her weekly since her admission to hospice and have difficulty accepting Jewel's terminal status. *She should not be dying. She is too young.* Working with Jewel is like being in a balancing pose: first, trying to align my head and my heart and, next, balancing the intensity of the visits with some humor and lightness alongside the strong emotional work. Then, there is balancing the realization that I am helping this young woman prepare for death. Balancing poses require the use of *drishti* or gaze to find stability; drishti is an intense, stabilizing focus on something still.

Pulling up in front of her modest home, I recall my first visit with Jewel. I can still picture her wearing a hand knit, striped, woolen hat pulled down over her eyebrows. She had the look of a young cancer patient: her face puffy from steroids, her eyes ringed with dark circles, her skin pasty—and a hat. Her stunning smile, her sense of humor, her pride at having purchased her own home when she was still working, and her love for her adopted animals also emerged that day.

During that initial visit with Jewel, we began our journey together not at the beginning of her life but at its end, as she was contemplating the end of her life and still trying to find ways to live meaningfully. In his essay "Broken Narratives," Kirmayer states, "For many illness episodes, narrative represents an end point, not a beginning" (2000, p. 153). Jewel's illness, while moving her toward an endpoint in reality, did not put an end to her ability to build narrative around her life and her illness journey. In that initial meeting, client-centered therapy, with its emphasis on active listening, accurate empathy, and reflecting client experiences (Rowe, 1996), was used to build therapeutic alliance, letting Jewel tell her story in the way she needed to, which tested me and my ability to sit and stay with her through her pain and loss, and to hold my gaze, despite what, for me, were feelings of intense sadness and anger that this young woman was dying.

During therapeutic work with Jewel, her hats served as primary carriers of meaning (Mattingly, 2000, p. 188). Jewel's hats were a jumping in point for her narrative as she spoke about the loss of her hair, which carried a strong metaphoric meaning for other losses she was experiencing and would come to discuss in relation to her life, her illness, and her impending death. Being with Jewel in her home, surrounded by her adopted animals, gave insight into her strengths and put her in a much larger context than that of Jewel as cancer patient.

Reflecting back on our second meeting, I recall Jewel sitting cross legged on her sofa, wearing a sapphire blue bandana that allowed her re-emerging hair, appearing like a soft, dark shadow, to stick out in small wisps. Because she was no longer undergoing chemotherapy, her hair was starting to grow back. "Doesn't seem so important anymore, but maybe I'll die with some hair" she had said, followed by a pained laugh, before adding, "funny how things go, huh?" We explored her feelings of sadness and regret that she would never marry, never have children, and never grow old. Jewel went on to say that another source of distress in her life was the inability to talk to her family about these losses, because it caused them so much pain. It can be difficult for the dying patient to discuss their experience with their loved ones, for fear of "upsetting them." According to Safran:

Often people hide the full intensity of their despair from others because of a belief that others will be alienated by it. They also hide the full intensity of their despair from themselves because it feels too painful to fully acknowledge. For such patients the first step in the process of cultivating faith [in the therapeutic relationship] often involves fully acknowledging and owning their despair and sharing it with another human being (1999, p. 6).

Over the course of our work together Jewel would continue to explore feelings of loss, and her hats continued to change. One day it was an emerald beret, and another day it had been a little topaz colored cap that sat on the crown of her head, exposing a little more of the dark, downy hair that continued to grow. While Jewel did not consider herself religious in the traditional sense, she had talked about her spiritual beliefs and how caring for her animals was a spiritual practice for her. I had brought her a prayer shawl at the previous visit, a physical representation of warmth and comfort.

Walking toward the door, I am thinking about Jewel and her hats, wondering what will be her hat *du jour*. She greets me at the door *sans chapeau*; instead, she is wrapped in the fuzzy shawl, and I know that she has become comfortable with our relationship. She jumps right in and talks about feelings of anger and loss, such as those for her friends who no longer know how to be with her because of the many complicated feelings related to her illness—the reality that they can return to their own lives with futures, the life she should be living but isn't. Then, she speaks about her boyfriend, who chose not to stay with her through the tough times.

"First, his visits started to become more and more infrequent, and then his phone calls did, too. At one time we were together daily," she says. "I could tell the last time we were together that he was having a real tough time with the changes that were going on for me. I guess I can't blame him." She looks down at her lap and pulls the shawl a little tighter around her thin body. "We had talked about getting married and having children. He didn't have the decency to face me with his decision to move on. He just did." Jewel is crying now.

We sit in silence, giving space to her hurt, her anger, her loneliness. In "Emergent Narratives," Mattingly claims, "Silence, too, when artfully deployed, may speak much more loudly than any words" (2000, p. 188). I have many thoughts going through my mind as I try to achieve balance in the moment; anger at her boyfriend while at the same time wondering what I would have done in his position at his age? I hold her in my gaze—my drishti—maintaining the connection and knowing that I have no words that can hold her feelings, but the therapeutic encounter does. We have created a container for her feelings and her falling tears.

The sounds of her animals begin to fill the spaces: the rustling of one of the dogs repositioning, the gentle purr of the cat at the other end of the sofa. I move to one of the cats and place it nearer to her. When the energy of the emotional exploration has shifted, I instruct her in some mindfulness techniques.

Leaving Jewel's house, I feel a desperate need to tell my children, who are so close to her age, how much I love them. I consider going to see Gloria, a patient in a nursing home with a quiet dementia, a visit that will not entail the intensity of the day's earlier visits, but the phone rings and I'm told Milton has just died.

Milton and Final Resting Pose

Milton had been on hospice for almost a year, a long slow decline from Chronic Obstructive Pulmonary Disease (COPD). Ninety-year-old Milton had been lovingly cared for by his 86-year-old wife, Hildene, whom he met in France at the end of World War II. Milton and Hildene were a case of the old caring for the older, a common phenomenon in hospice care that can be both heart breaking and heroic. Milton and Hildene's children and grandchildren live out of state and provided support when they could but that was not often. A few home care hours through his veteran's benefit helped to supplement what the hospice home health aide provided and assisted Milton and Hidene with all his activities of daily living. The hospice team supported Milton's last wish, to die at home.

Milton had been in the army, having enlisted as a young man, and he often downplayed his role and his war experience. Like so many WWII veterans, Milton was stoic and complained little about his discomfort throughout his time on hospice. It took time for Milton to talk about his time in the service, his feelings, and the losses he had incurred. So many veterans never talk about their service at all.

One day, during a visit, he began to talk about his wartime experience in Europe. I had learned when working with older veterans to listen, to validate, and to not to let any emotions register on my face as they retell pieces of their story, reflecting that stoicism that so many of the veterans themselves display. Milton had helped to transport the wounded. "There would be so many wounded, you wouldn't know what to do. Kids without limbs or with disfigured faces, with gaping wounds. There would be so much going on, so many wounded, the blood and the sounds of men crying out for help. And I couldn't help them all. I just couldn't. Sometimes when I close my eyes I still see some of them and hear them calling out for help." I saw him getting short of breath from talking but did not call attention to it. I sat quietly, giving him my full attention, not wanting to interrupt. "Sometimes it seemed endless, the wounded calling out for their mothers, calling out in pain, and I just kept going, as long as I could, helping as many as I could, but it was never enough." Milton's face appeared pained and tired. A tear trickled out. I knew that I have been given a glimpse of Milton that had been tucked away for years.

"How old were you," I asked.

"I was just a kid, a crazy young kid from New England with stars in my eyes when I enlisted, I had just turned eighteen," he replied.

"You were just a kid who didn't know what to do with all that with all that pain and suffering," I said.

"Yup, day in and day out sometimes, we would go on until we dropped from exhaustion and then start again the next day," he said matter-of-factly.

"That sounds like more than anybody could handle, let alone a young kid, and yet you did your job," I said.

"But it was never enough," he said, shaking his head and closing his eyes. I let the silence sit there for a minute, trying to maintain presence, focusing on my breath and on Milton.

Milton had been a hardworking man, his children, while away, kept in regular touch with him, and his wife seemed to care deeply for him, so I decided to tap into his love. "Milton, what would you say to your son or daughter if they were faced with that impossible job you were enlisted to do?"

I could see him searching his mind and his eyes softened a bit. "I would ask if they did the best they could," he said thoughtfully.

"Milton, did you do the best you could?" I asked.

"I tried, but feel like I failed some of those men," he said, again shaking his head.

"You know you could not have saved them all?"

"I know."

"What would you say to your children?" I asked again.

Again, he was quiet and thoughtful, "You could not have saved them all, but if you did your best, who could ask more?" he replied.

I was amazed at the sense of duty that had endured for so many years. I had heard similar feelings and stories from other veterans, how they often carried angst over those things they couldn't help or change. Together, we explored forgiveness. It is two weeks after that conversation, and Milton has just died.

The nurse, chaplain, and I arrive at the home within a few minutes of each other to find Hildene and other family members who had come, knowing Milton had moved into the actively dying phase a few days ago. The family is tearful, but comments about him being beyond his suffering are part of their conversation as they console themselves and each other. The nurse, chaplain, and I give hugs and handshakes and approach the family to lend our support. "He was calling out so many names during his last hours," Hildene says in her gently accented voice. "He was reaching out with his arms, staring at the corner of the room, and talking to people like they were there, and saying I need to go home. But you are home I told him."

"Yes, you kept him home, right where he wanted to be," I said. "A lot of people talk about going home, or on a trip, and talk to people we don't see during their last hours or days. Did it seem to comfort him?"

"It did," she replied.

The work of David Kessler (2010) has begun to quantify these deathbed visions, which have also come to be known by other names, "including *near-death awareness, deathbed phenomena* and *death-related sensory experiences*" (p. 4). According to Kessler, these experiences of the dying being visited by deceased others is "often a theme in end-of-life narrative. While this archetype has been around for a long time, it first appeared in scientific literature in 1924 in an article written…by Sir William Barrett, a physics professor at the Royal College of Science in Dublin" (p. 5). Kessler goes onto explain that while the phenomena have long been present in religious writings, they have had a difficult time finding "a legitimate place in medicine" (p. 7). Who and what the dying see at end of life is an experience that hospice workers regularly encounter or are told about by loved ones. While all dying patients do not experience it, it can be held as a legitimate part of the dying experience for some, one that often brings comfort to the dying and their survivors.

After giving the family time, we provide Milton with care. Postmortem care involves a gentle bathing of the deceased and includes helping the family get ready for their loved one to leave the home. It's an important part of the pronouncement process for the family and the interdisciplinary team, this last piece of physical care. The family is invited to support the care while also giving them permission to decline. Hildene, not surprisingly, wants to be part of the care, a final act of care and love.

Lavender essential oil aromatherapy is placed in the room. A favorite memorial poem and some other practical information are left for the family. When Hildene is ready, the funeral home is contacted. Based on Milton's faith tradition, the chaplain gathers the family and hospice team members around Milton and says a prayer. We say our goodbyes to the Milton, Hildene, and the rest of the family.

The final asana in a yoga practice is *shavasana*, also known as corpse pose or final relaxation. Lying on the back in a prone position, it ends a practice with the intent of integrating body, mind, and spirit while committing the practice to muscle memory. *Shavasana* is a recognition of the need for balance between activity and rest. For many who practice yoga, it can be the most difficult asana of the practice.

Care of the Practitioner

The daily reality of working with living and dying raises implications for care of the practitioner on the physical, emotional, and spiritual levels. Sanders, Bullock, and Broussard (2012) refer to the complex nature of death, dying, and grief, as well as the associated issues that accompany working with families in crisis when facing end-of-life issues. They state, "Emotionally charged situations professionals encounter can create feelings associated with their own morality and previous loss histories that can easily become barriers to the helping process" (p. 11). Quinn-Lee et al. report, "Hospice has been regarded as particularly stressful due to the complexity inherent in end-of-life care. Burnout and death anxiety are especially relevant to hospice social workers because they regularly function in a high-stress, high-loss environment" (p. 219). The work requires that clinicians be aware of their own feelings and limits on compassion.

The concept of death anxiety is explored by Quinn-Lee et al. and includes emotional, cognitive, experiential, developmental, sociocultural, spiritual, and motivational attributes (2014). It is reported that people who have lower levels of death anxiety have lower levels of apprehension about talking to the dying and that working with the dying decreased the phenomena of death anxiety (Quinn-Lee et al., 2014). I would suggest that Eastern philosophy, with its focus on life and death as a continuum, as well the view of personal and spiritual growth through the concept of letting go of attachments (Carrera, 2006) may help to mitigate the effects of death anxiety.

While acknowledging the challenges, there are also many rewards inherent to work in a hospice setting. Proulx and Jacelon (2004) captured the essence of this idea:

The intrinsic, philosophical view of dying with dignity reflects unconditional human worth. This form of dignity is synonymous with an individual's sense of identity and honors the being of each person. It emanates from the realm of spiritual transcendence and is demonstrated by the capacity for giving and receiving compassion and love, essential elements of the dying process. (p. 119)

The mutually supportive relationships that evolve within the interdisciplinary team, the autonomy to manage your time to maximize support to clients, opportunities to be challenged in your own belief system and clinical practice, and an ever-expanding awareness of the fragility of life and the need to live it fully are additional practical benefits to hospice social work. Sanders et al. (2012) also affirmed rewards inherent within hospice work while addressing self-care: "Most professionals choose hospice because of the more intimate nature of the work. However, it is this intimacy that can lead to both compassion fatigue and burnout if the professional is not able to balance professional boundaries and self-care" (p. 13). Slocum-Gori, Hemsworth, Chan, Carson, and Kazanjian (2011) further confirmed, "Research has pointed to self-care interventions as a resolution to reducing levels of compassion fatigue and increasing levels of Compassion Satisfaction" (p. 177). Physician Steven Baumrucker (2002) summed up this line of thinking when he wrote, "I could not give compassionate care to my patients until I was compassionate with myself" (p. 155). Acknowledging the rewards while balancing the challenges of work with the dying is an ongoing process that can be supported by yoga asana and contemplative practice.

Clinician self-care is not only a practical issue but also an ethical one. In her article, "The Ideological Dilemma of Subordination of Self versus Self-Care: Identity Construction of the 'Ethical Social Worker,'" Merlinda Weinberg (2014) discusses the inherent dilemmas encountered in this issue, stating, "In social work, one commonsense aspect of professional responsibility is to act for the benefit of others and to put the needs of those served ahead of one's own needs" (p. 87). The other side of this dilemma requires that social workers recognize that, "listening to the suffering of others and being exposed to traumatic situations on a daily basis is very difficult physically and psychologically.

While the need for self-care may not be the dominant side of this ideological dilemma, the interpretive repertoire of self care has emerged as a familiar trope in social work," (p. 88). She goes onto say, "Individual practitioners are expected to use behavioral strategies to avoid, or at least minimize, the effects of exposure to the pain of service users. They are held accountable for their own health, even though there is recognition of the significant impact that broader structural issues play in these psychological effects" (p. 88). For many of us, being a caregiver does not end at the end of a workday nor is it a function that can be turned on and off. Adopting self-care practices that speak to our physical, psychological, and spiritual needs is an important aspect in both personal and professional development. For me, yoga and meditation inform this need. The practice informs my living, and living informs the practice.

Decisions around self-care are personal but should be affirming and take commitment. Joan Halifax makes several suggestions for principles of self-care. These include: "See your limits with compassion. Set up a schedule that is sane. Know what practices and activities refresh you and make time for them. Actively involve, include, and support other caregivers. Develop a plan for doing your work in a way that is mindful, restorative, wholesome and healthy" (2009, p. 94). If we listen to our bodies, minds, and spirits to guide self-care practice, it will emerge.

While much has been written about mindfulness mediation for personal care (Slocum-Gori et al., 2011), the specific practice of yoga asana has garnered less attention. One of the aims of yoga asana is to prepare one for seated meditation and practices such as mindfulness. Organizational support for hospice workers is suggested by Quinn-Lee et al. (2014) and includes suggestions such as yoga, meditation, spiritual practices and spaces, education, and mentoring. I suggest that yoga asana itself has real applications and implications for practitioner self-care and processing the embodied experiences of countertransference and congruence. Shaw said, "Psychotherapy is an inherently embodied process. If psychotherapy is an investigation into the intersubjective space between client and therapist, then as a profession we need to take our bodily reactions much more seriously than we have so far because… the body is 'the very basis of human subjectivity'" (as cited in Schore & Schore, 2010, p. 67). Yoga asana brings you back to the body and helps to process and release the physical, mental, emotional, and spiritual effects of therapeutic work.

Returning home at the end of the day is a welcome relief. Joan Halifax (2009) wrote, "Especially when working with the dying, you need your home to be a refuge, a place in which to rest and restore yourself, a sanctuary in which you can be nourished and safe. If you try to cut corners by ignoring your personal or domestic needs, you might eventually pay with your health or your sanity" (p. 94). This can be extended to social workers in most areas of direct service, anyone who works daily with the pain, trauma, loss, and injustice that bring clients to our doors. I also return to the home that is my yoga mat, day after day, not just because of work with dying but because it is life affirming.

Conclusion: *Sa Ta Na Ma*

The encompassing philosophy associated with Eastern contemplative traditions and traditional social work ethics and values are both relevant and useful in work with the dying. The reductionist trend toward evidence-based practice does not provide the expanded set of resources needed to effectively work in a hospice setting. Relational approaches that focus first on the needs of the patient/client, along with a seamless fusion of theory-to-practice and practice-to-theory discourse, will best inform work with dying.

There is an opportunity for engagement in rich and meaningful education and research in the hospice and palliative care arena. Moving forward, the conversation in end-of-life care calls for expansion of the knowledge base to better inform cultural competence, as well as care of terminally ill patients with mental illness, trauma, or developmental delays. The added burden of illness, death, and dying for individuals and families with limited financial and material resources must be recognized and explored to better serve the already underserved. Complex situations with multiple, co-existing presentations are exacerbated by the dying process and require the practitioner to be making constant decisions and adjustments to guide theoretical frameworks and considerations for patient's physical, psychosocial, and spiritual well-being. Case studies can and should inform the interlocking perspective between theory and practice.

Some consider the Sanskrit mantra, *Sa Ta Na Ma*, to correspond to the circle of existence: birth, life, death, and rebirth (Yogapedia, n.d.). From an Eastern perspective, living and dying exist on the same spectrum. "We normally make a false dichotomy between living and dying, when in reality there is no separation between them, only interpretation and unity" (Halifax, 2009, p. xviii). Yoga, like fusion, translates to union. The fusion of practice perspectives, Eastern and Western philosophical frameworks, and the inseparable aspect of care of the practitioner best inform care in the hospice setting.

Epilogue

Nate's name eventually came up on the morning death report. I was sorry that he and his estranged children were not able to make peace or come to forgiveness in his living or dying, but I hoped that I had been able to help Nate process his lived experience of terminal illness and facing death. Milton was buried in a military cemetery a few days after he died. Hildene makes regular visits to be with her children and grandchildren. Jewel and I continued to work together for a few more weeks, and as she became weaker, helping her find homes for her pets became an important aspect of her end-of-life care. She died in the winter, hatless. I sat at her bedside a few hours before she took her last breath. Bea died surrounded by her dolls, presumably in her sleep, as her family found her gone one morning. I hoped that she died in comfort. John's journey ended a couple weeks after that first visit. Susan reported that he was talking to his wife, Della, during his final hours. Susan continues to see a bereavement counselor for support.

I continued to work on revolved triangle pose, knowing that despite the challenge, it has many benefits, including strengthening the legs, increasing flexibility in the hips, improving breathing, improving self-confidence, freeing energy through the spine and core, and improving balance and concentration (Schiffman, 1996, p. 46). The hips are thought to hold memory. Months after Bea's death, sitting on my yoga mat one day, I thought of her, and her room full of dolls. I had been aware of transference and countertransference in my work with her, but it was the haunting feeling that puzzled me. Suddenly, out of the blue, I was thinking about the brother I never knew. My brother had died in infancy in our home, two years before my birth. Next, my mind went to thoughts of my maternal grandmother, who I had never known. I looked back through family records to learn that my grandmother had died just months before my birth. I came to understand the unspoken losses in my own home in a new light. I had never thought, until that day on my yoga mat, that I had been dealing with grief and loss all my life, born into the loss experience of parents whose grief was always close by.

Existential psychotherapy utilizes the concept of *encounter,* an experience that occurs between the patient and the clinician. Encounter, as described by Ellenberger (1958), is the way in which, through the therapeutic experience, something totally new is revealed as a result of the relationship for one or both individuals in the alliance and can bring "a sudden liberation from ignorance or illusion, enlarge the spiritual horizon and give new meaning to life" (p. 119). Work with Bea had given rise to new realizations and had awakened a new understanding of my call to hospice social work, like the *fusion* of light elements resulting in a significant release of energy.

Acknowledgment

It would be an omission not to mention and thank the hospice interdisciplinary team members I have been privileged to work with for years, as well as the patients whose stories inform this case study. I have had the honor of supporting many hospice patients and their families through the end-of-life journey accompanied by the excellent work of doctors, nurses, chaplains, music therapists, home health aides, and volunteers. A special thanks to Kelli Stewart, MDiv, MSW, who journeyed with me through the hospice and yoga asana experience. Namaste.

Close Reading Questions

1. Ordille writes,

   Unlike Western thought, the Eastern philosophies of Hinduism and Buddhism view the scientific and the spiritual as inseparable and complementary. They also view the physical, emotional, mental, and spiritual aspects of being human as integrated components of a whole and recognize a connection between all living things. This parallels hospice philosophy in the holistic integration and attention to body, mind, and spirit.
       What specifics from Ordille's yoga practice parallel her hospice philosophy?

2. Ordille believes that people need love, touch, and communication in their final moments. How does the case material speak to and speak against Ordille's belief?
3. How might Saunders' concept of "total pain" connect to the sufferer's spirituality?

Prompts for Thinking and Writing

1. What would your ideal "practice fusion" look like? How is "practice fusion" different from eclectic practice?
2. How might one integrate spirituality into "legacy building activities"?
3. What connections do you find in the podcast on the spirituality of children, available on the E-Resources page, to the spirituality of Ordille's cases of adults?

References

Baumrucker, S. (2002). Palliative care, burnout, and the pursuit of happiness. *American Journal of Hospice and Palliative Care, 19*(3), 154–156.

Boccio, F. (2009). Taking mindfulness to the Mat. *Shambhala Sun Buddhism Culture Meditation Life,* 7, 43–47, 98.

Cain, A. C. (2002). Children of suicide: The telling and the knowing. *Psychiatry, 65*(2), 124–136.

Carrera, J. (2006). *Inside the Yoga Sutras a comprehensive sourcebook for the study and practice of Patanjali's Yoga Sutras.* Buckingham, VA: Integral Yoga Publications.

Centers for Disease Control and Prevention. (2015). Hospice care. Retrieved from https://www.cdc.gov/nchs/fastats/hospice-care.htm

Clark, D. (1999). 'Total pain', disciplinary power and the body in the work of Cicely Saunders, 1958–1967. *Science and Medicine, 49*, 727–736.

Ell, K. (1996). Crisis theory and social work practice. In F. Turner (Ed.), *Interlocking theoretical approaches social work treatment* (4th ed., pp. 168–190). New York, NY: Free Press.

Ellenberger, H. (1958). A clinical introduction to psychiatric phenomenology & existential analysis. In R. May, E. Angel, & H. F. Ellenberger (Eds.), *Existence: A new dimension in psychiatiry and psychology* (pp. 92–124). New York, NY: Simon & Schuster.

Halifax, J. (2009). *Being with dying cultivating compassion and fearlessness in the presence of death*. Boston, MA: Shambhala.

Kessler, D. (2010). *Visions, trips, and crowded rooms who and what you see before you die*. Carlsbad, CA: Hay House, Inc.

Kirmayer, L. (2000). Broken narratives: Clinical encounters and the poetics of illness experience. In C. Mattingly & L. Gerro (Eds.), *Narrative and the cultural constructions of illness and healing* (pp. 153–180). Berkeley, CA: University of California Press.

LaRowe, K. (2005). *Transforming compassion fatigue now to use movement & breath to change your life*. Eau Claire, WI: PESI.

Levant, R., & Schlien, J. (1984). Introduction. In R. Levant & J. Schlien (Eds.), *Client-centered therapy and the person-centered approach: New directions in theory, research and practice* (pp. 1–16). New York, NY: Praeger.

Mattingly, C. (2000). Emergent narratives. In C. Mattingly & L. Gerro (Eds.), *Narrative and the cultural constructions of illness and healing* (pp. 181–209). Berkeley, CA: University of California Press.

Miller, A. (2010, November). Swamis, stars & six-packs: Yoga's twisted history. *Shambhala Sun: Buddhism, Culture, Meditation, Life, 11*, 79–89.

Mithoefer, B. (2006). *The yin yoga kit: The practice of quiet power*. Rochester, VT: Healing Arts Press.

National Association of Social Workers. (2004). NASW standards for palliative and end of life care. Retrieved from www.socialworkers.org/practice/standards/Palliative.asp

National Hospice and Palliative Care Organization (NHPCO). (2012). History of hospice care. Retrieved from www.nhpco.org

Owen, I. R. (1999). Exploring the similarities and differences between person-centered and psychodynamic therapy. *British Journal of Guidance & Counseling, 27*(2), 165–177.

Proulx, K., & Jacelon, C. (2004). Dying with dignity: The good patient versus the good death. *American Journal of Hospice & Palliative Medicine, 21*(2), 116–120.

Quinn-Lee, L., Olson-McBride, L., & Unterberger, A. (2014). Burnout and death anxiety in hospice social workers. *Journal of Social Work in End-of-Life & Palliative Care, 10*(3), 219–239.

Rogers, C. R. (1951). *Client-centered therapy*. London, England: Constable & Robinson.

Rogers, C. R. (1980). *A way of being*. New York, NY: Houghton Mifflin.

Rogers, C. R. (2013). Significant aspects of client-centered therapy. *American Psychologist, 1*, 415–422.

Rowe, W. (1996). Client-centered theory: A person-centered approach. In F. Turner (Ed.), *Social work treatment: Interlocking theoretical approaches* (4th ed., pp. 69–93). New York, NY: Free Press.

Safran, J. D. (1999). Faith, despair, will and the paradox of acceptance. *Contemporary Psychoanalysis, 35*(1), 5–23.

Sanders, S., Bullock, K., & Broussard, C. (2012). Exploring professional boundaries in end-of-life care: Considerations for social workers and other team members. *Journal of Social Work in End-of-Life & Palliative Care, 8*(1), 10–28.

Schiffmann, E. (1996). *Yoga: The sprit and practice of moving into stillness*. New York, NY: Pocket Books.

Schore, A., & Schore, J. (2010). Clinical social work and regulation theory: Implications of neurobiological models of attachment. In S. Bennett & J. Nelson (Eds.), *Adult attachment in clinical social work: Practice, research and policy* (pp. 57–95). New York, NY: Springer.

Seife, C. (2008). *Sun in a bottle: The strange history of fusion and the science of wishful thinking*. London, England: Penguin Books.

Slocum-Gori, S., Hemsworth, D., Chan, W., Carson, A., & Kazanjian, A. (2011). Understanding compassion satisfaction, compassion fatigue and burnout: A survey of hospice palliative care workforce. *Palliative Medicine, 27*(2), 172–178.

Turner, F. J. (2011). *Social work treatment: Interlocking theoretical approaches* (5th ed.). Oxford, England: Oxford University Press.

Weinberg, M. (2014). The ideological dilemma of subordination of self versus self-care: Identity construction of the 'ethical social worker.' *Discourse & Society, 25*(1), 84–94.

Woods, M., & Robinson, H. (1996). Psychosocial theory and social work treatment. In F. Turner (Ed.), *Social work treatment: Interlocking theoretical approaches* (4th ed., pp. 555–580). New York, NY: Free Press.

Yogapedia. (n.d.). https://www.yogapedia.com/definition/10781/sa-ta-na-ma

10

THE SHARED SPIRITUAL ENERGY OF REIKI AND EARLY PSYCHOANALYTIC PRACTICE

Lynda Fabbo

Pre-Reading Questions

1. Before reading this chapter, tune into the podcast, located on the E-Resources page, featuring Reiki practitioner and author Karen Noe. What changed in your understanding of Reiki as a therapy and integrated medical approach?
2. What is an empath? What does a quick search online reveal about the public opinion and culture surrounding empaths?
3. How might a combination of Reiki and psychotherapy prove to be problematic?

The origins of psychoanalytic theory include ideas that unseen forces influence the human psyche. Jung and Jung (1963) said of psychiatry, "Here was the empirical field common to biological and spiritual facts, which I had everywhere sought and nowhere found. Here at last was the place where the collision of nature and spirit became a reality" (p. 108). Today, clinical social workers are trained in evidence-based therapies, derived from systemic research, designed to be solution focused to help a person achieve specific goals to improve their lives. The science driving this practice has been scrubbed clean of any mysticism that may have been present in its origins, and young clinicians are not encouraged to explore spirituality with their clients, in part, because psychology and psychiatry are fairly new sciences that want to establish and maintain the credibility of other empirical sciences (Fonagy, 2003; Thorton, 2019).

I started out as most clinical social workers do, employing the evidence-based therapies we learned in school to help my clients improve and maintain good mental health. I was later introduced to a healing technique called "Reiki," in which one person channels energy into another through gentle touch to restore physical and psychological balance. In this chapter, I will discuss my experiences both as a Reiki Healer and as a psychotherapist and how the skills I obtained from each of these very different treatment modalities positively influenced my work in both realms.

Reiki

I first heard about Reiki when I was in a prominent children's hospital rehabilitation center with my son. We didn't know it at the time, but he has a rare mitochondrial disease that caused him to have a stroke and subsequent life-long seizure disorder. He sustained significant injury to his brain, and after many weeks in an intensive care unit, he was moved to a rehabilitation center to receive intensive speech, occupational, and physical therapy treatment daily. During his stay there, he had many different roommates, one of whom had recently garnered a great deal of media attention at the time. This young man was in a drowning accident, and had been pulled underwater by a rushing stream in a nearby town. He was rescued by a doctor who lived by the stream from another hospital, who miraculously saved his life. In the various interviews and articles published at the time, the doctor characterized the rescue as "divine intervention." Because of this reference to the divine, the young man got the attention of many religious groups and healers who came to the hospital to help.

One day, a local Reiki Healer came to the room to offer a healing session. I had never heard of Reiki before, and trying to be a courteous hospital roommate, when the healer came into the room, I took my son for a walk so they could have privacy. This time in our lives was rather chaotic with our son's medical issues, and I never would have given Reiki another thought if it had burst back into my life. I was too consumed with the medical issues my son was experiencing. Until, that is, a month later when I was in a hospital recovery room after having a minor surgical procedure, and a woman came into my room and asked me if I wanted a Reiki treatment or Massage therapy.

What I hadn't known at the time was that most hospitals started offering alternative therapists as part of the Integrative Medical approach. Integrative Medicine, which emerged in response to the health crisis and consumer demand, incorporates various complementary and alternative therapies, which are provided in conjunction with traditional medical practices to improve overall health and wellness. These healing-oriented therapies are patient-centered and empowering, and they address the mind-body connection and spiritual aspects of illness (Maizes, Rakel, & Niemiec, 2009). I was curious about what it was, so I opted for the Reiki treatment.

The Reiki Healer took the remote control for the television, changed the channel to a music station featuring a peaceful waterfall in a green forest, and the room suddenly filled with an ethereal melody. She instructed me to close my eyes and asked me if she could gently lay her hands on my body. She assured me that if I wasn't comfortable with her direct touch, she would hold her hands a few inches above my body, which would also be effective. I told her that I was comfortable with her touching me, especially since I wanted to know what she was doing. She began the treatment by gently placing her hands on both of my ankles. I immediately felt a calming sensation wash over me, and as she changed the position of her hands, I felt a shift within my body. It started as a pulsing throughout my arms and legs, and then I was filled with an overwhelming sense of exhilaration and serenity. I hadn't expected to feel anything, to be honest, and I was surprised by the intensity of emotion I was feeling despite the little physical interaction we were actually having. When she finished the treatment, which took about 45 minutes, she asked me how I felt. I told her I actually wasn't sure, but I felt like I could leap out of my hospital bed and run down the hallway. There was a vitality coursing through my veins that I hadn't felt in quite some time, and for the first time in months, I felt grounded and strong enough to endure whatever was in store for me and my family.

After my son was discharged from the rehabilitation facility, our lives were slowly getting back to some semblance of normal. It had been a stressful time for our family, and we had a tremendous outpouring of support from our community. One particular person reached out to my husband and told him about someone that might be able to help with my son's condition, which was still somewhat of a medical mystery at the time. This person referred us to a Reiki Healer, Karen Noe, who was also known for her psychic mediumship. Reiki again was being brought into our lives, and because I had a positive first-hand experience with it, I accepted the recommendation and contacted Karen. At the time, Karen Noe's popularity was taking off with the publication of her second book, and she had a waiting list for appointments that was well over a year. Although she was not taking on new clients, out of desperation, we wrote to her of our son's recent health issues and asked her to put us on her waiting list for an appointment in the future and in case of a cancellation. She called us immediately and invited us in for a healing session with our son.

We took our son to her center, which was located in an office park off the highway. He looked around incredulously, wondering what kind of doctor we were bringing him to; he was used to visiting various specialists to determine what was causing his health issues. The center was warm and inviting, and there were angelic murals painted on the walls. Karen welcomed us in, and guided us to her healing room. She invited my son to lie down on her Reiki table, which is similar to a massage therapist's table. She gently placed her hands on his head and began the treatment continually placing her hands in strategic positions on his body, and he responded to her every touch. She explained that she was following the energy vortexes of his body, known as the Chakras (Beliefnet, 2017). He was definitely feeling something happening in his body, and he was vocal about his experience, which was quite positive and favorable. Karen said she felt tremendous energy surges in his head, and she helped balance this energy by drawing the excessive energy from his head down to his body so he wouldn't feel overwhelmed. This made sense to us, since the main manifestation his mitochondrial disease was seizures, and he seemed physically relieved as she worked. She had suggested that since he responded so well to the treatment, I should consider becoming an attuned healer myself so I can continue to provide him treatments as much as he needed. Later, I learned that she offered a series of certification classes for Reiki Healers, and I signed up and continued, becoming a Reiki Master and Teacher myself.

Becoming a Reiki Healer

Reiki is an alternative therapy used to promote overall well-being and balance. The practitioner channels healing energy through their hands by lightly touching certain areas of a recipient's body in order to restore the balance and flow of their energy. It is based on the belief that illness is caused by a disturbance in this energy, and Reiki will correct this balance, which will in turn promote healing. The healing energy that flows through the body is considered intelligent, and it travels to where it is needed most. A healer does not direct the energy, but acts as a conduit through which it travels. The word "Reiki" means "universal life energy," composed of the Japanese words for "spiritual," Rei, and "life energy," Ki. The traditional Reiki story begins in Japan with Mikao Usui in the early 20th century, although it was considered an ancient healing art then (Stein, 1995). This ancient healing technique has been passed down from teacher to student for hundreds of years, and although the symbols that are used are universal and constant, the training in how to perform the art is as unique as the instructor facilitating it.

As I mentioned before, my instructor, Karen Noe, was also a psychic medium. Karen discovered that her psychic ability was greatly enhanced while conducting Reiki with her clients. She found that connecting with her patient's energy through the Reiki process allowed her to "see" aspects of their lives that she had not known about previously. Therefore, the focus of Karen's training for her students had to do with the ability to quiet one's mind to sense energy from the client while conducting a Reiki treatment. She believed this energetic exchange between healer and patient would intuitively guide the healing session and maximize its effects. My Reiki training involved the mechanics of Reiki, as well as meditation and mindfulness. She had us focus on what our internal experiences were in conjunction with our client's internal experiences during the Reiki treatment which helped me open up and develop a new aspect of my understanding of human interaction. It forced me to recognize a whole other energetic realm that I had not previously not known about, through which I could connect with others.

Typically what occurs during a Reiki treatment is that the client lays on a table, either face up or down, and the Reiki practitioner gently lays her hands either on or right above the various energy vortexes, or Chakras, of the body. Each placement of the hands lasts about three minutes and then their position is changed to the next placement. Most often, there is ambient music playing in the background, created specifically for energy healing and treatment – meaning a gentle chime will ring every three minutes alerting the Reiki practitioner to change hand positions. This keeps the flow of treatment moving, and allows the healer, to attend and attune to her patient, rather than be concerned with watching the clock or timer. When all the Chakras have been treated, the patient rolls over, and the process is repeated again. There are specific hand positions suggested in various Reiki manuals, so the treatments are rather routine.

During treatment, I will occasionally ask people what they are feeling and compare it to my own inner experience. I am often shocked at the differences in our experiences. For instance, at times my hands would feel very warm to me, and when I would ask the client what they felt, expecting them to say they too felt warmth, they would respond that they feel a cooling sensation, and vice versa. I realized the energy that is coming through me as the healer, and going into them as the patient is uniquely felt and experienced by both of us simultaneously. I also noticed that patients would talk about certain aspects of their lives which seemed to correspond with the energy vortexes I was addressing at the time, and sometimes they would recall some sort of trauma that seemed connected.

One of my first Reiki patients was a woman who had several health issues. When I was working on her lower Chakras, she told me she was feeling relief in that particular area. She had been experiencing severe menstrual cramping that was slowing dissipating with my touch. She then went into a story about the first time she had ever gotten her menstrual cycle and what a traumatic experience it was for her when she was 12 years old. She had told her friend proudly about reaching this milestone in life, and for whatever reason, her young friend after hearing the news recoiled with disgust and humiliated my patient in a public place. This rejection caused my client to feel intensely ashamed and disgusted. Her memory was incredibly vivid, and she was shocked at how accessible it was to her during our treatment. She continued to say how she had always felt particularly ashamed to be a woman every month when her menstrual cycle came, and how she never saw this connection until that moment. As I continued the Reiki treatment, I suggested she go back to that moment in her mind when her friend humiliated her and speak to her younger self, reassuring her that being a woman wasn't something of which she should be ashamed. She closed her eyes and did this as I continued treatment, saying things to her young wounded self things a loving and understanding adult would, and when the treatment concluded, she looked completely different. Something had shifted in her, and it was actually visible on her face. There was a sense of relief around her, and her whole body looked and felt more relaxed. We discussed her experience after the treatment, and she said she had never before made the connection between the anguish she felt when her friend humiliated her and the pain she felt every month. My touching of her body allowed her access to this memory that she had been repressing for some time, harboring the pain of the experience in her body, and somehow the Reiki treatment released this from her body and her mind.

Bessel Van Der Kolk writes that the constant muscle tension is present in people who suffer chronically from emotions such as anger or fear but also often experience various forms of continual physical pain, and may be involved with multiple medical specialists who may provide temporary relief but fail to address the underlying cause of the patient's pain: "Their diagnosis will come to define their reality without every being identified as a symptom of their attempt to cope with trauma" (Van der Kolk, 2015, p. 266). For this reason, one of the methods he recommends for healing trauma is what he terms "bottom-up regulation." Traumatized people often have difficulty feeling relaxed and comfortable in their own bodies. Helping them to observe what is happening in their bodies, in a safe way, helps them feel more grounded and able to manage their emotions (Van der Kolk, 2015, p. 270). This grounding of a person's mental state into their physical body is what is considered "bottom-up." Although his research for this entailed yoga as the facilitator of this experience, I believe that Reiki had a similar effect on my patient. Laying my hands on her body, under her control, helped her to connect to that part of her body, and be grounded in her experience. This circumstance allowed her to tap into her pain and reveal and release her trauma.

First Intersection of Therapy and Reiki

Now that I was both a Reiki Healer and psychotherapist, I felt it important to keep these aspects separate in my practice. I was mindful of the way I advertised the services, booked appointments, and how each was administered. This separation was fairly easy to accomplish, since I offered the Reiki healing mostly in clients' home since they were often unable to travel due to health issues, and I provide psychotherapy in a traditional office setting. Although Reiki brought me a new awareness and appreciation for the energy exchange that exists between therapist and client during treatment, I never considered actually using Reiki in my psychotherapy practice with clients. My Reiki clients were mostly people interested in exploring alternative therapies for maladies that modern science could not effectively address for various reasons.

In addition to my traditional clinical social worker training in most of the evidence-based psychotherapies, I have undergone training in psychoanalysis, having completed a program in a Psychoanalytic Institute. My style of therapy is to fuse an amalgam of several theories depending on what is presented by the client during a session. I attempt to be fully present in the moment, listening to what people are saying, how they are saying it, what they are omitting, how their words affect their body movements and color. I try to discern what they may be feeling and what they are allowing me access to. I try to become a blank canvas on which their words and expressions create pictures and scenarios, to get as close to their experience as I can possibly be, and to be empathically attuned. I do not see a person seeking therapy as a set of problematic issues and behaviors that need to be addressed and changed, but as a person on a personal and spiritual journey. As a privileged, small part of their journey, it is my job to create a safe, sacred space for one to express and explore what one is feeling, being, and doing. I offer gentle reflection and another point of reference, or insight to help one make sense of what is happening. I try to provide an unconditional, all-loving lens because what often accompanies traumatic experiences are fragmented, painful berating voices of the past. Defense mechanisms generated from the little splintered pieces of the self that have gone rogue in order to survive, that are no longer needed, and need to be redirected or eradicated as they are causing emotional pain and anguish. This is where the true "work" is, in the realm of the unseen and unheard. It is not in the context of what is said, but in the context of impetus behind the words. Messaging works both ways; there is an exchange in the relationship on another level, which is similar to what occurs in Reiki.

To me, because of this, I understood how my background and philosophy in psychotherapy helped my Reiki work. However, I hadn't considered the reverse, until I started working with Billy.

Billy was a young college student who came for psychotherapy for panic attacks. He was a very successful high school student who was struggling terribly in his first year in college. He attended college in another state and was on the verge of failing and losing his scholarship. He had experienced his first panic attack in class, and he stopped attending for fear it would occur again. On the advice of his academic advisor, and in order to keep his scholarship, he took a medical leave of absence and came home to address his issues through therapy. Billy was the oldest in his family by seven years. His parents were divorced, and he lived with his mother and two younger sisters. His father struggled with addiction and had very limited contact with the family. When Billy was in high school, his father left the family, and he had to help his mother care for his younger sisters. In addition to going to school, he worked as much as possible and assumed many of the responsibilities in the home. Through our work, it was also revealed that Billy's mother suffered from depression, and oftentimes Billy had to care for her. This parentification was quite a lot of pressure for a 17-year-old to handle, but Billy seemed to rise to the occasion and not only helped care for his family and their home, but procured a significant academic scholarship for college. Although his mother encouraged him to go away to school, she was terrified of being left alone with her young daughters, and would often express this to Billy. She would tell him how proud she was of his accomplishments and how excited she was for him to go away to school, and then call him in the middle of the night because she heard a noise in the house. He grappled with whether or not he should stay in college, and at his mother's (reluctant) insistence, he stayed.

The first few months at school went very well for him, but after returning home from Christmas break, things started to fall apart, and he started having panic attacks in class. Much of the preliminary work we did together involved his feelings regarding his father's addiction, which he felt was at the heart of his emotional issues. He felt abandoned by him and he was angry at him for leaving the family the way he did, shirking his responsibilities to the family. Billy felt relieved when he talked about his father; however, he was still having panic attacks. During a session, I asked Billy to describe his first panic attack in class. I asked him to describe what was going on right before it happened, hoping to reveal what triggered the episode. He said it was a typical day, and he had been in a great mood. He couldn't identify anything that day that might have triggered this event, so I asked him to talk me through what a typical day looked like at that time for him, hoping this may jar some memory. He said he woke up, had breakfast in the dormitory cafeteria, and walked to class. On his way to class, his mom called to see how he was doing, and then he became silent in the room. At that moment I felt a tremendous wave of anxiety wash over me, which I had never experienced before. I continued focusing on Billy who remained quiet, except for his deep breathing, and then I was hit with another wave of emotion, and another. I realized Billy was having a panic attack in the office. His eyes were closed, and he was shaking uncontrollably and sweating profusely. He was breathing deeply, which was how he managed his episodes, and I gently reassured him until the episode was over. Could the waves of anxiety I was feeling be emanating from Billy's panic attack? When I realized this possibility, I was able to put aside what I was experiencing at the moment and help Billy process his experience. During the session Billy concluded that his anxiety was not generating from his anger toward his father, but stemming from his mother and the tremendous guilt he felt being away from her and his sisters. He felt that he, too, like his father, abandoned them, which caused him tremendous internal conflict and anxiety.

This was the first time I had actually felt an emotional energy from another during a psychotherapeutic session. I was experiencing Billy's anxiety. It wasn't being generated from a countertransferential experience I was having because it wasn't coming from me. It reminded me of how I felt when I was practicing Reiki with patients as I suspended my own internal experiences to be receptive to theirs, which I allowed to guide the treatment. I was having a pure empathic experience. "Empaths" have an ability to feel and sense the emotions of those around them. They are highly sensitive people, who make up about 20% of the population. Dr. Elaine Aron originated the concept that people with a heightened sensitivity tend to process information more thoroughly and be more reactive to positive and negative stimuli (Acevedo et al., 2014). Empaths can feel and sense others' emotions and energy as well as physical symptoms in the body without the usual psychological and social filters we often put in place. They are most often guided by emotions rather than logical thought (Orloff, 2017). Billy's extreme emotional condition in that moment overrode any emotional barrier I had in the session and I was swept into his experience. My training as a Reiki Healer heightened my sensitivity to others' feelings and experiences. Through this sensitivity, I was able to focus on the actual energy exchange that was occurring between Billy and myself, which brought my empathic attunement to a whole new level.

Other Examples of Heightened Empathic Attunement

After my intense empathic experience with Billy, I became acutely aware of the energetic exchanges that were going on in my therapy sessions. These exchanges are not to be confused with countertransference experiences. There is a vast amount of research on what countertransference is and how it can be used to further psychoanalytic treatment. Countertransference is best defined as the subjective experience a therapist is having triggered by an interaction with their patient or client. This interaction activates an internal conflict a therapist is experience that is brought to the surface during session (Hayes, 2004). This is different than the empathic experience I am describing because it is not something that is being generated inside of me, it is something being received, and it feels very differently. When I am experiencing an empathic energetic exchange, I am fully aware that whatever I am feeling is not generating from my experience. When I have countertransference experiences I can usually trace it back to some internal origin that is undoubtedly from my prior personal experience. I developed an ability to suspend my own personal emotional experience, and open myself up to whatever the person sitting across from me was emitting, literally removing my ego from the exchange and completely attuning to the other person. It was something I was easily able to do, until I began my work with Monica.

Monica was a woman in her 40s who seemed to have it all. She had a great job, great relationship with her partner, and was physically healthy. She came to therapy because she was not feeling connected to herself, and she was having moments of dissociation in social settings. She thought that this was due to the increasing stress she was experiencing at work, and sought treatment to cope and ameliorate her symptoms. Monica was an ideal patient. She was consistently on time every week, and would do whatever homework assigned with perfection. She was eager and insightful and generally a pleasant person to be around; however, I dreaded our therapy hour together. Why, I wondered? What was it about our session that I actually dreaded? During one of our sessions, as she was reading to me an entry in her journal, I let myself explore the energy in the room, and I realized I felt nothing. I was numb. I actually felt dead inside. And it hit me. Monica feels dead inside. She has suppressed her emotions so intensely, she couldn't feel them, and neither could I. I realized this as I came to pay attention to the words she was reading me from her journal. She was reading an entry she had written about an abusive incident she endured in her childhood. Her words were incredibly descriptive and powerful, yet the affect in which she read them with was cheerful and devoid of any emotion, as if she were reading a daily horoscope. She had completely numbed herself to her previous trauma for survival. She was devoid of energy and when we were together, so I had to expend energy for both of us, emotionally pulling her along. This was why I surmised, I always felt exhausted after our sessions together and subsequently dreaded our appointments. There wasn't an energy exchange in our work; it was one-sided. She did not have access to her own emotional energy, and she needed mine to move through her emotional experiences. This lack of access and need for a conduit is not an uncommon experience in our daily interpersonal experiences. Have you ever met someone who barely speaks? They give one word answers to your questions, no matter how cleverly you try to word them to elicit more information. It can be very taxing, and we often abandon conversations like there for that reason. They are draining. This anecdote explains what was happening on an energetic level with Monica in therapy.

Therefore, I started directing Monica's attention more to what she was actually feeling. Over time and a great deal of work on her part to reconnect with her emotions, she was able to resurrect her emotions and literally feel her life. As she progressed, I felt her energy levels increase and fill the room, no longer depending on mine to exist. Even her affect changed when she spoke: her cheeks flushed, and she would occasionally cry. She found her emotions and was able to feel them, and so could I.

Evidence of "Energy" in Psychoanalysis: Mystical Unseen Forces

One is hard pressed to find a singular definition of energy that does not require a degree in physics to understand. Some general definitions cull from my experience lead me to define energy as the strength and vitality required for sustained physical or mental activity – a fundamental entity of nature that is transferred between parts of a system, and available power. Mostly, "energy" is used in science to describe how much potential a physical system has to change. In physics, energy is a property of matter and space, objects and fields. It can be transferred between objects and can also be converted in form. In physics and chemistry, the law of conservation of energy states that the total energy of an isolated system remains constant; it is said to be conserved over time. After reviewing the various definitions, it can be surmised that energy is not created, nor destroyed, but it is something that can be transferred, shared, and accumulated. This I agree with, as I have experienced this in my private life and in my professional life as a Reiki Healer and psychotherapist. Two very different fields of work, or so I thought.

The origins of psychoanalytic theory include ideas that unseen forces were influencing the human psyche: "The greatest split in the depth psychology movement, between Freud and Jung, partly hinged on the way mystical experiences were understood" (Eigen, 1998). W.R. Bion (1962) suggested that a connection occurs between an infant and her mother when normal projective identification is able to take place through what he termed the alpha function. The baby projects sensory and affective data to the mother who receives the data and converts it to the baby's conscious or unconscious psyche: "It is a logical necessity to suppose that such a function exists if we are to assume that the self is able to be conscious of itself in the sense of knowing itself from experience of itself" (Bion, 1962, p. 308). Howard Levine, Reed, and Scarfone (2018) complicate Bion's ideas and proposed that the self-object construct is not in existence at all because the patient's capacity to think had not yet achieved a level of organization to be able to repress, and only exists as a spectrum of possibility that has yet to emerge. These unrepresented psychic states differ from the repressed states referenced in classical psychoanalysis as they do not have structure due to the disorganized thinking capacity of the patient. One cannot repress something that is not there, something unrepresented (Levine et al., 2018). But I think that these unrepresented and co-created states can be expressions of the energetic exchange that occurs between a healer and a patient.

A child's first relationship with her primary caregiver shapes the development of her personality as well as her adaptive capabilities and vulnerability to the potential development of pathology. This first relationship influences the organization of an integrated interpersonal construct whose stability and adaptability will determine the formation of the self (Schore, 2015). As our understanding of attachment patterns and neuroscience develops, it has been argued that "complex models of psychopathogenesis link early attachment stressors to the neurobiology of impaired emotional development, enduring deficits in affect dysregulation and the genesis of personality disorders" (Schore & Schore, 2010). When the basic physiological and psychological needs of the infant are recognized and met by her primary caregiver, she begins to feel a connection to another which validates the infant's existence. When this connection is not made because the primary caregiver is unwilling or unable to recognize and meet these needs, the infant is not sure of its own existence and therefore cannot be sure of another's. This connection is the shared energetic relationship which is evident in actual brain physiology. Allan Schore and Schore (2008) proposed this biphasic critical period in development as when the primary affect regulatory system is formed. The structure of the limbic system is organized hierarchically depending on the child's affect regulatory experiences with its primary caregiver (Hill, 2015). Emotional regulation develops when the psychobiologically attuned caregiver appraises the infant's positive and negative states of arousal and regulates these states through mutual affective communication helping the infant create resilience to stress. Although the infant is emotionally regulated by her caregiver, over the course of her early development she becomes increasingly self-regulated and develops flexible psychobiological states of emotions that will influence how she relates to others throughout her life (Schore & Schore, 2008). When the energy of the attachment system is activated and the attachment figure is perceived to be present by the child, she experiences a sense of security and exhibits strategies of affect regulation that are aimed at alleviating distress and strengthening personal adjustment through constructive, flexible, and reality-based mechanisms.

Empathic attunement, an energy connection generated by Heinz Kohut's (1978) theory of Self Psychology, describes the self as the essence of a person's psychological being. It is constructed through processes that organize subjective experiences consisting of sensations, feelings, thoughts, and attitudes toward oneself and the world. A cohesive self is achieved when one possesses a stable, positively valued, and congruent set of qualities, ambitions, ideals, and values, and is able to accomplish her goals without being rejected or isolated from significant others and important reference groups. It also provides a sense of inner security and resilience and repairs wounds to self-esteem (Kohut & Wolf, 1978). Difficulties in development can lead to disorders of the self that are characterized by an underlying lack of self-cohesion (Banai, Mikulincer, & Shaver, 2005). Crayton Rowe, Jr. (2014) further defines this concept through his interpretation of the undifferentiated self object. He describes the self as being undifferentiated or disorganized when an infant, who has not yet developed a sense of self, is not allowed to experience their world without excessive disruption. When the tolerance of the infant is exceeded by disruption, she will experience moments of non-existence which add to the psychological trauma of poor attachment (Rowe, 2014). Couldn't one also define these unrepresented psychic states as waves of undirected energy patterns looking for feedback or space to exist?

An empathic therapist must attune to and resonate with the shifting affective states of the patient in order to overcome the defenses and foster the emergence of memory. These attunement states of the right brain are unconsciously communicated nonverbally through facial expressions, tone of voice, and body posture. The affective connection between the therapist and the patient helps the patient to regulate their right-brain activity allowing the patient access to language to co-process subjective right-brain communication (Masterson, 2015). This is the work that is unseen. This is what is happening in the room energetically between the patient and the therapist.

When Worlds Collide: Reiki with a BPD Patient

Up to this point, I have described my experiences with energy as a Reiki Practitioner and as a psychotherapist. As I have explained, there are places where these two modalities overlap, and influence each other, significantly, and why this occurs. I have used what I have learned with Reiki patients in my therapeutic work with clients, and I have used my therapeutic knowledge to help with my healing Reiki work. But can they (and should they) exist in the same space? I will explore this concept with my work with Rachael.

Rachael was a woman in her 30s who had been diagnosed with borderline personality disorder (BDP) by her treating psychiatrist, and she was temporarily living with her elderly parents. I had been treating Rachael twice a week for four years when she asked me about my Reiki services. She had noticed them on my website, and said that she had been reading about Reiki. She wanted to know why I had never suggested using it with her. I explained to her that this was a separate service I offered to people facing chronic illness and not in psychotherapy. She said that she felt strongly that it could help her, and she wanted us to explore this possibility. Several things went through my mind. Would it be appropriate and ethical to provide this to her? Would my denying her this treatment modality that I offered to other destroy the progress made toward our therapeutic alliance? Would providing her the service also destroy the progress? Would offering her the Reiki advance our progress? Could it be something that could help?

As I began working with Rachael, I realized her internal self-experience was a whirlwind of confusion and I felt she may be too fragmented to be able to form a personal connection let alone a therapeutic alliance. The turbulence of her intersubjective experience prevented her from seeing the possibility that I could see her and could validate her existence. However, there was something in her that was reaching out looking for stability. Despite her chaotic presentation, there was a part of her that wanted to make a connection. As treatment progressed, I saw evidence of Rachael's self-construct emerging when she started to ask me questions about myself or about things in my office. She was noticing her separateness from those around her and hearing about others reinforced her own personhood. In her newfound separateness she was able to make a therapeutic connection. It was at this point in her treatment that she inquired about my doing Reiki with her.

After much introspection, and consultation with a clinical supervisor, I decided to provide her the Reiki treatment. I felt that doing so would nurture her need to further our connection, and more specifically her need to feel grounded in her world. Providing her this opportunity in her safe space might be the best way for her to experience this grounding, and if it proved to be too much for her emotionally, she was in a safe environment, with me, to process what she was feeling and to recover. In order to optimize the benefits, I decided I would have to make sure enough elements of the Reiki encounter were different than those of our usual therapy appointment, yet somewhat similar enough to offer her security and comfort. I facilitated this comfort by making the Reiki appointment on a different day and time then we usually met, and I explained to her extensively exactly what she should expect. I explained that we would not be talking like we normally do, and that there would be a table set up on which she would lay and soft music would be playing in the background. I explained how I would gently lay my hands on her body in specific places for three minutes each time and soft bell would chime indicating positions would shift.

When we met for the Reiki treatment, she remarked that she was surprised that I was dressed so casually, and we proceeded with the treatment. I started the music and hand placement, and she responded positively sharing what she was feeling as we progressed. There was nothing atypical about the session, and we spoke very little. She seemed content at its end. We saw each other later in the week and resumed our regular psychotherapy work together. At the following appointment, she told me she felt it helped her a great deal, but she did not like how we weren't talking as we usually did. She decided that she'd continue seeking Reiki from another healer, and we would continue our treatment as usual.

Although at first I was quite hesitant to provide a Reiki treatment for a psychotherapeutic patient, I believe that it helped advance our work. First and foremost, it did not disrupt the work we were doing indicating there was no breach in the therapeutic alliance. Because she *chose* to resume psychotherapy with me and made significant gains afterward. I believe that she felt satisfied that I was offering all I could to her, clinically and otherwise, to help her find peace and healing in her life. Also, her decision to seek and receive Reiki treatment with another practitioner indicated that it had some positive effect on her personally, and she wanted to explore this further. I also believe that her seeking someone else to provide the service indicated that she wanted to maintain the sacred space of our work together and perhaps recognized the importance and need to also talk and process.

Conclusion

The therapeutic process is a joint effort toward restoration and healing. A therapist and her patient reach toward each other, looking for a safe and secure connection creating the bond that is necessary to successfully weather the emotional storms that are ahead of her. Becoming a Reiki Healer and learning how to tap into my personal energetic realm helped me to become more attuned and aware of unseen forces and connections that exist between a healer and a patient, between people. The Reiki experience in my life taught me how to suspend my logical knowledge and open myself up to a higher experience. It enabled me to expand my empathic ability unfiltered and unrestricted, allowing me to truly connect to another to better understand her experiences. It has also allowed me to appreciate that there is an exchange that occurs. It is a partnership between two people who have agreed to journey together toward healing, which empowers both involved.

Clinical social workers are trained in evidence-based therapies, derived from systematic research, designed to be solution focused to help a person achieve specific goals to improve their lives, and the science driving this practice has been scrubbed clean of any mysticism that may have been present in its origins and young clinicians are not encouraged to explore spirituality with their clients. However, as technological advances afford empirical science the opportunity to expand its ability to observe what was once unobservable, perhaps this will change. As our understanding and acceptance of what energy is and how energy works deepens, our methods of utilizing it for healing will expand.

Close Reading Questions

1. Why does Fabbo reach back to older psychoanalytic texts?
2. What is empathetic attunement and how is it related to energy exchange?
3. What is the difference between empathy and countertransference?

Prompts for Thinking and Writing

1. What scares you or excites you about the prospect of undergoing Reiki and/or practicing it? In what ways would you prepare for this kind of energy exchange?
2. Write a narrative about the unseen or mystical forces in your therapeutic space.
3. How does the practice of Reiki in psychotherapy remind you of the yoga work that Ordille describes in "The Asana of Being with Living and Dying?"

References

Acevedo, B. P., Aron, E. N., Aron, A., Sangster, M. D., Collins, N., & Brown, L. L. (2014). The highly sensitive brain: An fMRI study of sensory processing sensitivity and response to others' emotions. *Brain and Behavior, 4*(4), 580–594.

Banai, E., Mikulincer, M., & Shaver, P. R. (2005). "Selfobject" needs in Kohut's self psychology. *Psychoanalytic Psychology, 22*(2), 224–260.

Beliefnet. (2017, March 27). Chakras – Your psychic energy centers. Retrieved from https://www.beliefnet.com/wellness/galleries/chakras-your-psychic-energy-centers.aspx

Bion, W. R. (1962). The psycho-analytic study of thinking. *International Journal Psycho-Analysis, 43*, 306–310.

Eigen, M. (1998). *The psychoanalytic mystic.* Binghamton, NY: esf Publishers.

Fonagy, P. (2003). Psychoanalysis today. *World Psychiatry, 2*(2), 73.

immersion in the opening phase of psychoanalytic treatment. *International Journal of Psychoanalytic Self Psychology, 2*(1), 1–26.

Hayes, J. A. (2004). The inner world of the psychotherapist: A program of research on countertransference. *Psychotherapy Research, 14*(1), 21–36.

Hill, D. (2015). *Affect regulation theory: A clinical model.* New York, NY and London, England: W.W. Norton & Company Incorporated.

Jung, C. G., & Jaffe, A. (1989). *Memories, dreams, reflections: Recorded and edited by Aniela Jaffe; translated from the German by Richard and Clara Winston.* New York, NY: Vintage.

Jung, C. G., & Jung, C. G. J. (1963). *Memories, dreams, reflections.* New York, NY: Vintage.

Kohut, H. (2009). *The restoration of the self.* University of Chicago Press.

Kohut, H., & Wolf, E. S. (1978). The disorders of the self and their treatment: An outline. *International Journal of Psychoanalysis, 59*(4), 413–425.

Levine, H. B., Reed, G. S., & Scarfone, D. (Eds.). (2018). *Unrepresented states and the construction of meaning: Clinical and theoretical contributions.* Routledge.

Maizes, V., Rakel, D., & Niemiec, C. (2009). Integrative medicine and patient-centered care. *Explore: The Journal of Science and Healing, 5*(5), 277–289.

Masterson, J. F. (2015). *The personality disorders through the lens of attachment theory and the neurobiologic development of the self: A clinical integration.* Phoenix, AZ: Zeig, Tucker & Thiesen.

Orloff, J. (2017). *The empath's survival guide: Life strategies for sensitive people.* Boulder, CO: Sounds True. Kindle location: 99.

Rowe, Jr, C. E. (2014). Disorders as undifferentiated selfobject formations: Treatment of a multidisordered patient. *Psychoanalytic Review, 101*(3), 341.

Schore, A. N. (2015). *Affect regulation and the origin of the self: The neurobiology of emotional development.* New York, NY: Routledge.

Schore, J. R., & Schore, A. N. (2008). Modern attachment theory: The central role of affect regulation in development and treatment. *Clinical Social Work Journal, 36*(1), 9–20.

Schore, J. R., & Schore, A. N. (2010). Clinical social work and regulation theory: Implications of neurobiological models of attachment. In S. Bennett & J. Nelson (Eds.), *Adult attachment in clinical social work* (pp. 57–75). New York, NY: Springer.

Stein, D. (1995). *Essential reiki: A complete guide to an ancient healing art.* New York, NY: Ten Speed Press.

Thorton, S. P. (2019). Sigmund Freud (1856–1939): Critical evaluation of freud. *The Internet Encyclopedia of Philosophy.* ISSN 2161-0002. Retrieved from https://www.iep.utm.edu/

Van der Kolk, B. A. (2015). *The body keeps the score: Brain, mind, and body in the healing of trauma.* New York, NY: Penguin Books.

Index

For Product Safety Concerns and Information please contact our EU
representative GPSR@taylorandfrancis.com
Taylor & Francis Verlag GmbH, Kaufingerstraße 24, 80331 München, Germany

www.ingramcontent.com/pod-product-compliance
Lightning Source LLC
Chambersburg PA
CBHW070412270326
41926CB00014B/2792